Engendering social policy

Engendering social policy

edited by
Sophie Watson and **Lesley Doyal**

Open University Press
Buckingham · Philadelphia

Open University Press
Celtic Court
22 Ballmoor
Buckingham
MK18 1XW

email: enquiries@openup.co.uk
world wide web: http://www.openup.co.uk

and
325 Chestnut Street
Philadelphia, PA 19106, USA

First Published 1999

A catalogue record of this book is available from the British Library

ISBN 0 335 20113 X (pb)   0 335 20114 8 (hb)

Library of Congress Cataloging-in-Publication Data
Engendering social policy / Sophie Watson and Lesley Doyal (eds.).
        p.   cm.
    Includes bibliographical references and index.
    ISBN 0-335-20114-8. – ISBN 0-335-20113-X (pbk.)
    1. Great Britain–Social policy–1979–   2. Welfare state–History.
  3. Sex discrimination against women–Great Britain.   4. Sex role.
  I. Watson, Sophie.   II. Doyal, Lesley.
  HN390.E54   1998
  361.6'1'0941–dc21   98-17036
                                                                 CIP

Typeset by Graphicraft Limited, Hong Kong
Printed in Great Britain by Biddles Ltd, Guildford and King's Lynn

Contents

The editors and contributors

Margaret Boushel, Elaine Farmer, Gill Hague, Marianne Hester, Hilary Land, Christina Pantazis, Sarah Payne, Teresa Rees and *Imogen Taylor* are academics in the School for Policy Studies, University of Bristol. Many of the contributors also have a long history working in feminist organizations and as advisors to local and national governments on questions of social policy reform, women's issues and equal opportunity policies.

Sophie Watson is Professor of Urban Cultures in the Department of Cultural Studies, University of East London. At the time the book was conceived, she was a professor in the Centre for Urban Studies at the School for Policy Studies.

Lesley Doyal is Professor in Health and Social Care at the School for Social Policy Studies, University of Bristol.

Introduction

Sophie Watson

This book represents an attempt to bring new and fresh perspectives to a range of issues in social policy. While there are now several feminist analyses of the impact of the welfare state on women (from the early work of Wilson 1977 to more recent studies such as Maclean and Groves 1991) the focus has tended to be on women rather than on gender. This book represents a new departure in that many of the chapters are concerned with unpacking how social policy constructs gendered social relations. Other chapters draw on recent feminist analysis to cast old problems in a new light in the hope that different solutions and strategies for change emerge.

The book draws on the current research and work of a group of feminist scholars at the School of Policy Studies at the University of Bristol. Thus it does not aim to cover comprehensively the checklist of social policy issues that readers may expect to find in such a text, but rather to bring together a range of different theoretical and methodological approaches to, and analyses of, some of the key issues facing social policy analysts today. Despite the intervening 20 years since Elizabeth Wilson (1977) drew attention to the many ways in which the welfare state both constructed, and was underpinned by, delineated roles for women, mainstream social policy analysis remains sadly uninformed by questions of gender. Fiona Williams' (1989) book *Social Policy: A Critical Introduction* probably remains the best attempt to integrate a feminist analysis with other perspectives on welfare, but inevitably many of the debates have moved on.

Engendering Social Policy goes to press at a strange and depressing moment for those committed to progressive notions of welfare, and arguably feminism. Blair's Labour Party was elected to power in the summer of 1997 after nearly 20 years of a Conservative government which had restructured the welfare state and made swingeing cuts under a rhetoric of, on the one hand, individualism and the end of society, and on the other, a return to traditional gender roles and the patriarchal nuclear family. Many old Labour supporters joined with Liberal and Conservative voters disaffected with growing inequalities between the rich and the poor, and with a society driven by material gain rather than notions of social citizenship, to vote-in a New Labour government which seemingly stood for social justice and 'one nation'. The Blair proposals to restructure the welfare state were to be expected and in some quarters were welcomed by those who saw welfare as too bureaucratic, as a disincentive to entering the labour force or simply as providing for groups who were not in need. The shock came with the first group to be targetted: single parents' benefit was to be reduced by £10 with a view to encouraging them back into work. The outcry from the Labour backbench and community activists alike was immediate, with vociferous arguments that the cut would only plunge single parents – 90 per cent of whom are women – further into poverty since employment opportunities, especially in poorer regions of the country, simply were not available. Though the Chancellor, Gordon Brown, insisted that the move was intended to save £300m to expand childcare his announcement came too late to check the growing rebellion in the ranks.

The fact that such policies are being devised by the Labour government at the time this book goes to press underlines the urgent need firmly to reintroduce and re-emphasize the importance of gender to the social policy debate. Despite 30 years of renewed feminist activism the inequalities of gender persist: women still take major responsibility for childcare, dependants in the family and domestic work. Women are also still concentrated in lower-paid jobs, occupy lower positions in almost all organizations and professions, are more likely to be in part-time work and if in full-time employment are paid approximately two-thirds of the male full-time wage.

While these material realities persist, young feminists are now arguing that it is time to retrieve femininity (Natasha Walter 1998 tells of the pretty silk dresses in her wardrobe) and that women are simply different – keen on self-adornment, more intuitive and nurturing, less competitive and more attuned to personal issues. As far as Walter is concerned these qualities, which earlier feminists have argued to be socially and psychically constructed, are innate. We are not arguing here against pleasure in self-adornment and fashion nor against the qualities historically associated with women, rather that a reductive notion of femininity has underpinned many of the exclusions women face, and in arguing that some attributes are inherently feminine we find ourselves on weak ground when arguing that others are not. Gender either is or is not a social construct, whatever the complexities of interplay between bodies, psyches and the social.

Feminist politics and gender analysis does however have to confront some thorny theoretical questions as well as address a new social/economic terrain constructed by global and local interconnections. Arguably the space for new feminisms that sideline the force of gender analysis has opened up as a result of feminist theory sometimes described as post-modernist or post-structural (which we discuss shortly), which has also been influenced by ideas from French feminism and psychoanalysis.

Earlier feminist social policy perspectives could largely be categorized in four ways (Williams 1989). Liberal feminism has a long history which dates back to Mary Wollstonecraft's *A Vindication of the Rights of Women* 1792. This politics of equal rights advocates equal participation of women in the public sphere. Thus the policy focus is around equal employment opportunities, an end to discriminatory practices, and sex equality legislation. Differences between men and women are seen to be of little relevance and the fact that women bear children can be mediated by reforms in the public arena. The private sphere is left intact and the emphasis shifts to finding ways to enable women to be active social citizens.

Welfare feminism stands in sharp contrast and largely describes the approach of social reformers like Beatrice Webb in the early 1900s, Eleanor Rathbone in the 1930s and, more recently, Beveridge. Within this paradigm the differences between men and women are taken as given: women's biology is their destiny and motherhood must be revered and protected. The role of social policy is thus to provide reforms to ease women's lives as wives and mothers by providing family allowances and other provisions such as maternity benefits and care. The emphasis, then, is on the private sphere and enhancing women's position within it.

Both radical feminist and Marxist/socialist feminist arguments came later and were particularly dominant throughout the 1970s. For radical feminism patriarchy is a universal system of oppression within which men hold power (Firestone 1970). Men as a class exploit women in every area of life, both private and public. Thus all institutions, laws and policies are seen to act in men's interests and men hold the dominant positions in society (Mackinnon 1983). The policy focus is on issues of domestic violence, rape and pornography. Marxist feminist analysis on the other hand was concerned to develop an analysis of the welfare state which was formed in the context of both patriarchal and capitalist relations (Wilson 1977; McIntosh 1978; Barrett 1980). The welfare state, it was argued, not only served the interests of men but also the interests of capital. Capital needed women in the home to reproduce labour power – that is, to feed, look after and service the needs of their husbands and families – for free, thereby enabling capitalists to pay lower wages. Women were thus also situated as a reserve army of labour who could be drawn in and out of the labour force when needed. The patriarchal nuclear family, and women's role within it, was also argued to have an important ideological function in reproducing class relations and maintaining social stability.

This is not the place to discuss any of these perspectives in detail since this has been well accomplished elsewhere (Williams 1989). Rather the purpose has been briefly to chart the shifts that have taken place in order to situate this collection. The first major critique to these positions came from Black feminists and arguably prepared the ground for some of the postmodern ideas which followed. Again the debate was far more complex than can be sketched here. Black feminists argued that each of the feminist perspectives ignored and overlooked the position of Black women. In their view the welfare state could not easily be mobilized in women's interests as liberal feminists and welfare feminists had argued since the state was a racist one which discriminated on racial grounds towards Black people. Similarly the Marxist feminist argument that the patriarchal capitalist state had an interest in maintaining the family made no sense in the context of racist immigration laws which kept Black families apart (Bhavnani and Coulson 1986). These arguments opened up the space to listen to the voices of the 'Other' – or voices from the margins (hooks 1982), an idea which has been central to postmodernism.

By the late 1980s postmodern ideas were shifting the focus to illuminate notions of difference, fragmentation, subjectivity and the construction of meaning (see Hillyard and Watson 1996). In *Destabilising Theory* Michele Barrett and Anne Phillips (1992) argue for theory that challenges the universalizing, generalizing and overambitious models of liberalism, humanism and Marxism which have characterized social policy thinking. Instead many feminists have turned their attention to the local, specific and the particular. Thus challenging the universal system of patriarchy (Walby 1992), Rosemary Pringle (1995) in another more contemporary collection of feminist writings (Caine and Pringle 1995) argues that treating patriarchy as a monolithic logic of oppression ignores the more complex and fluid ways in which power operates and thus reinforces our sense that we cannot change it or get outside of it. Instead it is more useful, she suggests, to look at the concrete instances of gender domination and its intersection with class, race and sexuality. Drawing first on Foucault and second on psychoanalysis, she points to the importance of analysing the power-knowledge relations within which subjectivities are constituted and through which girls and boys take their place in a gendered symbolic order (Coward 1993). In *The End of Capitalism (as we knew it)* Gibson-Graham (1996) similarly unpacks this well-worn shibboleth and argues for a more complex understanding of class, power and political subjectivity.

The contributors to this collection would differ in their degree of sympathy with the postmodern approach and some chapters are more influenced by these ideas than others. While earlier feminisms differed in their focus on the sphere of reproduction and the family, or on economic structures or cultural representation, or sexuality or motherhood as the primary locus of oppression, what they shared was an attachment to the fundamentals of an original and founding cause (Barrett and Phillips 1992). With the interventions of Black women and women of different minority cultures, including lesbians and women with disabilities, the dominant feminist paradigms came to be criticized for their racism, ethnocentrism and heterosexism. 'Other' voices came to be heard and these destabilized old certainties and understandings. At the same time a growing interest in questions of subjectivity, sexual difference and identity illuminated the theoretical problems of distinguishing biology and social construction and the sex/gender distinction (Gatens 1992). Subjectivities came to be seen as being fragmented, fluid, shifting, and constituted within a variety of discourses.

Attention was also focused on how public, political and policy discourses constructed different subject positions for men and women which themselves had important effects. Carol Smart (1992) for example, distinguished between woman and Woman arguing that the latter was a gendered subject position which legal discourse brought into being. Thus legal discourse produces not only different types of Woman – the female criminal, the prostitute and the infanticidal mother – it also constructs Woman in contradistinction to Man. Developing the critique of the sex/gender distinction other critiques deconstructed, challenged and subverted such gendered binary oppositions as private/public, nature/culture and home/work.

Earlier theories of the state also came under challenge. Feminists have had an uneasy relation to the state for many years. In part the tension was around what the state can do for us, expressed well in an early text 'In and Against the State' written on a train by a group known as the London Edinburgh Return Group, since the participants travelled between the two cities. Both radical feminists and Marxist feminists have critiqued the state as not acting in women's interests and reinforcing relations of power. The former position would see the state as reinforcing men's power through the criminal justice system, the courts, the medical professions and so on. As MacKinnon (1983: 682) has forcefully argued: 'The question for feminism for the first time in its own terms is: What is this state from women's point of view? . . . [t]he state, in part through law, institutionalises male power. If male power is systemic, it is the regime'. Marxist feminists in contrast attempted to analyse the part played by the state in establishing and maintaining women's dependence within the family household and wage labour as interrelated systems. Marrying an analysis of patriarchy with an analysis of capitalism McIntosh (1978: 259) wrote: 'it is a society in which the dominant class is composed mainly of men, yet it is not as men but as capitalists that they are dominant . . . The state must be seen as a capitalist one or at least one that is to be understood primarily in relation to the capitalist mode of production'.

Liberal feminists clearly thought otherwise believing that the state could be mobilized to represent and respond to women's interests. This view was much more prevalent in the United States, Scandinavia and Australia (Watson 1990) where progressive reforms were gained (and also taken away by Conservative governments) far earlier than in Britain. One explanation for this was the dominance of socialist feminism within the British women's movement which was not matched elsewhere. Where women did enter the arenas of the state in Britain it tended to be at the local or metropolitan level – the Greater London Council and left Labour local authorities – and there was some suspicion as to whether radical views would thereby become co-opted and lose their critical edge. A similar fear was evident in Australia where the feminists who developed policy for women within government bureaucracies were called 'femocrats' and described jokingly in one article as 'bosses in beige suits' (Lynch 1984).

A post-structuralist/postmodernist approach to the state was developed by Pringle and Watson (1990, 1992). In this work earlier formulations of the state were criticized for being too functionalist and for presenting the state as either unified in its intentions or contradictory: in this case reflecting a presumption of unity and intentionality which has been disrupted. Instead Pringle and Watson argued that the state should be seen as erratic and disconnected rather than contradictory; as a set of arenas or in Yeatman's terms 'a plurality of discursive forms' (1990: 170). In this analysis the practices and discourses which construct the 'state' are not structurally pre-given but are a historical product of struggles and interventions which may be partial and temporary. Earlier feminist accounts tended to take women and men as unified categories each with their shared interests, rather than recognizing that interests are actively constructed in the process of engagement with the arenas of the state (Pringle and Watson 1992).

There are two related strands to the feminist challenges to these ideas which are of particular relevance to social policy. First there is a concern that a critique of such universalisms as social justice and social citizenship – notwithstanding the embeddedness of women's exclusion in these concepts (Pateman 1988) – leads to a vacuum where no clear goal, set of standards or progressive universal system of reform can be established. If each instance of power relations is to be investigated in its specificity how can we combat widespread inequalities or establish common grounds for change? For some feminist theorists post-structuralist ideas take us down a path of relativism where no values or progressive norms can be established. The other critique focuses on new feminist ideas around subjectivity and identity. Here the argument is that as soon as women gained strength and power to fight oppression from the subject position of woman, then postmodernist theorists came along and deconstructed the notion of the subject. In a famous quote Nancy Harstock (1990: 163–4) argues:

Why is it that just at the moment when so many of us who have been silenced begin to demand the right to name ourselves, to act as subjects rather than objects of history, that just then the concept of subjecthood becomes problematic? Just when we are forming our own theories about the world, uncertainty emerges about whether the world can be theorised. Just when we are talking about the changes we want, ideas of progress and the possibility of systematically and rationally organising human society become dubious and suspect.

Certainly the equality/difference debate has preoccupied feminists for more than a decade, sometimes with disabling effects. Joan Scott (1990: 138) provides a useful way of avoiding the dilemma: 'the antithesis itself hides the interdependence of the two terms, for equality is not the elimination of difference, and difference does not preclude equality'. We are left then with an argument that we should build a notion of equality that rests on, and embodies, difference. As for the problems with universalistic thought and a plea for attention to the particular and local instances of gender power relations, this also is a tricky path to tread for those concerned with feminist social policy. Yet almost unwittingly this collection finds itself precisely at the intersection of the local and the particular with some generalized, sometimes implicit rather than explicit, notions of gender. The majority of the chapters examine specific instances of gender relations in a diverse range of social policy arenas. There is no claim to producing a totalizing overview of gender and social policy but rather to elucidating the ways in which gender is embedded in issues as diverse as crime and health. It is hoped that this book will thus provide new analyses and insights on social policy which will seep (or hopefully gush) their way into the arenas of the state, and shift the dominant discourses and policies that have for too long been embedded in disabling gendered practices.

Themes and debates

A number of different themes and debates are implicitly or explicitly addressed in this collection. Many of the earlier feminist discussions of social policy have analysed how social policies have produced and reinforced traditional gendered patterns of work, domestic labour and caring, and these questions are also addressed here. For example, in Chapter 3, I consider how cities are structured on the assumption that men work full-time in the centre of the city, while women maintain the suburban home, looking after children and dependants, and possibly work part-time. Farmer and Boushel (Chapter 5) look at how the management of risk by the state has been a profoundly gendered activity directed primarily at poor and disadvantaged mothers, and Land (Chapter 1) analyses the way in which the benefit system has reinforced the dependence of single mothers.

A related issue, but one which has been subject to greater attention in recent years with the influence of postmodern ideas, is the representation of gender. Here the focus is on how women, and men, are conceived in models of social policy, how different family forms are represented and the discursive practices which produce the gendered assumptions underpinning social policy. In her chapter on the reconstructions of madness in the 1990s and the role of mental health policy, Payne (Chapter 10) charts shifts in the discursive constructions of the mentally ill whereby young dangerous men have become central figures in the landscape of madness, and analyses how mental health policy has played a part in the creation of this new spectre and in the subsequent re-creation of the danger posed by this figure. Pantazis (Chapter 6) addresses the criminalization of female poverty and challenges the view that women's increased involvement in criminal activity is linked to changing gender roles, arguing that the rise in poverty among women is at least as important an explanation.

A further issue which emerges is the vexed question of the restructuring of domestic gender roles. For decades feminists have argued for greater involvement by men and fathers in the domestic sphere, particularly in child-rearing. But as others have pointed out this is a double-edged sword. First, because the domestic arena represents one site of women's power, albeit a complex one, not least because it is a site of their labour. Second, in the context of male violence towards women and children, from which they often have little protection, the concept of domestic equality is a meaningless one. Though there have been minor shifts in gendered attitudes to domestic labour and child-rearing and some signs of change among certain social groups particularly inner-city 'thirty-something' heterosexual couples, the overall statistical evidence suggests that these changes are marginal. Despite growing numbers of women in the paid labour force, women also still take the major responsibility for domestic tasks. Several chapters in this book consider these complexities. In 'Fatherhood, children and violence' (Chapter 8) Hester and Harne suggest that while incorporating fathers in the lives of children has been presented as bettering children's lives in some circumstances, at the same time it has provided a vehicle for abusive fathers to extend their power over children and their mothers. Taylor (Chapter 4), in contrast, considers gender and caring in the context of a rural community and how to develop non-sexist models of community care which meet the needs of both men and women carers.

The equality/difference debate is addressed in various ways throughout the book but is particularly central to Rees's chapter, 'Mainstreaming equality' (Chapter 9), though the emphasis here is on the equality side of the equation. Rees argues that mainstreaming is about integrating equality into all policies, programmes and actions from the earliest stage of their formulation to their implementation and review. Building equality into all policy making from the start represents, she suggests, a paradigm shift in the context of both employment, and service and product delivery. Mainstreaming has so far been focused on gender relations and the implications for other forms of inequality such as race and ethnicity have not yet been developed.

These kinds of approaches are also situated in an analysis of gender as a social construction where the body or sex falls out of the picture. Recent debates have challenged the sex/gender distinction (Gatens 1992) and the body has become a central site of feminist analysis (Bordo 1988). In Chapter 2 Doyal takes up this theme arguing for a clearer understanding of the relationship between the biological and social shaping of human beings, while at the same time recognizing that gender divisions shape the health of both men and women. On a related tack we find an argument in Doyal's and Payne's chapters for the need to develop services for women that explicitly incorporate gender awareness. The 'problem of men' is addressed in various chapters taking up the premise of the book that feminist social policy analysts have moved beyond an analysis of women to an analysis of gender. In Chapter 7, for example, Gill Hague discusses abusers' programmes which operate a curriculum, based on a gendered analysis of power and control in relationships. This shift implies looking at how traditional gendered assumptions embedded in social policy can also have damaging effects on men. There are implications here for the kinds of strategies to pursue. Within feminist pragmatic practices there has always been a tension between short- and long-term goals. For example, in Chapter 3 I refer to the feminist architects who were caught in the dilemma of whether to emphasize changes in the design of housing which enabled women in their domestic role, or whether to argue for more profound changes in the built environment. This links with arguments relating to restructuring the domestic arena mentioned earlier. It also relates to the question of what kinds of expectations we have of the 'state' and whether it is more helpful to adopt Pringle and Watson's (1990, 1992) arguments for local strategic interventions in different state arenas. In the context of persistent anti-public rhetoric and traditional familism, it seems to us important to find different ways of strategic intervention into policy discourse, debate and formulation. The diverse ways of thinking about these interventions form one of the strengths of this collection.

Finally, in an increasingly globalized world it makes less and less sense to think about social policy in a simply national context. This is for a number of reasons. On the one hand international political and economic shifts are having profound effects on national labour and housing markets and on social and cultural trends particularly as a result of migration and the resultant racial and ethnic diversity in most large cities. Households are becoming more and more diverse and resemble less and less the white patriarchal nuclear family on which the British welfare state was predicated. On the other hand, there are many areas of social policy which are affected by supra-national agencies either at the European level, as illustrated in Rees's chapter, or at the level of international agencies as shown by Doyal. For many British people who have suffered discrimination the European Court has provided the main source of redress and compensation. At the same time more progressive models of social policy and welfare reform, particularly from the Scandinavian countries, have been useful in giving us different ways of viewing and tackling old problems.

The research in this book varies in its sources. Some chapters draw on studies which are local and specific while others are written at a more general level. Similarly some of the chapters have a British focus while others adopt a more international framework. It is hoped that this collection will illustrate the diversity of current feminist methods and theories as well as reasserting the importance of analysing social policy from a gendered perspective.

With thanks to Lesley Doyal for her input and comments.

References

Barrett, M. (1980) *Women's Oppression Today: Problems in Marxist-feminist Analysis*. London: Verso.

Barrett, M. and Phillips, A. (eds) (1992) *Destabilising Theory: Contemporary Feminist Debates*. Cambridge: Polity Press.

Beveridge Report, the (1942) *Report of the Social and Allied Services Committee*, Cmd 6404. London: HMSO.

Bhavnani, K. and Coulson, M. (1986) Transforming socialist-feminism: the challenge of racism. *Feminist Review*, 23.

Bordo, S. (1988) Anorexia nervosa: psychopathology as the crystallization of culture, in I. Diamond and L. Quinby (eds) *Feminism and Foucault*. Boston MA: North Eastern University Press.

Caine, B. and Pringle, R. (eds) (1995) *Transitions: New Australian Feminisms*. Sydney: Allen & Unwin.

Coward, R. (1993) *Our Treacherous Hearts*. London: Faber & Faber.

Firestone, S. (1970) *The Dialectic of Sex: the Case for Feminist Revolution*. New York: Bantam Books.

Gatens, M. (1992) Power, bodies and difference, in M. Barrett and A. Phillips (eds) *Destabilising Theory: Contemporary Feminist Debates*. Cambridge: Polity Press.

Gibson-Graham, J.K. (1996) *The End of Capitalism (as we knew it)*. Oxford: Blackwell.

Harstock, N. (1990) Foucault on power: a theory for women? in L. Nicholson (ed.) *Feminism/Postmodernism*. London: Routledge.

Hillyard, P. and Watson, S. (1996) Postmodern social policy: a contradiction in terms? *Journal of Social Policy*, 25 (3): 321–346.

hooks, b. (1982) *Ain't I a Woman: Black Women and Feminism*. London: Pluto Press.

Lynch, L. (1984) Bureaucratuc feminisms: bosses in beige suits. *Refractory Girl*, May.

McIntosh, M. (1978) The state and the oppression of women, in A. Kuhn and A. Wolpe (eds) *Feminism and Materialism*. London: Routledge.

Mackinnon, C. (1983) Feminism, Marxism, method and the state: an agenda for theory. *Signs*, 7 (3): 515–44.

Maclean, M. and Groves, D. (1991) *Women's Issues in Social Policy*. London: Routledge.

Pateman, C. (1988) *The Sexual Contract*. Cambridge: Polity Press.

Pringle, R. (1995) Destabilising patriarchy, in B. Caine and R. Pringle (eds) *Transitions: New Australian Feminisms*. Sydney: Allen & Unwin.

Pringle, R. and Watson, S. (1990) Fathers, brothers, mates, in S. Watson (ed.) *Playing the State*. London: Verso.

Pringle, R. and Watson, S. (1992) Women's interests and the post-structuralist state, in M. Barrett and A. Phillips (eds) *Destabilising Theory: Contemporary Feminist Debates*. Cambridge: Polity Press.

Scott, J. (1990) Deconstructing equality-versus-difference, in M. Hirsch and E. Fox Keller (eds) *Conflicts in Feminism*. London and New York: Routledge.

Smart, C. (1992) The woman of legal discourses. *Social and Legal Studies: An International Journal*, (1): 29–44.

Walby, S. (1992) Post-post modernism? Theorising social complexity, in M. Barrett and A. Phillips (eds) *Destabilising Theory: Contemporary Feminist Debates*. Cambridge: Polity Press.

Walter, N. (1998) *The New Feminism*. London: Little, Brown.

Watson, S. (1990) *Playing the State: Australian Feminist Interventions*. London: Verso.

Williams, F. (1989) *Social Policy: A Critical Introduction*. Oxford: Blackwell.

Wilson, E. (1977) *Women and the Welfare State*. London: Tavistock.

Wollstonecraft, M. ([1792] 1967) *The Vindication of the Rights of Women*. New York: W.W. Norton & Co.

Yeatman, A. (1990) *Femocrats, Bureaucrats, Technocrats*. Sydney: Allen & Unwin.

The changing worlds of work and families

Hilary Land

This chapter explores shifts in family and household structures over the last 50 years. Many assumptions and ideologies underpin family policy which are neither made explicit nor fully examined for their effects. Increasingly families are recognized to be diverse, yet it is also clear that this is not such a new phenomenon as many people would have us believe. There has been a long-standing diversity among families and households, but in the past it has been more hidden and difficult to quantify.

In the last ten years there has been an increasing emphasis in family policy on biological origins and various attempts have been made to attach parental responsibilities to biological parents. Yet the social meaning of parenthood remains confused, and gaining greater and greater knowledge at the genetic level does not clarify the more important questions of how to understand either motherhood or fatherhood. With growing numbers of single mothers, governments have sought to attach women to the biological fathers of their children on the one hand, or 'encourage' them back into the labour market on the other. Not only does this not recognize the value of women's work as mothers, it also fails to recognize the complexities of women's relationships to the fathers of their children. Other reactionary and regressive trends in family policy are also evident although overall current trends in policy are contradictory. In poorer families we see attempts by the government to reimpose the male breadwinner model on the family at the same time as recognizing the costs of childcare. More generally proposals that the tax system should privilege legal marriage over cohabiting relationships are still on the agenda, but the Chancellor of the Exchequer, Gordon Brown's first Budget agreed that the level of family resources should be determined more by the presence of children than by the marital status of their parents. Through looking more specifically at the employment and benefit systems, and their gendered effects, this chapter explores some of these trends.

Families, households and labour markets in many countries have undergone profound changes since the end of the Second World War and in particular in the last 20 years. These socio-economic changes are not confined to the UK but are worldwide and are being driven by the transition to a new stage of 'global capitalism' combined with, and facilitated by, the revolution in information and communication systems. In advanced economies, following the deregulation of financial markets and the free movement of capital at the end of the 1970s, capital has moved to find cheaper labour in developing countries. As technology has replaced human labour the number of jobs in the manufacturing sector as well as in parts of the service sector (e.g. banking) has declined.

In the UK a million jobs were lost from manufacturing between 1979 and 1989 alone. Overall by the mid-1990s there were half the number of jobs in this sector compared with the late 1950s. Most of the jobs lost were full-time and were found in the traditionally male sectors: shipbuilding, steel, coal and the railways. Women however were also affected and in the mid-1990s only one in ten women's jobs in the UK was in manufacturing compared with one in three in 1960. The collapse of the textile industry, as cheap clothes were imported from the Far East, particularly affected women. However, in contrast to men, growing numbers of women, particularly in the UK, have found part-time employment in the expanding public and private service sectors.

In autumn 1997, for the first time, the official employment count in the UK enumerated more women than men active in the labour market, although men still contribute many more hours of paid work because part-time employment is still largely confined to women. (The growing number of men in part-time jobs are either young men in full-time education or older men who have taken early retirement.) It is unskilled male manual workers who have no place in this very different labour market and find themselves trapped in the de-industrialized areas of the country. During the 1980s there was a shift in the occupational structure of the employed population towards highly paid non-manual occupations and away from low paid manual occupations. The 1992 General Household Survey showed that between 1981 and 1992 while the proportion of people in semi-skilled and unskilled manual occupations fell from 32 per cent to 26 per cent, the proportion in professional and managerial occupations rose from 11 per cent to 18 per cent. In the 1960s five out of six young people left school at the minimum school leaving age (then 15) and went straight into a full-time job. Today only a minority enter full-time employment at 16, and far fewer men will experience an unbroken employment record between the end of full-time further or higher education and their early or mid-sixties. Women's employment patterns are also different from their mothers because they

Table 1.1 Historical trends in British part-time and full-time employment

Year	Full-time (000s)		Part-time* (000s)	
	Total	Of which female	Total	Of which female
1951	19,239	6,041	832	779
1961	19,794	5,698	1,999	1,851
1971	18,308	5,413	3,341	2,757
1981	16,407	5,481	4,442	3,789
1991	16,307	5,802	5,539	4,593
1995	15,348	5,728	5,890	4,780

Source: Select Committee on the European Communities 1982; Employment Committee 1990; ONS 1997(b): 109.
*Note: except for 1951, part-time work defined as working less than 30 hours per week.

will spend less time out of the labour market as full-time wives and mothers and more time in part-time paid work. See Table 1.1.

Since the early 1980s structural unemployment has been a problem not only in the UK, but all over Western Europe. For example, as the directorate general for Employment, Industrial Relations and Social Affairs of the European Communities stated in the Green Paper on Social Policy:

> There can be no doubt that the causes and consequences of high and rising unemployment in Europe represent the single most serious challenge facing member states today . . . Increased unemployment to a forecast community average of around 12% in 1994, following an already high structural unemployment level has reached the point where it is socially dangerous as well as politically and economically unacceptable.
>
> (Commission of the EU 1993: 34)

The support of unemployed people makes heavy demands on social security systems. At the same time, state revenue from social security contributions and taxes is reduced, thus putting a double pressure on public expenditure. It also makes demands on family support systems, altering patterns of dependency between the generations as well as between men and women. However, government responses to unemployment have not been uniform between countries and as will be discussed below, both recent British Conservative and Labour governments have looked to the USA and Australasia for policy models rather than to fellow members of the EU.

Family life and family structures have also changed, and there are some features of change which are shared across Europe and in other industrialized societies. An International Labour Office (ILO) report on demographic change in Europe, called appropriately *From Pyramid to*

Pillar (1989), described the radical changes in the shape of demographic structures and graphically demonstrated the extent to which a growing proportion of the population in nearly every European country, north and south, east and west, is over 65, while, as fertility has fallen, the population in younger age groups is declining. Overall, Europe has an ageing population mitigated only a little by net immigration rates over the past 30 years. If the forces behind 'Fortress' Europe succeed in constraining the movement of labour into Europe from outside, there is less likelihood that an imbalance in the age structure within the EU will be reduced by immigration, at least not legally.

This is how the ILO report summed up the characteristics of families today:

> The nuclear family is still the core. However, the parents may not have a marriage certificate or they may have two or more certificates: marriage, divorce, remarriage. At times the family may consist only of mother and child; however single parenthood tends in most cases to be a temporary phase rather than a permanent state. One child families are more common than in the past and large families are declining fast. Families with children from previous as well as present partnerships are becoming more common. At the same time, it is worth noting that class and income differences, which may not affect external characteristics of families, still have a fundamental influence on the standard of living of the family. While demographic developments have meant that the European family may well be characterised by increasing change and diversity, there is little evidence that it is characterised by crisis.
>
> (International Labour Office 1989: 51)

This picture means, among many things, that family life, like working life has become more uncertain. Fewer women can expect to find lifelong economic security by remaining faithful wives. Although at any point in time in the UK four out of five children are living with both their natural parents, a third of children are living with both parents who are not married to each other. It is estimated that at least one in four children will experience the divorce of their parents before they reach the age of 16. Fewer fathers can expect to earn a family wage and those who do are more likely to have a partner active in full-time employment. Children are more likely to be living in households with either no earners or two earning parents. Between 1979 and 1991 the proportion of children living in a family with no one in full-time employment rose from 19 per cent to 26 per cent (DSS 1993). However, children in families with one employed parent were also more likely to be poor and altogether the proportion of children in the UK growing up in poverty (defined as a household with below half the average household income) increased from one in ten to over one in three. In 1996 there were nearly 750,000 families with children claiming Family Credit, the means-tested benefit for poor working families. Nearly half were lone parents. This represents a threefold increase in ten years.

Parents must now support their children for longer as older teenagers stay on in full-time education after the compulsory school-leaving age in larger numbers. The proportion of 16–18-year-olds in full-time education doubled from 28 per cent to 56 per cent between 1981 and 1995 in response (at least in part) to their inability to find employment. (These proportions however are still low compared with the USA, Japan and many member countries in the EU.) The brief respite from financial hardship which traditionally British working-class families had experienced while their employed adult children lived at home and before they themselves become dependent on a pension, disappeared. Unemployment, like paid work and wages, is not distributed evenly among households and unemployed young people are more likely to be living in households with unemployed parents. In the current jargon there are 'work rich' households and 'work poor' households. At the same time inequalities between high earners and low earners has grown (e.g. the rates of the lowest decile to the highest decile of gross hourly earnings for women changed from 2.6 to 3.2 between 1983 and 1993).

The growth of the numbers of lone mothers in the UK and, in particular, the proportions dependent on social security benefits, has attracted much attention in the UK in the past ten years. However, it is important to note that there is evidence that women-headed households have been growing in numbers worldwide. The same economic forces which shape the structure of labour markets and wage systems also have an impact on the capacity of families and households to support their members. As Sylvia Chant concluded on the basis of her comparative study of women-headed households, drawing in particular on case studies in Mexico, Costa Rica and the Philippines:

> Women-headed households in many countries of the developed and developing world would seem to be increasing, even if the data on which rises are calculated are often wanting and need to be interpreted with caution. Global factors which might have an impact on widespread increases include economic development, the internationalisation of production and global moves towards neo-liberal strategies (under the influence of First World financial institutions), world population change, and the growing exposure of gender inequities through national and global initiatives by and for women.
>
> (Chant 1997: 87)

Chant makes a very useful distinction between 'women-maintained' households where, for example, the father may be absent because he has migrated to the city or to another country, but is remitting money home, and 'women-headed' households meaning a household detached from a man. She examines the impact that those macroeconomic forces outlined above are having on family relationships and the allocation of

resources both within and between households, as well as on arrangements for the care of children. At the same time she draws attention to
the complex political and cultural as well as economic processes involved.

Chant's study together with the work of economists such as Sylvia
Hewlett (1997) and Nancy Folbre (1994) shows how important it is to
place any detailed analysis of the changes in the worlds of family and
employment in any one country, and the policy responses to these
changes, in a broad context. In other words, for example, the search for
explanations for such trends as the growth in lone motherhood especially among never-married mothers and in the case of the UK, their heavy
reliance on state benefits in the past decade, must look beyond the
'dependency culture' identified in the 1980s by the Secretary of State,
John Moore and his successors at the Department of Social Security (see
Land 1989). This culture allegedly arose from an over-generous welfare
state which had been swept along by the tide of decadence and irrespons-
ibility let loose in the swinging sixties and boosted by the re-emergence
of the women's movement in the 1970s.

The growing diversity, inequalities and uncertainties in family and
working life raise very important questions about collective and individual responsibilities as well as about the appropriate division between
them both for personal and social welfare. The response of Conservative
governments and in the late 1990s the New Labour government has
been to attempt to rework the claims for maintenance and care which
men and women have on each other and which children have on their
mothers and fathers as well as the claims which all citizens have on the
State. An integral part of these debates has been a discussion of the
extent to which men *and* women should look first to paid employment
in order to support themselves and their children. It is no surprise that
such attempts have been controversial, for as well as trying to shift the
boundaries between the (so-called) public and private spheres, they challenge the relationship of the State to individual citizens.

The debates over the last ten years show that we have become less
certain either of the meaning of 'public' and the meaning of 'private' or
where the boundary between these spheres should be drawn. As the
social historian Michael Anderson recently wrote, 'perhaps what is new-
est of all about the modern family is the extent of moral and behavioural uncertainty which surrounds it' (Anderson 1994: 4). Certainly the
heated controversy triggered in 1993 by the implementation of the 1991
Child Support Act in Britain, concerning the support of lone parents,
shows there are deep-seated but conflicting attitudes both towards what
constitutes legitimate state intervention in these families and towards
appropriate patterns of responsibility and dependency within them. More
recently the strategy of allocating more resources towards services to
help lone mothers in paid work while withdrawing resources from those
dependent on benefit, reveals that the meaning of work and care and
the value placed on them especially if they happen outside the wages

system, are also in a state of flux. Before discussing these issues and the policy responses to these changes this chapter will describe some of the key changes in families, households and employment.

Families and households

Recent debates about the size and structure of the population in the UK have been particularly dominated by concern about the growth of lone parenthood associated with the rise in divorce and with the growth in the proportion of the population over retirement age. This has particular relevance for women because nine out of ten lone parents are lone mothers and there are twice as many women over retirement age as men. The decline in the average size of family since the 1960s and the growing proportion of women remaining childless into their thirties, some of whom may never have children, has attracted rather less attention in the UK than these trends have attracted in other European countries such as Scandinavia, France and Italy. To some commentators the growing separation of sexual activity from marriage, followed in the 1980s by the separation of parenthood from marriage as cohabitation increased, signifies the breakdown of traditional marriage and family life. While there is no question that the numbers and proportions of mothers and children living in households on their own is greater in the 1990s compared with the 1950s and 1960s, interpreting these changes must be done with care. Similarly, in discussing pensions policies it is important to look at both the economic determinants of the size of the economically active population – in particular levels of unemployment and levels of economic activity among women – and the demographic determinants, namely the size of different generations.

First, lone mothers have become more *visible* in the official statistics. For example the Finer Committee, set up by the Labour government at the end of the 1960s to examine the needs of one-parent families, found that the census underestimated the number of unmarried mothers by half, because 'never-married' adult children living with their parent(s) were counted as members of their parents' family, resulting in illegitimate grandchildren being counted as the children of their grandparents. This also accorded with practice in some cases, for history and literature provide many examples of children being brought up believing their mother was their sister and their grandmother their mother. The UK census definition of 'family' extending only to two generations also underestimated the numbers of families caring for an elderly parent. However, rather than hiding a 'problem' this fed a long-standing fear (finding expression for example in the 1834 Poor Law Commission's Report), that adult children no longer care as much as they once did for frail elderly parents.

Second, because of the greater stigma associated in former times with divorce, separation or unmarried motherhood, women were more likely than at the present time to describe themselves as married when they were not. As a result most twentieth-century UK censuses have enumerated more married women than married men. For similar reasons there was much greater pressure throughout the twentieth century until the end of the 1960s to get married if pregnant. Forty per cent of teenage brides in the 1960s were pregnant on their wedding day. However, 'shotgun' marriages, particularly those involving young brides, were more likely to end in divorce and so a proportion showed up in the statistics as divorced or separated lone mothers a decade later, by which time divorce law had been reformed and divorce was more acceptable.

In contrast the unmarried woman in the 1990s who becomes pregnant is less likely to marry although she may be cohabiting and, if she does not have an abortion, more likely to keep the child. She will be counted as a 'never-married' lone mother and her child will be illegitimate. The growing proportion of lone mothers described as 'never-married' therefore needs interpreting with caution. Kathleen Kiernan's work shows that the proportion of women having children either by decision or accident without a man has remained *constant* for the past 30 years (see Kiernan, *et al.* 1998). The conclusion that growing numbers of women are *choosing* to have children independently of men, thus challenging the very fabric of family life based on the heterosexual couple is not based as firmly on the official statistics as it would seem at first glance. In contrast to the 1950s therefore, current definitions of unmarried motherhood exaggerate what is seen to be a 'problem', perhaps because their greater numbers together with reductions in inequalities between men and women in other respects seem more threatening to the 'traditional' family.

Third, adoption is a way of avoiding lone motherhood, although not a painless one as more recent accounts of women who gave up children for adoption in the 1950s and 1960s show (see Howe *et al.* 1992). Until the end of the 1960s a significant minority of unmarried mothers, encouraged by social workers, took this route. Legal adoption only became possible in England and Wales in 1926 but informal and often clandestine adoption by childless relatives and neighbours has a long history and again, examples can be found in literature. Margaret Forster's account of the lives of her grandmother and mother in *Hidden Lives* (1995) shows how unmarried motherhood could be handled with extreme secrecy so that not even the closest relatives knew about it. Moreover, the official records revealed very little of her grandmother's story. However, the State in England and Wales has never been as willing, as is the case still in France for example, to give total anonymity to the mother of an illegitimate child. Since the mid-nineteenth century, in order to discourage abortion, and because of concern about the overall size of the birth rate, French women both married and unmarried have had the right to give birth to a child completely anonymously and to abandon it to be brought up by the State. On the other hand, the anonymity of sperm donors in the UK has been taken for granted in contrast to Sweden, for example. In the UK the legalization of abortion following the 1967 Abortion Law Reform Act and the reduction at that time in the legal discrimination between legitimate and illegitimate children are no doubt two of the reasons why the number of adoptions in the UK fell rapidly after peaking in 1968, although more liberal attitudes towards illegitimacy were also important.

During the 1970s not only were unmarried mothers more likely to keep their children but they began to leave the parental home and establish their own households, assisted first by changes in housing benefit schemes and second by the route into local authority rented housing opened up by the 1977 Housing (Homeless) Act which for the first time gave local authority housing departments the duty to house homeless families. This duty included lone parent families, for the debates about homelessness in the 1970s had taken place against the background of the 'rediscovery' of domestic violence which the women's movement had succeeded in getting on to the policy agenda. Married mothers were also leaving the marital home as divorce and separation became more common. Lone parents were therefore becoming more visible as separate households in the official statistics, but this cannot be attributed simply to demographic changes.

It is also important therefore to discuss how both families *and* households have changed. For example, in the UK, 'family' (meaning biological family) has become more important than 'household' following the Child Support Act 1991, as far as responsibility for children is concerned. Prior to 1993, marital and household status were the determinants of a woman's claims to means-tested benefits. Since then her claims depend more on active motherhood i.e. being a 'parent with care' than on either her legal relationship to the father or on her living arrangements. It is therefore important to distinguish carefully between 'family' and 'household'. As Sylvia Chant (1997: 218) points out:

> While writers on developing countries more commonly discuss 'households', those writing on households in advanced economies often work with the term 'family'. This is an interesting difference considering that a greater proportion of households in developing economies are family-based units than in the advanced regions. One possible reason why 'household' has been the preferred term in developing societies is because the members of individual residential units are often embedded within strong networks of wider family and kin and it accordingly makes little sense to confine 'family' to small domestic groups. Alternatively, people in Northern countries often have less contact with relatives beyond the immediate household or their natal families and so the concept of family becomes prioritised in a household setting. Another possibility is that 'family' becomes more relevant in contexts where there are more established social policy frameworks.

Table 1.2 Household by type of household and family in Britain (percentages)

	1961	1971	1981	1991	1995–6
One person					
Under pensionable age	4	6	8	11	13
Over pensionable age	7	12	14	16	15
Two or more unrelated adults	5	4	5	3	2
One family					
Married couple,[1] with no children	26	27	26	28	29
1–2 dependent children[2]	30	26	25	20	19
3 or more dependent children[1]	8	9	6	5	4
Non-dependent children only	10	8	8	8	6
Lone parent[1] with dependent children[2]	2	3	5	6	7
Non-dependent children only	4	4	4	4	3
Two or more families	3	1	1	1	1
All households (millions)	16.3	18.6	20.2	22.4	23.5

Source: ONS 1997(a) Table 2.3.
Notes:
1 Other individuals who were not family members may also be included.
2 Households may also include non-dependent children.

The numbers and proportions of single person adult households has grown among both younger and older members of the population. As table 2 shows, in 1971, fewer than one in five households in Britain were one person households, twenty years later this had increased to one in three. This change does not just reflect the increase in the proportion of the population over retirement age because a growing number of one person households are younger – 40% under 60 years of age in England and Wales in 1971 compared with 32% in 1971. The increase among those aged 20–40 has been the most rapid, from 10 per cent to 20 per cent over the same period. In contrast to the past, living alone among the younger age groups in England and Wales is associated with owner occupation, particularly for women. For these groups it is also an urban phenomenon associated with high rates of geographical mobility which in turn are associated with upward social mobility into professional occupational groups. As Hall and Ogden concluded from their study of one person households in England and Wales and France (a study in the ESRC Population and Household Change research programme 1995–1998):

'The continued atomisation of society into smaller and smaller households has wider social implications since their patterns of social interaction and welfare needs may well differ from those family households'.

The issues concerned do not just affect older people currently living alone and considerations of their welfare needs, but may affect the *future* obligations established *between* family members for these may be different if the transition to an independent household, at least for some groups, occurs at an earlier age. There are important differences between social classes and between income groups concerning age at leaving home, with a growing number moving away and then returning to the parental home. Moreover the housing benefit system encourages young adults to leave home if their parents are unemployed or low earners because their presence substantially reduces the amount of benefit paid. Conversely changes in the funding of higher education may result in more young people, especially working class girls, and young people from some minority ethnic groups living at home while they study.

Women and men in the labour market

Governments of both political parties until the mid 1970s were committed to maintain full employment – at least for men. Women's claims to a paid job have always been weaker than men's and attitudes and policies affecting the employment of women were and still are, complex. On the one hand the post-war social insurance and social assistance schemes followed the Beveridge Report's recommendations and were based firmly on the model of the family, which comprised a male breadwinner and a dependent wife who put her responsibilities as housewife and mother above all others (Cmd, 6404, 1942). A woman's marital, rather than employment status determined her eligibility to benefits. This model was not seriously challenged within the benefit system until the mid-1970s. Independent taxation was not introduced until 1990. Prior to that a married woman's income belonged to her husband for tax purposes. On the other hand, the marriage bar in teaching was abolished in 1944 and in the civil service in 1946. There was a shortage of labour following the end of the war and many women wanted to stay in, or return to, paid employment. In particular there was a shortage in those services associated with the expansion of the welfare state, especially the health and education services.

Government departments therefore did not have entirely consistent policies towards women's employment. For example, the Ministry of Health together with the Ministry of Labour developed strategies which included encouraging the development of part-time jobs for women with 'domestic duties'. There was ambivalence towards *mothers* taking paid employment, particularly outside the home, an ambivalence which goes back at least to the turn of the century. Prevailing wisdom among health and welfare professionals was that young children fared best with mothers who remained at home full-time and did not take even part-time employment until the children were in school. At least this was the case for married mothers; lone mothers were expected to take paid work when their children were younger. Day-care services to enable mothers to take up paid employment were therefore left to family and friends and from the 1980s onwards, to the market. Lone mothers had priority to what local authority provision there was until child abuse was redis-covered in the 1970s and local authority day nursery places were taken by children 'at risk'. Lone mothers were also more likely to be living with or near relatives who could and did provide childcare. Only a minority of lone mothers (a fifth in 1960 increasing to two-fifths in 1980) were dependent on means-tested benefits.

The post-war shortage of labour was not as temporary as was thought at first (see Ministry of Labour 1947) and should be seen in the context of a country which still had an empire and therefore a rather different position in global markets than today. In addition to the growing demand for women's labour as the welfare state became established, British involvement in the Korean War, rearmament policies and the introduction of national service for all young men in their late teens made women's labour rather less disposable than Beveridge had envis-aged. National service did not end until the late 1950s.

Women continued to be drawn into the labour market throughout the 1950s and by 1961 there were 4.4m married women in paid work, including 1.5m wives and mothers who had part-time employment. The proportion of mothers combining full-time paid employment with responsibility for preschool children declined slightly during the 1950s in contrast to the growth in those working part-time. Among mothers of school-age children the growth in employment was also largely part-time.

Health, education and welfare services continued to expand in the 1960s and the rising number of births, which peaked at nearly one million in 1964, guaranteed that demands for these services would con-tinue. Concern about shortages in nursing and teaching remained and recruitment campaigns for nurses and other health workers continued in the British West Indies and other former British colonies. At the beginning of the decade immigration was a matter of employment policy and therefore a concern of the Ministry of Labour. By the middle of the decade responsibility for controlling immigration had moved to the Home Office because limiting the number of immigrants, particularly from the new Commonwealth countries, had become an issue.

While the debates about women's employment in the 1950s and 1960s focused mainly on working *wives*, throughout the 1970s the debates encompassed working *mothers*, including lone as well as married mothers. The decade had started with the Equal Pay Act which was phased in over a period of five years between 1970 and 1975. The 1975 Sex Dis-crimination Act, while leaving untouched discrimination against women in the social security and income tax systems and in family law, did tackle discrimination against girls and women in education and training.

The Equal Opportunities Commission was established. Maternity leave and pay were introduced in the 1975 Employment Protection Act giving certain maternity leave entitlements for the first time. In other words, girls and women's claims to education, training and employment changed both in principle and in practice in the 1970s. Provided women behaved like men in the labour market they would be subject to less discrimination.

However, the majority of married mothers who combined paid employment with the care of young children did so on a part-time basis because responsibility for the care of children remained firmly with their mothers and their families. Day-care provision and full-time nursery education for preschool children grew very slowly although the subject was much more widely debated throughout the 1970s than in previous decades, not least because it was high on the women's movement agenda. It remained a controversial topic:

> The related questions of women's employment and childcare facilities raises strong emotions and it is clear that while social attitudes are changing, there is still widespread disagreement in society at large and an ambivalence in Government circles as to whether it is desirable for the mothers of young children to work outside the home.
>
> (TUC Working Party 1976: 6)

The labour market of the 1980s was very different. Unemployment rates which had remained below 2.5 per cent throughout the 1950s and 1960s increased during the 1970s, falling slightly in 1979 to 4 per cent. With the abandonment of government commitment to the maintenance of full employment, far higher levels of unemployment became acceptable in the 1980s. During this decade the unemployment rate increased rapidly reaching over 11 per cent by the mid-1980s followed by a fall until the early 1990s. After that it rose to reach double figures again in 1992 but has subsequently fallen. Official measures of unemployment have always underestimated the numbers of unemployed, particularly women, and the government deliberately and repeatedly redefined measures of unemployment throughout the 1980s (see Atkinson and Micklewright 1989). The unemployed, rather than unemployment, have been a matter of major concern for the past 20 years. In the mid-1990s concern focused increasingly on the poor employment prospects of young, unqualified men, especially those from minority ethnic groups and those living in deprived urban housing estates.

The fall in demand for their labour compared with better-qualified men *and* women reflects the further restructuring of the labour market, following the deliberate strategy of creating a more 'flexible' labour market and a deregulated wages system. In order to encourage young people into paid work, their benefits were reduced and in the case of 16- and 17-year-olds withdrawn altogether in 1988.

Policy consequences

By the end of the 1980s the majority of lone mothers were dependent on means-tested benefits and in contrast to the past and to other EU countries, the economic activity rates were lower than those of married mothers. Just as the growth of youth unemployment earlier in the decade forced the question of parental responsibility for older children onto the political agenda, the dependence of lone mothers on state support raised the question of the responsibility of fathers for their children. The 1991 Child Support Act was an attempt in the words of the then Secretary of State for the Department of Social Security, Peter Lilley, 'to reverse the inadvertent nationalisation of fatherhood' (BBC *World at One*, 23 March 1993). The determination of maintenance for lone mothers and their children was taken out of the courts and put into the hands of the new Child Support Agency. Drawing on similar policy innovations in the USA and Australia, a formula was used to calculate the amount absent parents (usually fathers) should pay. The implementation was controversial because the mother was required to name the biological father unless she had 'good cause' not to do so and he was held to be responsible for the maintenance of his children *and* their mother if she was caring for them and dependent on benefits. Moreover, no account was taken of responsibilities for stepchildren or the children of a second family; in other words 'first' families' claims for maintenance took priority over 'second' families' claims. While the development of DNA testing can identify the biological father with a level of certainty which was impossible in the past, this change of policy met enormous opposition, particularly from fathers.

Responsible fatherhood is not genetically determined as socio-biologists sometimes imply. Thus, identifying the biological father does not settle the question of who *will* or indeed, who *should* maintain the child. As the anthropologist Edmund Leach warned in the early 1970s just as reproductive technology was beginning to make big advances and shortly before the first 'test tube' baby Louise Brown was born:

> We have been modifying our traditional rules in such a way that the social status of the child comes to be defined more and more by biological rather than by legal criteria . . . Our modern society is so heavily dependent upon artificial contrivances that it might well have been expected that we would be moving into an era of intensified legal fiction whereby we could recognise all sorts of new categories of foster fathers, foster mothers, deputy parents and so on. Instead we actually seem to be moving more and more in the direction of literal biological definition. This may get us into a dilemma. The flexibility implicit in legal fictions can be very valuable but we may deprive ourselves of this flexibility if we insist on identifying legal parenthood with biological parenthood.
>
> (Leach 1970: 97)

The Child Support Agency was forced to modify the formula within months but the administrative problems resulting in unacceptably high levels of error continued. After only two years the government was forced to reconsider its strategy for reducing the cost of lone mothers to the social security system. Attention shifted away from fathers and back onto mothers. First the penalties substantially increased so they could lose 40 per cent of their benefit if they failed to name the father without 'good cause', second, their level of benefit was reduced by abolishing the one parent premium. More attention was paid to getting lone mothers off benefits by moving them into paid employment. Again the government has looked to policies in the US. It is against this background that the new Labour government's policy of 'welfare to work' must be seen. The only difference between the policies of the Labour government and their predecessors is that greater recognition is given to the need to provide childcare.

While both Conservative and Labour government policies towards lone mothers are driven by a determination to cut public expenditure on the social security system, other considerations are important. The passage of the 1996 Family Law Act was a stormy one and at times it seemed that it might not even reach the Statute book. This Act was the first time that a government had sponsored a bill regulating marriage and divorce. Previously these had been left to a private member to introduce, albeit with the tacit support of the government of the day. The controversy surrounding this Act shows that the increasing incidence of cohabitation and lone motherhood is seen as a threat to 'traditional' marriage and family life. It was argued that the tax and benefit system no longer privilege the married couple over the cohabiting couple or lone parent. The cuts in benefits to lone mothers which the new Labour government willingly inherited from their predecessors are consistent with a belief that the benefit system should not 'encourage' (or at least be seen to be encouraging) women to have children on their own. More recently in January 1998 the Law Commission published proposals to give cohabitees some of the same legal rights as married couples. A leader in *The Times* warned ministers that if they value marriage they 'should be careful not to remove every advantage that it brings'. However, *The Times* supported proposals to recognize homosexual relationships because 'they are logically the most deserving. Some gay couples live together as if married, and feel an equivalent commitment towards each other. Yet they are unable by law to finalise that commitment . . . At least heterosexual couples have the choice of marrying or not' (*The Times*, 'Happy Families', 5 January, 1998).

The 'welfare to work' programme raises other questions in addition to those concerning how responsibilities for the maintenance of children and their carers should be shared between fathers and mothers as well as between parents and the wider society. The past decade has seen a renegotiation of the claims which women have on husbands for maintenance, not least because they are more likely to have access to an income of their own in the form of earnings. However, less attention has been given to renegotiating responsibilities for caring for children between men and women. As shown above, mothers are more likely to be in paid employment even with young children than was the case in earlier decades. Increasing numbers are purchasing substitute care in the private sector, and New Labour's childcare policies will still rely heavily on the expanding private sector rather than on public provision. Pay is low and the vast majority of the workers in this sector are women. Attitudes towards, and the practice of, combining paid employment with responsibility for preschool children have changed for mothers. However, men still work their longest hours when they have children, especially young children, and their hours have increased in the 1990s. In the 1970s men overall were contributing three times as many hours of paid work as women. This has fallen to twice as many in the 1990s.

Although overall, women are contributing more hours of work in employment than previously, this does not mean men are contributing more hours of unpaid work in the home. The Family and Working Lives Survey conducted in 1994/5 found that whereas two out of three women said their working arrangements were affected by the presence of children in the household only one in six men were affected. Time-budget surveys suggest that although men are doing more domestic work and childcare than their fathers did, the increase is slow and small. In other words it is still women who take on the major responsibility for caring for children. As a result in the UK the typical mother of two children has only half the lifetime earnings of her childless sister. The greater emphasis on an earnings-related pension system will perpetuate this disadvantage into old age.

The new national childcare strategy at the time of writing is still to be revealed in detail, but if it becomes easier for women to combine paid work with the responsibilities for children the depleting effect on their earnings should decline. However the focus in 1998 is to get *lone* mothers back into employment, and by insisting that they ought to take paid employment and describing claimants as 'passive' and 'dependent', caring when it takes place unpaid in the home is devalued. Indeed it is rendered invisible. At least in the post-war Beveridge model the work of wives and mothers was recognized as 'vital' to the nation's future. It is not yet clear what the pay and conditions of the new childcare workers are going to be. Some will be young people trained under the 'New Deal' for the unemployed, others will be lone mothers in the 'welfare to work' programme. However, the minimum wage may not apply to the under 25-year-olds so this expansion in the childcare labour force already numbering half a million workers may not raise childcare workers from their position among the lowest paid.

Women's paid and unpaid work as carers is poorly recognized. Children are almost invisible in the debates about childcare. There will be no subsidy for children looked after in their own homes or cared for by their mother or other relatives, because the childcare tax credit can only be used for formal *registered* day care. The provision of day care is presented as a means to an end: to get mothers back into paid work. When children's needs are discussed the focus is largely on 'education' which will continue to be provided free for 4-year-olds, while 'care' must be paid for. The false dichotomy between the care and education of under fives, present in the structures of government at both the local and central government level, still persists.

Patterns of dependency between young and old and men and women are changing and are different from the early post-war years in the UK, although some of the differences are not as great as they appear at first sight. There are continuities as well as discontinuities. The values placed on 'work' and 'care' are still determined by who does them and where they are located. 'Work' is a gendered construct and the rewards of activities which take place within the home and family are less than those which take place in the public arena. Women are more visible in the world of paid employment but the current debates about the future of the welfare state render their contribution as wives and mothers to their families and to the wider society invisible. Women and children have much to lose if the meaning of social citizenship is further devalued in these debates.

References

Anderson, M. (1994) The family in an historical context. Paper presented at JRF seminar, *'Parents and Children'*, February 1994.

Atkinson, A.B. and Micklewright, J. (1989) Turning the screw, in Dilnot, A. (ed.) *The Economics of Social Security*. Oxford: Oxford University Press.

Beveridge, W.H. (1942) *Report on Social Insurance and Allied Services* (the Beveridge Report), Cmd 6404. London: HMSO.

Central Statistical Office (1993) *General Household Survey 1992*. London: HMSO.

Chant, S. (1997) *Women-Headed Households*. London: Routledge.

Commission of the EU (1993) *Green Paper on Social Policy*. Brussels: EU.

DSS (Department of Social Security) (1993) *Low Income Households 1979–1990/91*. London: HMSO.

Folbre, N. (1994) *Who Pays for the Kids?* London: Routledge.

Forster, M. (1995) *Hidden Lives*. London: Viking.

HC 122-ii (1990/1) Employment Committee, *Part-Time Work*, Vol. 2. London: HMSO.

HL 216 (1981/2) Select Committee on the European Communities, *Voluntary Part-Time Work*. London: HMSO.

Hall, R. and Ogden, P. (1997) One person households in England and Wales and France, in *Research Results No. 7 ESRC Programme an Population and Household Change*. Swindon: ESRC.

Hewlett, S. (1997) *Children in Rich Countries*. Geneva: UNESCO.

Holterman, S. (1995) *All Our Futures*. Barking: Barnardos.

Howe, D., Sawbridge, P. and Hinings, D. (1992) *Half a Million Women*. London: Penguin.

International Labour Office (ILO) (1989) From Pyramid to Pillar. Geneva: ILO.

Kiernan, K., Land, H. and Lewis, J. (1998) *Lone Motherhood in Twentieth-Century Britain*. Oxford: Oxford University Press.

Land, H. (1989) The construction of dependence, in H. Glennerster, J. Lewis, and D. Piachaud (eds) *Goals of Social Policy*. London: Unwin.

Leach, E. (1970) in K. Elliott (ed.) Ciba Foundation symposium, *The Family and its Future*. London: Churchill.

Ministry of Labour (1947) *Economic Survey 1947*, Cmd 7046. London: HMSO.

Office of National Statistics (1997a) *Social Trends 27*. London: Stationery Office.

Office of National Statistics (1997b) *Labour Market Trends, March*. London: Stationery Office.

TUC Working Party (1976) *Day Care for the Under-Fives*. London. TUC.

2

Sex, gender and health: a new approach

Lesley Doyal

Differences between men and women are now beginning to receive greater attention in the planning of public services. This has been especially apparent in the health sector with women around the world drawing attention both to the specificity of their particular health needs and also to the discrimination they often experience in their medical encounters. These are important concerns with immediate practical implications for women's well-being. However a more theoretical analysis is also emerging which has wider political and theoretical significance for feminist thinking. In this chapter we will be considering two issues in particular that emerge from these deliberations. The first is the need for a clearer understanding of the relationship between the biological and the social in the shaping of human well-being and the second is the recognition that gender divisions shape the health of men as well as that of women.

The relationship between the social and the biological – between sex and gender – has been a central theme in feminist debates for many years. Not surprisingly perhaps, the emphasis has increasingly been on the social with some writers arguing that biology itself is of very little value in explaining the differences between 'maleness' and 'femaleness'. It is certainly clear that biology is socially constructed in a whole variety of ways and that we can never treat it unproblematically. But at the same time, we cannot afford to ignore the material reality of biology as a fundamental determinant of well-being. Millions of women (and men) around the world still suffer from avoidable sickness, disability and early death and, as we shall see, both biological and social factors play a central part in this.

Feminist debate over the past few years has shifted from what has been called a 'women and' to a 'gender' approach – to an exploration of the dynamics of the relations between men and women. For the most part this has involved the uncovering of gender inequalities that clearly damage women's well-being. However, analysis of this kind has also led to the recognition that despite their overall dominance, the form of existing gender relations can sometimes be hazardous for men too (Sabo and Gordon 1993). For those involved in feminist health advocacy this can raise difficult questions which have yet to be fully discussed. This chapter will spell out some of these concerns in more detail through an account of current debates on the relationship between sex, gender and health, returning at the end to a brief discussion of their wider political significance.

Men, women and well-being: historical trends and contemporary patterns

Patterns of health and illness in men and women show marked differences. Most obviously, women as a group tend to have longer life expectancy than men in the same socio-economic circumstances as themselves. Yet despite their greater longevity women in most communities report more illness and distress than men (Blaxter 1990; Rodin and Ickovics 1990; US National Institutes of Health 1992; Rahman *et al.* 1994). The precise details of this excess in female morbidity and the factors that lie behind it will vary in different social groups but the broad picture is one where women's lives seem to be less healthy than those of men (Macintyre *et al.* 1996). The explanation for this apparent paradox lies in the complex relationship between biological and social influences in the determination of human health and illness.

Part of women's advantage in relation to life expectancy is biological in origin. Far from being the 'weaker sex' they seem to be more robust than men at all ages (Waldron 1986). In all societies significantly more male foetuses are spontaneously aborted or stillborn and in most societies this pattern of excess male mortality continues to be marked during the first six months of life (Hassold *et al.* 1983). The reasons for this greater 'robustness' of girl babies need further investigation but they seem to include sex differences in chromosomal structures and possibly a slower maturing of boys' lungs due to the effects of testosterone (Waldron 1986). In adult life too, women may have a biological advantage at least until menopause as endogenous hormones protect them from ischaemic heart disease.

Sex differences in inherent susceptibilities and in immunities to particular pathogens are just beginning to be explored and it is likely that women will be found to be more vulnerable than men to particular diseases. We know for instance that they are more likely to suffer (and die) from osteoporosis, diabetes, hypertension, arthritis and most immune disorders, and biological factors are likely to play some part in this. But overall, their innate constitution appears to give women an advantage over men, at least in relation to life expectancy. When this female potential for greater longevity is not realized it is an indication of serious health hazards in their immediate environment.

Women have not always lived longer than men. In Europe and America the female advantage over males first became apparent in the latter part of the nineteenth century as the life expectancy of both sexes increased (Hart 1988). This gap between the sexes has continued to widen ever since with the size of the female advantage being proportional to the life expectancy of the population as a whole. Thus in most of the developed countries the gap is now about 6.5 years while in Latin America and the Caribbean it is about 5.0 years, in Africa 3.5 years and in Asia about 3.0 years (United Nations 1991). Only in a few countries in Asia do women have a shorter life expectancy than men.

European experience suggests that the gap between male and female life expectancy grew as economic development and social change removed two of the major risks to women's health. As food became more widely available most women were assured of adequate diets. This improved nutrition contributed to a reduction in female mortality from infectious diseases such as tuberculosis which had previously affected them disproportionately. At the same time the introduction of new birth control techniques alongside changing values gave women greater control over family size while general improvements in living standards and the introduction of maternity services led to a significant reduction in maternal mortality rates. Thus a range of social factors combined to enhance women's inherent biological advantage.

Even before these female hazards began to decline, changes in the gender division of labour meant that men were taking on new risks (Hart 1988). The emergence of the male 'breadwinner' in industrial economies required men to take on life-threatening jobs in much greater numbers than women. As a result male deaths from occupational causes have historically been higher than those among females and that pattern continues today (Waldron 1995). At the same time, men's increased access to resources and their growing freedom from religious and other constraints led many to take up potentially dangerous pursuits including the consumption of a number of dangerous substances (Waldron 1995). Increasingly these new habits came to be defined as inherently 'masculine' pursuits that had to be pursued by those who wanted to be regarded by their peers as 'real' men (Kimmel and Messner 1993).

While these defining characteristics of masculinity vary in different cultures there are few societies in which risk-taking of various kinds does not play a significant part (Pleck and Sonenstein 1991; Canaan 1996). In most parts of the world young men now run a much greater risk than young women of dying from accidents and violence. This includes large numbers of deaths in motor vehicles, often with alcohol involved. Later in life the greater numbers of premature deaths among males from heart disease reflect not only their greater biological vulnerability but also what have traditionally been higher rates of smoking. Smoking, along with men's greater exposure to occupational carcinogens is also responsible for the much higher numbers of male deaths from lung cancer. According to one estimate, 50 per cent of the entire sex differential in life expectancy in the United States and Sweden today can be attributed to (past) gender differences in smoking patterns (Waldron 1986).

It would appear therefore, that as many societies have undergone economic and industrial development, a variety of social and cultural factors have combined to allow women's inherent biological advantage to emerge. The hazards of infectious diseases and the perils of childbearing have been reduced while certain risks associated with masculinity have increased, giving women longer – but not necessarily healthier – lives than men. These processes continue to be evident today but progress towards improved life expectancy for women differs markedly between societies. In some of the richest countries in the world the gap between male and female life expectancy is now extremely wide, although it may even be starting to narrow again as the consequences of increased female smoking rates become apparent. However, in other countries the picture is very different with gender discrimination continuing to prevent women from realizing their potential for greater longevity.

In Bangladesh, for example, men outlive women, while in India and Pakistan the two sexes have almost equal life expectancy (United Nations 1991). In these societies there is an excess of female deaths both in childhood and in the childbearing years and most can be attributed to material and cultural discrimination against girls and women (UNICEF 1990; WHO 1992). In some populations this has reached the point where the ratio between men and women has become unbalanced. In India for instance the sex ratio fell from 972 women per thousand men in 1901 to 935 per thousand in 1981 while the ratio of women to men was increasing in most other parts of the world (Sen 1990). These are societies in which the biological advantage of the majority of women is entirely cancelled out by their social disadvantage, offering a sharp reminder that economic development alone will not necessarily allow women greater opportunity to flourish.

Even when women's potential for greater longevity is realized, this rarely results in them being healthier than men during their lifetime. Again, the reasons for this are partly biological, but social influences also play a major role. Most research on gender differences in health and illness have been carried out in the developed countries and the pattern is a consistent one. Women's own assessment of their health is worse than that of men. In the United States for example, women are 25 per cent more likely than men to report that their activities are restricted by health problems and they are bedridden for 35 per cent more days than men because of acute conditions (US National Institutes of Health 1992).

In community surveys women also report twice as much anxiety and depression as men (Paykel 1991; Desjarlais *et al.* 1995). Though data on female morbidity in the developing countries is extremely sparse, a roughly similar pattern emerges (Rahman *et al.* 1994).

These very broad gender differences in self-reported illness are obviously difficult to interpret. The patterns themselves may vary slightly between age groups and across societies as may the different factors causing them (Macintyre *et al.* 1996). To some extent they may simply reflect gender differences in illness behaviour with males less willing than females to admit weakness or distress. However, most commentators agree that in a wide range of social groups women experience higher levels of illness and disability than men. The reasons for this are complex but we can identify three contributory factors.

First, women's greater longevity is itself a cause of their higher rates of morbidity. As we have seen this has both social and biological dimensions. Deteriorating health is a frequent though not an inevitable part of the ageing process for both sexes and women make up the majority of elderly people in the world, especially the 'old, old' (WHO 1996). Moreover, the ageing process itself is a highly gendered one and the experience differs for men and women in a number of ways. Older women are biologically more susceptible than men to certain disabling diseases including arthritis, diabetes, osteoporosis and Alzheimer's disease. Because of inequalities in income and wealth in earlier life, older women are also likely to have fewer material resources at their disposal and are less likely than men to receive assistance from relatives and friends (WHO 1996).

Second, women are more likely than men to suffer health problems connected with their reproductive systems. Throughout their lifetime, both men and women are at risk from sex-specific diseases. For example, only women need screening for cancer of the cervix, and breast cancer is almost entirely a female problem while only men can develop prostate cancer. Overall however, women bear a heavier burden of reproductive health problems than men and this vulnerability is exacerbated during their childbearing years.

Women's capacity to conceive and bear children brings them into the arena of the healthcare system more often than men. Very often they are perfectly healthy and are either seeking access to fertility control services or support during a normal pregnancy. However these 'natural' processes will sometimes go wrong causing problems that require expert care. Though these difficulties take the form of biological disorders, social factors often play a major part in causing them with gender discrimination in nutrition, heathcare and social support all heightening women's vulnerability during the reproductive process.

Third, studies from many parts of the world show that women are more likely than men to report symptoms of mental distress (Desjarlais *et al.* 1995). At most stages in the life cycle, women report higher levels of anxiety and depression than men and, in the developed countries at least, they are more likely to receive treatment for these conditions. Men, on the other hand are more likely to suffer from schizophrenia and other serious psychoses and are more likely to commit suicide (Desjarlais *et al.* 1995).

Attempts to explain these differences in terms of biology have met with little success and answers are increasingly being sought in the daily lives of those who become mentally ill. For instance, the increasing rates of suicide among young men in many of the developed countries have been linked with rising rates of unemployment and a loss of identity and sense of self-respect (Charlton *et al.* 1993; Aggleton 1995). Similarly the higher rates of anxiety and depression found among women in so many parts of the world have been linked on the one hand to the stresses and strains of daily life, especially in conditions of poverty, and on the other to the gender socialization that leads so many women to put little value on themselves and their potential (Desjarlais *et al.* 1995).

Gender and risk: three case studies

We have seen that being 'male' or being 'female' has a major effect on an individual's health and well-being. The combination of their biological sex and the gendered nature of their cultural, economic and social lives will put them at risk of developing some health problems while protecting them from others. Furthermore, the subsequent effect of these problems on the individuals concerned will also be influenced by both their sex and their gender. The 'natural' course of a disease may be different in men and women, men and women themselves often respond differently to illness, while the wider society may respond differently to sick males and sick females. These are complex processes that are not easy to disentangle but three case studies will be used here to illustrate them.

Tropical infectious diseases

Worldwide, the so-called tropical diseases continue to be major causes of disability and death, causing between a half and a third of all deaths among young adults in sub-Saharan Africa (Howson *et al.* 1996). Though they are closely linked with certain climatic conditions they are also diseases of poverty found almost entirely in the least developed countries. Malaria causes the most damage with around 270m people infected worldwide and about 110 clinical cases identified annually (WHO/TDR 1991). Schistosomiasis is prevalent in more than 76 countries with 200 million individuals affected each year and around 200,000 deaths (WHO/ TDR 1991). Leprosy, filiariasis (onchocerciasis and elephantiasis), trypano-somiases (African sleeping sickness and Chagas disease), Leishmaniasis and trachoma also cause extensive morbidity and mortality in tropical countries.

Any differences between male and female prevalence rates are difficult to measure since cases in women are more likely be undetected due to their less frequent use of malaria clinics and other health services (Vlassoff and Bonilla 1994). However, there appear to be roughly equal numbers of men and women or a slight predominance of males among those affected (Vlassoff and Bonilla 1994; Howson *et al.* 1996). Despite these similarities in incidence there are significant differences between the sexes in both the causes and the impact of tropical diseases.

Inherent biological factors can affect both susceptibility and immunity to these diseases and these will vary between the sexes. At the same time, gender differences in patterns of behaviour and in access to resources will influence both the degree of exposure to the relevant vectors and also the options available to those who become infected (Manderson *et al.* 1993; Rathgeber and Vlassoff 1993). There is now considerable evidence to show that since women are generally the poorest and most disadvantaged in many of the countries where tropical diseases are prevalent, they are also likely to be the group most severely affected by them (Vlassoff and Bonilla 1994).

Until recently researchers had paid very little attention to either sex or gender issues in the field of tropical diseases. If differences between males and females were considered at all, the focus was very clearly on women's reproductive lives, assessing the effects of tropical diseases on fertility and pregnancy outcomes (Manderson *et al.* 1993). Few studies had explored either the impact of wider biological variations between the sexes or the influence of gender inequalities on the incidence or outcomes of infection. However, this gap is now beginning to be filled due in large part to the continuing efforts of the Special Programme for Research and Training in Tropical Diseases (TDR) at the World Health Organization (WHO).

Looking first at the biological dimension, in the case of malaria it appears that men are inherently more vulnerable to the disease than women. However women's immunity is somehow compromised during pregnancy, making them more likely to catch the disease and also worsening its effects. These sex differences in vulnerability and their variability with women's reproductive status have received little attention from researchers despite the fact that malaria is one of the most important causes of death in pregnant women in endemic areas. Further work is urgently needed to clarify the particular issues relating to malaria as well as the more general question of sex differences in susceptibility to a range of infectious diseases including measles and tuberculosis (Hudelson 1996).

Moving on to social or gender influences, it is clear that differences in the daily lives of women and men lead to differential exposure to disease vectors and hence to varying degrees of risk of contracting tropical diseases. Research thus far has concentrated mainly on the greater exposure of males to these vectors through their more active participation in the public arena including their higher rates of paid employment. However, more recent findings are now highlighting women's domestic labours as potential sources of exposure along with their increasing involvement in work previously done by men (Michelson 1993).

Some cultural practices do seem to protect women. Those who remain in seclusion for instance are less likely to be exposed to mosquitoes and therefore less likely to contract malaria (Reuben 1993). Women's more extensive clothing can also have protective effects. However, domestic labour itself may increase exposure to other vectors (Vlassoff and Bonilla 1994). A recent review of studies from a number of African countries suggested that the prevalence of schistosomiasis peaks in adolescent girls around the age of 15 when they become fully involved in water-related domestic work such as agricultural tasks and clothes washing (Sims 1994). While the rate in males drops after late adolescence that of females remains stable, reflecting the fact that men grow out of playing around water but women's duties require continued exposure (Michelson 1993). Care of dependants too may increase women's risk of contracting particular diseases. The excess of trachoma among females has been linked to their greater involvement with children who bring the disease home from school (Howson *et al.* 1996).

As well as affecting exposure to disease vectors, gender divisions are also important in understanding the effects of tropical illnesses. There is considerable evidence to show that women are often constrained in their use of the appropriate health services by lack of transport, by inadequate resources or even by their husband's refusal to grant permission (Parker 1992). The social interpretation of particular diseases may also be important. In the case of disfiguring problems such as leprosy, for instance, women may be especially reluctant to expose themselves to healthcare providers, fearing subsequent stigmatization (Duncan 1993; Ulrich *et al.* 1993). Similarly, some cultures have a double standard equating schistosomiasis with immoral sexual behaviour in women but with virility in men (Sims 1994). These gender differences in illness behaviour and in societal responses to male and female patients mean that the progress of tropical diseases can sometimes be speeded up in women especially those with the least resources and the lowest levels of support.

Sexually transmitted diseases and HIV/AIDS

Around the world, sexually transmitted diseases continue to be a major cause of distress, disability and sometimes death for both sexes (Dixon-Mueller and Wasserheit 1991; Germain *et al.* 1992). HIV/AIDS in particular is continuing to spread, killing millions of men and women in the prime of life. Current estimates suggest that around 30m adults and more than a million children are now living with the HIV virus or with full-blown AIDS (UNAIDS 1998). This pandemic is concentrated in the poorest parts of the world with around one-third of those who are HIV positive living in sub-Saharan Africa.

Though both sexes are affected, AIDS is becoming an increasingly female affair (Berer and Ray 1993). In the initial stages, few women were among those directly affected but this pattern has changed dramatically. Heterosexual transmission is now dominant in many parts of the world and recent figures suggest that over 40 per cent of those who died from AIDS in 1997 were female (UNAIDS 1998). In the United States HIV infection has now supplanted heart disease as the third major killer of women aged 25 to 44, following cancer and unintentional injuries (Zierler and Krieger 1997: 402). This increase in the numbers of HIV-positive women reflects their greater biological vulnerability to the disease. However it is also a consequence of the social construction of male and female sexuality as well as the profound inequalities that continue to characterize many heterosexual relationships (du Guerney and Sjoberg 1993; Zierler and Krieger 1997).

It is now clear that women are inherently at greater risk than men of contracting HIV and other sexually transmitted pathogens from a single act of intercourse with an infected partner. This is because in females a larger area of surface mucosa is exposed to a greater concentration of pathogens for a longer period of time. This high level of risk will be enhanced still further in the presence of other sexually transmitted diseases and these often remain undetected in women for longer periods. Thus women are biologically more vulnerable than men to infection from HIV during a potentially dangerous sexual encounter. This biological vulnerability is too often reinforced by socially constructed constraints on their ability to protect themselves.

Heterosexual encounters are not simply natural and instinctive events. They are socially shaped with certain modes of behaviour seen as appropriate for each partner. Though the precise pattern will vary between societies, in most the male is defined as the dominant actor. As a result, men are expected to be the initiators, to be powerful and to be risk-takers. Some men will find it difficult to conform to this stereotype of masculinity and may themselves feel damaged by their failure to match up to expectations (Segal 1990). Others will conform but as a result may put themselves and their partners at risk through failing to practise safer sex (Ringheim 1993; *Reproductive Health Matters* 1986).

Not surprisingly, many women find the heterosexual relationship a difficult one in which to negotiate a strategy for their own safety. In many societies sex continues to be defined primarily in terms of male desire with women the relatively passive recipients of male passions (Richgels 1992; Gavey 1993). Under these circumstances women may find it difficult to articulate their own needs and desires and their own pleasure may be of little concern (Holland *et al.* 1990; Weeks *et al.* 1996). They will find it difficult to assert their wish for safer sex, for their partner's fidelity or for no sex at all and as a result their own health and that of others may be put at grave risk. This applies in particular to very young women who are often sought out by older men because of their presumed passivity and freedom from infection (Bassett and Mhloyi 1991; DeBruin 1992).

Cultural pressures of this kind are reinforced by gender inequalities in income and wealth. For many women, their economic and social security – sometimes even their very survival – is dependent on the support of a male partner (Worth 1989; Seidel 1993). Sexual intercourse done in the way he desires may well be the price that has to be paid for that continuing support. In some instances this bargain will be explicit as social pressures in many parts of the world push women towards selling sex for subsistence (Ford and Koetsawang 1991; Jochelson et al. 1991; Panos Institute 1992). In other situations it may only be implicit but the fear of abandonment can be a powerful force especially in those societies where few roles exist for a woman outside marriage and motherhood.

As well as economic and social insecurity many women also have to face the threat of physical violence if they are not sufficiently responsive to a partner's desires. Under these circumstances many will prefer to risk unsafe sex in the face of more immediate threats to their well-being. Thus women's sexual behaviour is rarely spontaneous. It is the outcome of complex interpersonal negotiations in which the social constraints of gender inequality play a key role. Not surprisingly, it is often the poorest women who have the fewest choices, run the most frequent risks and are most likely to become infected (Zierler and Krieger 1997).

If a woman does become infected with HIV or with any sexually transmitted disease, gender inequalities may affect the progression of the illness and possibly her survival chances. In those parts of the world where AIDS is commonest, healthcare budgets are often so small that neither sex can expect sophisticated treatment. However, funds are still spent disproportionately on men (Seidel 1993). Even in the United States where resources are more abundant there appears to be a gender bias in their allocation (Kurth 1993). Moreover, women have often been excluded from clinical trials even when this represented their only hope for survival (Denenberg 1990; Korvick 1993).

This exclusion of women from many research studies has had the additional effect of prolonging the male bias in research into the disease, so that key questions concerning biological differences in male and female experiences of AIDS remain unanswered (Kurth 1993; WHO 1990; Anastos and Vermund 1993). Researchers are beginning to address this lack of information but it still affects some women's ability to get an accurate prognosis and may exacerbate the uncertainties they face in making choices about their reproductive future. In the final analysis the combination of unequal access to care and the gender gap in medical knowledge contributes to a situation where women in both rich countries and poor countries have a shorter life expectancy than men after a diagnosis of AIDS (Richie 1990; Anastos and Vermund 1993; DeBruin 1994).

Injuries and violence

Both intentional and unintentional injuries are among the major causes of morbidity and mortality for men and women at all ages and across all societies. Again, precise figures are difficult to estimate but we know that in the developed countries they account for more deaths in people aged 1–44 than all infectious diseases combined. Even in developing countries they are usually among the top five causes of death at all ages (Howson *et al.* 1996). Both unintentional and intentional injuries are more common among men.

Starting with unintentional injuries, we have already seen that men are more likely than women to die in car accidents or to suffer death or disability as a result of occupational hazards. The latter reflects their historical role as the main economic supporters of their households as well as their more frequent employment in the most dangerous industries. Though women have lower rates of unintentional injuries overall, their domestic responsibilities mean that they are more likely than men to suffer injuries at home. These have so far received little attention but there is growing evidence that occupational injuries may be as real here as they are in more conventional workplaces.

As noted above, intentional injuries are also more common among men, with much of this violence being directly connected to what is defined as 'masculine' behaviour, to risk-taking, to aggression and to the consumption of drugs and alcohol (Staples 1995). In the inner cities in the United States for example, young black males have been referred to as an endangered species because they are the only group in the population with a life expectancy that is actually declining (Gibbs 1988). However it is not just themselves that men can damage through this type of behaviour. Certain types of intentional injury are more common among women but are perpetrated by men and these lie at the heart of the debate about gender inequalities.

All acts of violence are 'gendered' irrespective of whether the victim is male or female. In general those who commit the violence are male. Both sexes can be the victims of violence but men and women are likely to experience the attack in distinct ways: they are likely to have a different relationship to the perpetrator and the type of harm inflicted is likely to reflect the sex of the person being attacked. When women are the objects of the attack, the perpetrator may well be motivated directly by the desire to demonstrate his own masculinity and enforce his (male) power. This has led many experts to adopt the term 'gender violence' to describe these intentional injuries to women.

Reliable, epidemiological data on the extent of these injuries are sparse, particularly in the developing countries. Not surprisingly women are often extremely reluctant to report attacks and those who do so may not be believed. However, some progress has been made in recent years in estimating the scope of the problem. A recent review of evidence from

40 of the best population-based studies suggested that between 25 and 50 per cent of women around the world report being the victims of physical abuse by men at some point in their lives (Heise *et al.* 1994). Estimates from the World Bank suggest that rape and domestic violence together account for 5 per cent of the total disease burden for women in the developing countries and 19 per cent in the developed countries (World Bank 1993).

This violence is more common in some communities than in others but there are none in which women can feel entirely safe (Brown 1992). In most, women appear to be at greatest risk from intimate male partners or other men that they know and the violence happens most frequently in the 'haven' of the family. The damaging effects on women's well-being can be extremely pervasive. A physical battering may include pushing, clubbing, stabbing or shooting. The injuries inflicted may be severe and for some women will be fatal. If the attack also includes rape then it may lead to unwanted pregnancy, gynaecological problems or a range of sexually transmitted diseases.

As well as causing physical damage, gender violence can also lead to psychological distress and trauma with the resulting distress often lasting a lifetime. Those who are sexually abused as young girls may be especially damaged and some are never able to make a full recovery (Browne and Finkelhor 1986; de Chesney 1989). Women who have been abused are often debilitated by anxiety about the next attack and many suffer post-traumatic stress disorder (Koss 1990). They have increased rates of depression and substance abuse and some see suicide as the only way out (Andrews and Brown 1988; Plichta 1992). A recent study in the United States found that between 30 and 40 per cent of all battered women attempted to kill themselves at some point in their lives (Stark and Flitcraft 1991: 123).

Emerging evidence of the high rates of intentional injuries imposed on women has put them high on the agenda of women's health advocates. However, successful prevention requires a much clearer understanding of the reasons behind these injuries. Violence is an overwhelmingly male pursuit but it is unclear whether this is the result of biology, social conditioning or a combination of these. The answer to this question is still the subject of considerable debate, but there is now a growing consensus that male violence is neither an entirely biological phenom- enon nor solely a product of culture (Heise *et al.* 1994). Hence the greater propensity of some (but not all) men to commit acts of violence may not be immutable and is potentially reducible through community and/or individual interventions.

These case studies have explored the complex relationship between sex and gender in the patterning of health problems among women and men. They have identified both biological and social influences on well-being and identified some of the constraints imposed by gender stereotyping on each sex. However, it has been evident throughout the analysis that despite their (usually) greater longevity it is women who are most disadvantaged by current patterns of social organization. They are less valued than men, have less access to a range of resources and less capacity to realize their potential for health. At the same time, the biological characteristics associated with their reproductive capacities give them particular needs additional to those of men. The next section explores the implications of these issues for women by examining the impact of their daily lives on their health. It describes their roles in both biological and social reproduction, in domestic labour, childbearing and waged work and explores the cumulative effects of these different activities on their well-being.

The impact of daily life on women's well-being

Around the world, the central focus of most women's existence is their responsibility for home, family and household labour: for the care of others. The gender division of labour locates them firmly within the domestic arena and this is a continuing thread across the life cycle. In the developed countries, women are responsible for what is traditionally referred to as 'housework'. In other parts of the world they may also have to grow food as well as acquiring fuel, water and other physical necessities. Any attempt to make sense of the social dimensions of health and illness in women must therefore include a systematic analysis of the impact of domestic labour on their well-being (Doyal 1995, Ch. 2).

Houses in poor condition affect the health of all their inhabitants but women are most at risk. For them a home is not just a shelter. It is also a workplace, and damp and dilapidated houses require extra labour to keep clean as well as causing increased levels of asthma, respiratory disease and chest problems (McCarthy et al. 1985; Hyndman 1990). Looking after a home and its inhabitants can bring women into contact with a range of hazardous chemicals including bleaches and detergents that are largely unregulated (Dowie et al. 1982; Rosenberg 1984). Rural women may also be at risk from agrochemicals used or stored close to the house. Domestic fuels used for cooking can be major sources of pollution, contributing to the very high levels of respiratory disease found among women in some of the world's poorest countries (WHO 1984; Chen et al. 1990; Mishra et al. 1990; Behera et al. 1991; Grobbelaar and Bateman 1991; Norboo et al. 1991; Sims 1994, Section 4).

As well as exposing women to chemical hazards domestic work itself may be damaging to health. The labour can be extremely hard, requiring intense effort sometimes in extremely difficult conditions and often during pregnancy (Kishwar 1984; Cecelski 1987; Ferro-Luzzi 1990; Kabeer 1991; Lado 1992). Those women engaged in subsistence agriculture, for example, may have to work very long hours in severe heat with little food or water to sustain them while further domestic labours await their return. In some cases their household responsibilities also require women to carry heavy loads of fuel and water that would not be permitted for either sex in countries with occupational health and safety legislation (Chatterjee 1991; Rodda 1991).

The nature of women's domestic lives may also be dangerous for their mental health. A considerable body of evidence from the developed countries indicates that depression is an occupational hazard among the dwindling numbers of women who stay home alone to look after small children (Brown and Harris 1978). In community surveys many full-time 'housewives' and carers report feelings of emptiness, sadness and worthlessness. Though research is sparse, it is increasingly evident that in other cultures too, women's domestic lives are often the cause of considerable anxiety and depression (Davis and Guarnaccia 1989; Chakraborty 1990; Malik et al. 1992; Desjarlais et al. 1995, Ch. 8). The reasons for this are complex but include the low status awarded to domestic work, as well as isolation and lack of economic and social support (Reichenheim and Harpham 1991; Belle 1990; Dennerstein et al. 1993; Desjarlais et al. 1995, Ch. 8).

As well as being the main workplace for many women, their home is also the place from which they receive many of the material and emotional resources needed to sustain health. Yet there is substantial evidence to show that despite the 'caring' image of the family, items such as medical care and food may not be distributed according to need (Dwyer and Bruce 1988; Sen 1988; Sundari Ravindran 1986; Sims 1994, Section II; Kurz and Prather 1995). In many societies, cultural norms dictate that males in the household are entitled to the majority share of income and wealth as well as higher status and greater decision-making power.

These inequalities in influence and power within the household can also affect women's reproductive lives, constraining their ability to make fully informed choices about sexual practices or about fertility control. All societies operate with a set of moral beliefs about the nature of men and women, the purposes of sexual activity and the meaning of parenthood and family life (Caplan 1982; Snitow et al. 1984; Vance 1984; Segal 1987). As a result, many women find themselves locked into complex webs of duties and obligation which may severely limit their ability to make autonomous decisions that are central to their future lives.

For some this will mean parenting that has not been actively chosen and possibly a dangerously high number of pregnancies. Others may be forced to take the risk of an unsafe termination. At least 200,000 women die each year as a result of induced abortion, not because of technical problems but because others have decided it is not appropriate for them to end their own pregnancy (Henshaw 1990; Jacobson 1990). If contraceptives are available women may have little choice about methods, forcing them to make complex trade-offs between the risks of the

However, alterations in power relations, and in traditional notions of masculinity and power, are likely to have more contradictory effects on men's health. On the one hand many lives would be saved if men stopped killing each other or killing themselves through indulgence in what are defined as 'masculine' activities. On the other hand, loss of control over material resources might be damaging to their health just as loss of status and of control over women might have a negative effect on their mental health. Women in many different settings have developed a clear and cogent analysis of the impact of gender relations on their health and are campaigning for change. For men the analysis is just beginning and the resulting politics can only be guessed at. It remains to be seen therefore, whether the majority of men will need to accept some loss of power and privilege as a reasonable price to pay for better health both for themselves and for the women in their lives.

References

Aggleton, P. (1995) *Young Men Speak Out*. London: Health Education Authority.

Anastos, K. and Vermund, S. (1993) Epidemiology and natural history, in A. Kurth (ed.) *Until the Cure: Caring for Women with HIV*. London and New Haven: Yale University Press.

Andrews, B. and Brown, G. (1988) Violence in the community: a biographical approach. *British Journal of Psychiatry*, 153: 305–12.

Bartley, M., Popay, J. and Plewis, J. (1992) Domestic conditions, paid employment and women's experiences of ill health. *Sociology of Health and Illness*, 14 (3): 313–41.

Bassett, M. and Mhloyi, M. (1991) Women and AIDS in Zimbabwe: the making of an epidemic. *International Journal of Health Services*, 21 (1): 143–56.

Behera, D., Dash, S. and Yadar, S. (1991) Carboxyhaemoglobin in women exposed to different cooking fuels. *Thorax*, 46: 344–6.

Belle, D. (1990) Poverty and women's mental health. *American Psychologist*, 45: 385–9.

Berer, M. and Ray, S. (1993) *Women and HIV/AIDS: An International Resource Book*. London: Pandora.

Blaxter, M. (1990) *Health and Lifestyles*. London: Routledge.

Brown, G. and Harris, T. (1978) *Social Origins of Depression*. London: Tavistock.

Brown, J. (1992) Introduction, definitions, assumptions, themes and issues, in D. Counts, J. Brown and J. Campbell (eds) *Sanctions and Sanctuary: Cultural Perspectives on the Beating of Wives*. Boulder, CO: Westview Press.

Browne, N. and Finkelhor, D. (1986) The impact of child sexual abuse: a review of the research. *Psychological Bulletin*, 99 (1): 66–77.

Canaan, J. (1996) One thing leads to another: drinking, fighting and working class masculinities, in M. Mac an Ghaill (ed.) *Understanding Masculinities*. Buckingham: Open University Press.

Caplan, P. (1982) *The Cultural Construction of Sexuality*. London: Tavistock.

Cecelski, E. (1987) Energy and rural women's work: crisis response and policy alternatives. *International Labour Review*, 126 (1): 41–6.

Chakraborty, A. (1990) *Social Stress and Mental Health: A Social-psychiatric Field Study of Calcutta*. New Delhi: Sage Publications.

Charlton, J., Kelly, S., Dunnell, K., Evans, B. and Jenkins, R. (1993) Suicide deaths in England and Wales: trends in factors associated with suicide deaths. *Population Trends*, 71 (spring): 34–42.

Chatterjee, M. (1991) *Indian Women: Their Health and Productivity*. Washington DC: World Bank.

Chen, B., Hong, C., Pandey, M. and Smith, K. (1990) Indoor air pollution in developing countries. *World Health Statistics Quarterly*, 43: 127–38.

Davis, D. and Guarnaccia, D. (1989) Health, culture and the nature of nerves: an introduction. *Medical Anthropology*, 11: 1–13.

de Chesney, M. (1989) Child sexual abuse as an international health problem. *International Nurses Review*, 36 (5): 149–53.

Denenberg, R. (1990) Treatment and trials, in The ACT UP/NY Women and AIDS Book Group, *Women, AIDS and Activism*. Boston, MA: South End Press.

Dennerstein, L., Astbury, J. and Morse, C. (1993) *Psychosocial and Mental Health Aspects of Women's Health*. Geneva: WHO.

Desjarlais, R., Eisenberg, L., Good, B. and Kleinman, A. (1995) *World Mental Health: Problems and Priorities in Low-income Countries*. Oxford: Oxford University Press.

Dixon-Mueller, R. and Wasserheit, J. (1991) *The Culture of Silence: Reproductive Tract Infections Among Women in the Third World*. New York: International Women's Health Coalition.

Dowie, M., Foster, D., Marshall, C., Weir, D. and King, J. (1982) The illusion of safety. *Mother Jones*, June: 38–48.

Doyal, L. (1995) *What Makes Women Sick: Gender and the Political Economy of Health*. London: Macmillan.

du Guerny, J. and Sjoberg, E. (1993) Interrelationship between gender relations and the HIV/AIDS epidemic: some possible considerations for policies and programmes. *AIDS*, 7: 1027–34.

Duncan, M. (1993) A historical and clinical review of the interaction of leprosy and pregnancy: a cycle to be broken. *Social Science and Medicine*, 37 (4): 457–63.

Dwyer, D. and Bruce, J. (eds) (1988) *A Home Divided: Women and Income in the Third World*. Stanford, CA: Stanford University Press.

Ferro-Luzzi, A. (1990) Seasonal energy stress in marginally nourished rural women: interpretation and integrated conclusions of a multicentre study in three developing countries. *European Journal of Clinical Nutrition*, 44 (supplement 1): 41–6.

Ford, N. and Koetsawang, S. (1991) The sociocultural context of the transmission of HIV in Thailand. *Social Science and Medicine*, 33 (4): 405–14.

Frankenhaueser, M., Lundberg, U. and Chesney, M. (eds) (1991) *Women, Work and Health: stress and opportunities*. New York: Plenum Press.

Gavey, N. (1993) Technologies and effects of heterosexual coercion, in S. Wilkinson and C. Kitzinger (eds) *Heterosexuality: A Feminism and Psychology Reader*. London: Sage.

Germain, A., Holmes, K., Piot, P. and Wasserheit, J. (1992) *Reproductive Tract Infections: Global Impact and Priorities for Women's Reproductive Health*. New York: Plenum Press.

Gibbs, J. (1988) *Young, Black and Male in America: An Endangered Species*. Dover, MA: Auburn House.

Grobbelaar, J. and Bateman, E. (1991) Hut lung: a domestically acquired pneumoconiosis of mixed aetiology in rural women. *Thorax*, 46: 334–40.

Hart, N. (1988) Sex, gender and survival: inequalities of life chances between European men and women, in A.J. Fox (ed.) *Inequality in Health Within Europe*. Aldershot: Gower.

Hassold, T., Quillen, S. and Yaman, J. (1983) Sex ratio in spontaneous abortions. *Annals of Human Genetics*, 47 (1): 39–47.

Haynes, S. (1991) The effect of job demands, job control and new technologies on the health of employed women: a review, in M. Frankenhaueser, U. Lundberg and M. Chesney (eds) *Women, Work and Health: Stress and Opportunities*. New York: Plenum Press.

Haynes, S., LaCroix, A. and Lippin, T. (1987) The effect of high job demands and low control on the health of employed women, in J. Quick, R. Bhagat, J. Dalton and J. Quick (eds) *Work, Stress and Health Care*. New York: Praeger.

Heise, L., Pitanguy, J. and Germain, A. (1994) *Violence Against Women: The Hidden Health Burden*. Washington DC: World Bank.

Henshaw, S. (1990) Induced abortion: a world review, 1990. *Family Planning Perspectives*, 22 (2): 76–89.

Holland, J., Ramazanoglou, C., Scott, S., Sharpe, S. and Thomson, R. (1990) Sex, gender and power: young women's sexuality in the shadow of AIDS. *Sociology of Health and Illness*, 12 (3): 336–50.

Howson, C., Harrison, P., Hotra, D. and Law, M. (eds) (1996) *In Her Lifetime: Female Morbidity and Mortality in Sub-Saharan Africa*. Washington DC: National Academy Press.

Hyndman, S. (1990) Housing, damp and health among British Bengalis in East London. *Social Science and Medicine*, 30 (1): 131–41.

Jacobson, J. (1990) *The Global Politics of Abortion*, Worldwatch Paper 97. Washington DC: Worldwatch Institute.

Jacobson, J. (1991) *Women's Reproductive Health: The Silent Emergency*, Worldwatch Paper 102. Washington DC: Worldwatch Institute.

Jochelson, K., Mothibeli, M. and Leger, J.P. (1991) Human Immunodeficiency Virus and migrant labour in South Africa. *International Journal of Health Services*, 21 (1): 157–73.

Kabeer, N. (1991) *Gender, Production and Wellbeing: Rethinking the Household Economy*, Discussion Paper 288. Brighton: Institute of Development Studies, University of Sussex.

Kimmel, M. and Messner, M. (eds) (1993) *Men's Lives*. New York: Macmillan.

Kishwar, M. (1984) Introduction, in M. Kishwar and R. Vanita (eds) *In Search of Answers: Indian Women's Voices from Manushi*. London: Zed Press.

Korvick, J. (1993) Trends in federally sponsored clinical trials, in A. Kurth (ed.) *Until the Cure: Caring for Women with HIV*. London and New Haven: Yale University Press.

Koss, M. (1990) The women's mental health research agenda: violence against women. *American Psychologist*, 45 (3): 374–80.

Kurth, A. (1993) Introduction: an overview of women and HIV disease, in A. Kurth (ed.) *Until the Cure: Caring for Women with HIV*. London and New Haven: Yale University Press.

Kurz, K. and Prather, L. (1995) *Improving the Quality of Life of Girls*. New York: UNICEF.

Lado, C. (1992) Female labour force participation in agricultural production and the implications for nutrition and health in rural Africa. *Social Science and Medicine*, 34 (7): 789–807.

McCarthy, P. *et al.* (1985) Respiratory conditions: effects of housing and other factors. *Journal of Epidemiology and Community Health*, 39 (1): 15–19.

Macintyre, S., Hunt, K. and Sweeting, H. (1996) Gender difference in health: are they really as they seem? *Social Science and Medicine*, 42 (4): 617–62.

Malik, I., Bukhtiari, N. and Good, M-J., (1992) Mothers' fear of child death: a study in urban and rural communities in Northern Punjab, Pakistan. *Social Science and Medicine*, 35: 1043–53.

Manderson, L., Jenkins, J. and Tanner, M. (1993) Women and tropical diseases: introduction. *Social Science and Medicine*, 37 (4): 441–3.

Messing, K., Neis, B. and Dumais, L. (1995) *Invisible: Issues in Women's Occupational Health*, Charlottetown P.E.I. Canada: Gynergy Books.

Michelson, E. (1993) Adam's vib awry? Women and schistosomiasis. *Social Science and Medicine*, 37 (4): 493–9.

Mishra, V., Malhotra, M. and Gupta, S. (1990) Chronic respiratory disorders in females of Delhi. *Journal of the Indian Medical Association*, 88 (3): 77–80.

Norboo, T., Yahya, M., Bruce, N., Heady, J. and Ball, K. (1991) Domestic pollution and respiratory illness in a Himalayan village. *International Journal of Epidemiology*, 20 (3): 749–57.

Panos Institute (1992) *The Hidden Cost of AIDS: The Challenge of HIV to Development*. London: Panos Publications.

Parker, M. (1992) Reassessing disability: the impact of schistosomal infection on daily activities among women in Gezira province, Sudan. *Social Science and Medicine*, 35 (7): 877–90.

Paykel, E. (1991) Depression in women. *British Journal of Psychiatry*, 158 (suppl. 10): 22–9.

Pleck, J. and Sonenstein, F. (eds) (1991) *Adolescent Problem Behaviours*. Hillsdale, NJ: Lawrence Erlbaum.

Plichta, S. (1992) The effects of woman abuse on health care utilisation and health status. *Women's Health*, Jacobs Institute, 2 (3): 154–62.

Rahman, O., Strauss, J., Geurtler, P., Ashley, D. and Fox, K. (1994) Gender differences in adult health: an international comparison. *The Gerontological Society of America*, 34 (4): 463–9.

Rathgeber, E. and Vlassoff, C. (1993) Gender and tropical disease: a new research focus. *Social Science and Medicine*, 37 (4): 513–20.

Reichenheim, M. and Harpham, T. (1991) Maternal mental health in a squatter settlement in Rio de Janeiro. *British Journal of Psychiatry*, 159: 683–90.

Repetti, R., Matthews, K. and Waldron, I. (1989) Employment and women's health: effects of paid employment on women's mental and physical health. *American Psychologist*, 44 (11): 1394–401.

Reuben, R. (1993) Women and malaria: special risks and appropriate control strategy. *Social Science and Medicine*, 37 (4): 473–80.

Richgels, P. (1992) Hypoactive sexual desire in heterosexual women: a feminist analysis. *Women and Therapy*, 12 (1/2): 123–35.

Richie, B. (1990) AIDS: in living color, in E. White (ed.) *The Black Women's Health Handbook*. Seattle, WA: Seal Press.

Ringheim, K. (1993) Factors that determine the prevalence of use of contraceptive methods for men. *Studies in Family Planning*, 24 (2): 87–99.

Rodda, A. (1991) *Women and the Environment*. London: Zed Press.

Rodin, J. and Ickovics, J. (1990) Women's health: review and research agenda as we approach the 21st century. *American Psychologist*, 45 (9): 1018–34.

Rooney, D. (1992) *Antenatal Care and Maternal Health: How Effective Is It? A Review of the Evidence*. Geneva: WHO.

Rosenberg, H. (1984) The home is the workplace: hazards, stress and pollutants in the household, in W. Chavkin (ed.) *Double Exposure: Women's Health Hazards on the Job and at Home*. New York: Monthly Review Press.

Rosenfeld, J. (1992) Maternal work outside the home and its effect on women and their families. *Journal of the American Women's Association*, 47 (2): 47–53.

Royston, E. (ed.) (1991) *Maternal Mortality: A Global Factbook*. Geneva: WHO.

Royston, E. and Armstrong, S. (1989) *Preventing Maternal Deaths*. Geneva: WHO.

Sabo, D. and Gordon, G. (1993) *Men's Health and Illness: Gender, Power and the Body*. London: Sage Publications.

Segal, L. (1987) *Slow Motion: Changing Masculinities, Changing Men*. London: Virago.

Seidel, G. (1993) The competing discourses of HIV/AIDS in sub-Saharan Africa: discourses of rights and empowerment vs. discourses of control and exclusion. *Social Science and Medicine*, 36 (3): 175–94.

Sen, A. (1988) Family and food: sex bias in poverty, in T. Srinivasan and P. Bardham (eds) *Rural Poverty in South Asia*. New York: Columbia University Press.

Sen, A. (1990) More than 100 million women are missing. *New York Review of Books*, 20 December: 61–66.

Sims, J. (1994) *Women, Health and Environment: An Anthology*. Geneva: WHO.

Snitow, A., Stansell, C. and Thompson, S. (1984) *Powers of Desire: The Politics of Sexuality*. London: Virago.

Staples, R. (1995) Health among African American males, in D. Sabo and D. Gordon (eds) *Men's Health and Illness: Gender, Power and the Body*. London: Sage Publications.

Stark, E. and Flitcraft, A. (1991) Spouse abuse, in M. Roseberg and M. Fenley (eds) *Violence in America: A Public Health Approach*. Oxford: Oxford University Press.

Sundari Ravindran, T. (1986) *Health Implications of Sex Discrimination in Childhood: A Review Paper and Annotated Bibliography Prepared for WHO/UNICEF*. Geneva: WHO.

Thaddeus, S. and Maine, D. (1991) *Too Far to Walk: Maternal Mortality in Context*. New York: Centre for Population and Family Health, Faculty of Medicine, Columbia University.

Ulrich, M., Zuyleta, A., Caceres-Dittmar, G., Sampson, C., Pinard, M., Rada, E. and Nacarid, A. (1993) Leprosy in women: characteristics and repercussions. *Social Science and Medicine*, 37 (4): 445–56.

UNAIDS Organisation (1998) *Report on the Global HIV/AIDS Epidemic*. Geneva: WHO.

UNICEF (1990) *The State of the World's Children 1989*. Oxford: Oxford University Press.

United Nations (1991) The world's women 1970–1990: trends and statistics. *Social Statistics and Indicators*, series K. no. 8. New York: UN.

US National Institutes of Health (1992) *Opportunity for Research on Women's Health*, (NIH publication no. 92–3457). Washington DC: US Department of Health and Human Services.

Vance, C. (ed.) (1984) *Pleasure and Danger: Exploring Female Sexuality*. London: Routledge.

Vlassoff, C. and Bonilla, E. (1994) Gender related differences in the impact of tropical diseases on women: what do we know? *Journal of Biosocial Science*, 26: 37–53.

Waldron, I. (1986) What do we know about the causes of sex differences in mortality? *Population Bulletin of the United Nations*, 18: 59.

Waldron, I. (1995) Contributions of changing gender differentials in behaviour to changing gender differences in mortality, in D. Sabo and D. Gordon (eds) *Men's Health and Illness: Gender, Power and the Body*. London: Sage Publications.

Waldron, I. and Jacobs, J. (1989) Effects of labor force participation on women's health: new evidence from a longitudinal study. *Journal of Occupational Medicine*, 30 (12): 977–83.

Weeks, M., Singer, M., Grier, M. and Schensul, J. (1996) Gender relations, sexuality and AIDS risk among African American and Latina women, in C. Sargent and C. Brettell (eds) *Gender and Health: An International Perspective*. Upper Saddle River, NJ: Prentice Hall.

WHO (World Health Organization) (1984) *Biomass Fuel Combustion and Health*. Geneva: WHO.

WHO (World Health Organization) (1990) *Global Programme on AIDS: Report of the Meeting on Research Priorities Relating to Women and HIV/AIDS*, 19–20 November. Geneva: WHO.

WHO (World Health Organization) (1992) *The World Health Report 1995: Bridging the Gaps*. Geneva: WHO.

WHO (World Health Organization) (1996) *Women, Ageing and Health: Achieving Health Across the Life Span*. Geneva: WHO.

WHO (World Health Organization)/TDR (1991) *Progress in Research 1989–1990, Tenth Programme Report of the UNDP/World Bank/WHO Special Programme for Research and Training in Topical Diseases (TDR)*. Geneva: WHO.

World Bank (1993) *World Development Report 1993: Investing in Health*. Oxford: Oxford University Press.

Worth, D. (1989) Sexual decision making and AIDS: why condom promotion among vulnerable women is likely to fail. *Studies in Family Planning*, 20 (6): 297–307.

Zierler, S. and Krieger, N. (1997) Reframing women's risk: social inequalities and HIV infection. *Annual Review of Public Health*, 18: 401–36.

3

City A/genders

Sophie Watson

It is 20 years since feminists first challenged radical urban theorists for failing to see the ways in which their analysis of urban processes and urban social movements ignored women (IJURR 1978). Feminist activists of the 1970s were quicker to latch onto city politics as a crucial site of gender divisions than their sisters in academia – probably reflecting the then limited number of women in the traditionally masculine spatial disciplines of geography, planning and architecture. In the so-called grass roots movements of the city, feminists were involved in squatters groups, tenants and residents associations, community transport, and refuges developing an analysis of how the provision of urban services and the distribution of resources were marked by patriarchal assumptions and gender divisions. In the public spaces of the city, feminists were campaigning around issues of women's safety. In London, Leeds and other large cities women organized large 'reclaim the night' demonstrations carrying candles and torches through areas designated as unsafe. There were though, some tensions in the choices of locality for the marches, since these often coincided with spaces of sex work or spaces with a high proportion of Black residents, and feminists were concerned not to be seen to be antagonistic to people who were marginalized in these places.

This chapter first explores briefly some ways in which cities are gendered. Earlier themes in feminist analysis of cities and their political implications are then considered, before suggesting new ways of thinking cities from a feminist perspective. The second part of the chapter looks at some crucial contemporary issues and their implications for a more gender-nuanced urban policy.

Gendered cities

How does space matter to the construction of gender in material and symbolic ways? At the macro level how cities are organized has real effects on women's lives. Urban development and planning have tended to reflect, and also reinforce, traditional assumptions about gender. Traditionally, employment has been concentrated in the centre of cities separated out from residence in the suburbs. The transport system is constructed to support the needs of the worker leaving home in the morning and returning in the evening on a radial system which links centres with peripheries but rarely links suburbs to each other. Services and facilities are dispersed throughout the suburbs and the taking of children to school or the doctor, doing the shopping and other household chores operate on different temporal and spatial scales such that the complexity of running a home and bringing up children militates against participation in the labour force, at least on a full-time basis.

Transport links seldom connect schools, shops, services, employment and shopping centres and many women do not have the use of a car during the day. The assumption underpinning this spatial organization is that the man of the household goes out to work while the woman stays at home and looks after the children. This kind of city form, combined with the lack of childcare facilities, in part explains the concentration of women in part-time or home-based work. As the Marxist urban theorist Manuel Castells wrote as early as 1977, the city could not function without the unpaid labour of women to oil its wheels.

The lack of safety associated with the public spaces of the city, the lack of street lighting and the imagined and real dangers of public transport, particularly at night, curtail women's easy movement, particularly older and younger women and migrants from rural areas in the UK and overseas, who may have little experience of city life. Urban design and built forms, though implicitly imbued with gendered assumptions, at the same time are rarely sensitive to the needs of women with children. Roads are difficult to cross with prams, safe play areas are few and far between, and designated public spaces are often more suited to the needs of young adolescent men than women with young children. Studies of the central business districts of cities have shown that the majority of women are afraid to walk through them at night.

The home, while seen as the domain of women, particularly in middle-class homes, offers each member of the household their own space except the woman. Children often have a playroom, men have the study, garage, shed or workshop. The women's space is a site of labour – the kitchen, while the 'master' bedroom suggests a sexual sleeping area where men have control. Virginia Woolf was an early advocate of the need for autonomous space in *A Room of One's Own* (1929).

The suburbs are not simply gendered in the sense that women spend more time at home and its locality, they are also gendered in a symbolic sense. With the increasing separation of home and work associated with industrialization, femininity was mapped onto the home, the local, and a sense of place. The suburban home came to represent the 'haven in the heartless world', the warm and cosy space to which men returned after a hard day at work in the hurly burly of the city. Thus women were constituted in the home as nurturing, passive, subordinate mothers, while men were powerful, public, active and even aggressive. At the same time this haven has been unpacked to reveal the suburban home as a site of violence, isolation and work for women, but its gendered symbolic force remains.

Feminist urban theory

The early feminist interest in space developed out of geography and related disciplines. In the UK, a geography and gender group was initiated in the early 1980s (McDowell 1983). Initially feminists sought to address women's absence from urban planning literature and policy and attempted to reinsert them into the frame. The emphasis was on the ways in which women were marginalized within urban systems either via constraints or lack of access to goods and services. A central argument was that city forms and structures and urban institutions created and reinforced women's dependence, consigned them to the domestic arena and disabled them from fully entering public life and spaces. Theoretically the work was underpinned by different forms of analysis each of which had very different implications for policy and change.

The most pragmatic approach derived from Weberian or institutional approaches which saw women's exclusion or marginalization in terms of institutional failures and regulatory systems (e.g. Brion and Tinker 1980; Coles 1980). On the one hand policies were seen to favour masculine patterns of responsibility and work, such as the public transport system being organized around the needs of suburban dwellers travelling to the city centres for work, rather than the mobility requirements and patterns of women at home trying to combine domestic and paid employment. Over the following decade these arguments seeped into policy discussions in radical local and metropolitan authorities like the Greater London Council which had its own women and planning group (Hamilton and Jenkins 1989). But changing the physical structure of cities proved to be more difficult and expensive than changing the regulations or procedures that marginalize women.

Alternatively the problem was seen to lie with the 'gatekeepers' in the urban system who allocated public goods, such as housing or finance, according to prejudice or discriminatory practices. Thus single parents were allocated poorer quality housing than nuclear families, or single women had difficulty gaining access to mortgage finance when lenders

constructions of space which were too homogenized, continuous, objective, Cartesian and knowable. In postmodern versions space is seen as
fragmented, imploding, imaginative, subjective, unknowable and fantastic.
Space is linked with power and difference. These feminist approaches to
Space have opened up possibilities of a new politics and way of thinking
space have opened up possibilities of a new politics and way of thinking
about gender and the city which earlier approaches foreclosed.

One path takes the construction of meaning in the sexed and gendered
spaces and places of the city as its starting point for rethinking the
urban, planning and housing. This kind of work draws on qualitative
research methodologies. Thus, Susan Thompson (1994), for example,
showed how the home for migrant women represents a site of power,
or atonement for loss or a sign of success. Challenging earlier feminist
urban analysis which viewed the process of suburbanization as controlling and subjugating women, and locking them into domestic roles, she
suggests that suburban discourse is fractured. Thompson thus explores
how stereotypical representations of suburbia tell only half the story.
Other work (Duruz 1994; Mee 1994) has looked at how women now
redraw the post-war suburbs in memory and imagination and what
meanings are encoded. What this allows for politically are possibilities
for a rethinking of the 'private' domain and constructing suburbs of the
future. It offers a more textured way of intervening into urban policy
debates around the compact city versus the suburban city, or development on greenfield versus brownfield sites. Instead of crude caricatures
of what constitutes suburban or inner-city life, different meanings are
examined. Australian feminist activists have drawn on these ideas to
develop new models of local planning which acknowledge different
cultural practices.

Foucault's notion of the Panopticon whereby conditions of uncertainty and invisibility of surveillance produce self-socialization, surveillance and regulation, has also influenced feminist work. As Margo Huxley
(1994) has shown, the zoning of cities can be read in terms of strategies
of social control which are resisted by multiple intersecting practices
such as the setting up of gay and lesbian households or legal appeals
through the planning system. These resistances challenge dominant forms
of divisions and the regulation of space, and can contribute to strategies
to create a more participatory, less discriminatory planning system and
alternative uses and development of social space.

Sexuality, which has long been central to feminist thought and analysis and, indeed, present in the early debates around the home and
suburbia, has re-emerged in a contemporary guise. Elizabeth Wilson
(1995) highlights the crucial influence of sexuality on spatial structure,
regulation and behaviour, and explores how the male gaze in the late
nineteenth century eroticized city life and sexualized the spaces it viewed.
Designating prostitutes as the public face of woman in the city, the
respectable woman's movements in urban space became a subject for
regulation. Such work is helpful in illustrating the ways in which women

made assumptions about their repayment potential. In 1983 lone women
borrowers accounted for 8 per cent of all borrowers compared to an
equivalent figure of 17 per cent for men (CML 1983). In British cities
many single parents were housed in the poorer quality public housing
(DHSS 1974). The political and policy solutions suggested by these kinds
of analyses lay in legal or institutional reforms or in education or training of the actors involved, and there was no fundamental challenge to
the status quo.

A more radical critique came from Marxist feminists who saw the
source of women's spatial marginality or exclusion as patriarchal capitalism where the city was structured to reinforce the place of women as
domestic labourers and men as waged labourers (McDowell 1983; Watson
1988). Keeping women in the home meant cities could run more
smoothly as women carried out the necessary reproductive activities and
wages could be kept lower since these activities were being performed
for free. The argument's weaknesses lay in its sometimes conspiratorial
flavour and its rather functionalist analysis. These debates were more
oriented to critique than to reform. The policy implications were unclear
and the political solution was ultimately to overthrow capitalism, which
was constructed at this time as a monolithic unified system. In a similar
vein radical feminists posed the problem as patriarchy (Wekerle et al.,
1980). The city, they suggested, worked in men's interests, men controlled space, they were the gatekeepers of resources and they had a lot
to lose if things changed. The solution implied here lay in more women
entering the policy-making arenas and the professions of architecture
and planning, or in subverting the gatekeepers of the system – those
who controlled the resources.

Through the 1980s a growing number of women entered planning
and architecture schools and the professions. Others took the route of
the manual trades, challenging one of the more gendered labour forces
and skills. These women, who mostly took advantage of government
training schemes to become carpenters and builders, formed the 'women
in manual trades' collective. There were strong parallels with the early
utopian feminists and communitarians excavated by Dolores Hayden
(1981) in *The Grand Domestic Revolution*, who saw the reorganization of
space as a route to the freedom of women and the subversion of gender
divisions. A group of women architects and builders set up a collective
'Matrix'. The aim was to examine how spatial forms limited, defined or
constrained women's lives: underpasses with no ramps, poorly lit streets,
poorly designed kitchens. There was a tension between short-term goals
trying to facilitate women's lives as carers, and a recognition that focusing on women's needs as such could ossify them in a domestic role. In
some senses the analysis was deterministic in that it assumed a changed
built environment would mean changed social relations, and space
was treated as a homogeneous category which had visible and clear-cut
effects. The goal of getting more women into the design professions

and the building trades was predicated on an assumption that women would understand their own needs better.

In the less specifically spatial disciplines feminist sociologists, cultural and social historians and anthropologists from the 1970s (e.g. Davidoff 1979; Pringle 1983) continued to develop analyses of how different meanings were produced spatially, and this was a precursor to contemporary postmodern accounts. Suburbs were analysed in terms of discourses of 'female', 'safe', 'haven', 'sexual', etc. versus the urban as 'male' 'aggressive' and 'assertive' and these were mapped onto a consumption/production binary. Other work deconstructed notions of home and homelessness and its sexed differentiation (Watson 1986). Though framed also by earlier Marxist ideas, the ideological underpinning of the production of space was 'foregrounded': that is, space was not simply seen as a blank undifferentiated surface which has no effects. The terrain of political intervention implied was thus also at the level of subverting and challenging meaning and discursive practices. A related body of work came out of geography and allied disciplines which looked at the spatialization of gender relations. Feminist geographers used techniques such as local empirical studies to explore, for example, how capital shifted to localities where women's supposed docile and cheap labour could be exploited (McDowell and Massey 1984). The potential political dimension to these analyses lay in developing links with the trade union movement and in strategic interventions in arenas like the local economic development strategies initiated by authorities such as the radical Greater London Council.

Feminist perspectives over the first ten years or so came from different quarters and had different strategic potential. One area where the analysis was limited was in developing links between gender, race and space. By the late 1980s, the impact of new theory and an interest in space across a range of disciplines (notably cultural studies and philosophy) brought new ways of thinking about space. These have enabled a different form of politics which takes account of the imaginary and the importance of meaning, on the one hand, and which brings together diverse players, for example community artists with planners, on the other. These shifts offer exciting possibilities for rethinking and reshaping space. Though the early debates were important for raising issues of inequality and marginalization, which still need to be addressed, feminists need also to think about what kind of cities and spaces might offer new ways of living which accommodate the diversity of women's and men's lives on the one hand, and the huge social and economic shifts on the other. Taking the urban system as given and trying to accommodate it to women, or dismantling it entirely – as was suggested by some analyses – have proved limited routes.

More recent feminist urban theory draws on post-structuralist or postmodernist ideas and theories of subjectivity, identity and meaning. In these new discourses earlier notions of space have come under scrutiny for

have been denied an urban sociality and civic subjectivity. Further shifts in the debate have questioned the ways in which queer sexualities are located in specific geographical sites (Probyn 1996). These approaches take us away from the earlier feminist analyses which see the state as the solution to women's exclusion from the city and suggest new and transgressive ways of inhabiting postmodern spaces.

Contemporary feminist interest in the body has also been mapped onto space. In *Space Time and Perversion* Elizabeth Grosz (1995) considers questions of spatiality, space and the design professions of architecture and planning, and their relationship to subjectivity, corporeality and thought. Grosz argues that an understanding of the ways in which women occupy space is predicated on an exploration of the appropriation and disenfranchisement of femininity within dominant knowledge systems. New ways of dwelling must acknowledge the invaded nature of bodies and spaces as we know them. She sees bodies as formed by the city spaces they inhabit. The model is based on a productive notion of bodies and cities defining each other. Again a new politics of space is suggested by her work. In this there is no ideal environment for the body or perfect city in terms of the potential it offers for well-being. The question then becomes how to distinguish conducive and unconducive environments – physical and socio-cultural – and how these produce different bodies. The city is the locus for the production and circulation of power and the city leaves traces on the subject's corporeality; the dramatic information revolution will thus have its corporeal effects. This way of thinking shifts the focus of the lens and suggests new struggles and possibilities.

Kathie Gibson and Sophie Watson, drawing out some of the implications of these debates (Gibson and Watson 1994; Watson and Gibson 1995), have suggested that postmodern feminist theory has much to offer conventional notions of planning and urban policy. The heroic visions of modernist politics and mass mobilization of the exploited masses have eclipsed other strategic possibilities, especially for women. Modernist planning was underpinned by the notion of a rational and clear solution to city chaos and inequality which was predicated on gendered social relations and patterns of movement. It assumed a linearity of progress and reform that was fixed and not easily open to change and fluidity. A recognition of difference and embodiment challenges the universalist and normative assumptions and principles of planners acting in the public good. This notion of planning for difference is compatible with new theories of the state which see the state as a set of discursive arenas where different interests are constructed and contested (Pringle and Watson 1992). In this formulation ebbs and flows of power are embedded in the planning system and are not fixed.

New possibilities for feminist strategies, both theoretically and practically, are thus beginning to emerge. Planning in this frame can take account of the local and the specific, and can be flexible and allow for change, recognizing that there is no one solution for all time, and that any so-called solution will itself later represent a node of power and be contested. Postmodern urban politics suggests a shift from the old class politics around space to an assertion of multiple forms of resistances and alliances articulated at different sites and at different times (Gibson-Graham 1996). This is important since it allows for a politics of difference across race, gender and sexuality and recognizes that there is no one strategy which will provide the solution. It means taking account of identities and how these are formed in urban spaces and in the interstices of the city. It implies rethinking public and private and recognizing that these too are shifting and not fixed.

Feminist perspectives on space have moved a long way from their early preoccupation with gendered forms of exclusion and marginality in the city. Over time these have become less and less located in the simple binaries of public and private and home and work, and less and less analysed in terms of a simple functionalism. Important new directions are opened up as feminists like J.K. Gibson-Graham (1996) start to dismantle the monolithic categories of class and capitalism. By attacking these shibboleths, spaces are freed up in which to move. In this new terrain subjectivity, sexuality, corporeality and the place of the imaginary come to the fore. The reforms sought have also shifted. Though feminists are still keen to campaign for a greater provision of urban services which are sensitive to women's lived experiences in the city and also for an end to discriminatory practices, there is a greater complexity in forms of analysis and outcomes sought. My argument here is not that earlier forms of analysis are no longer important, rather that new perspectives bring a fresh light to old problems.

The city out there

The new theoretical approaches, in particular those emphasizing complexity, difference and flexibility are especially relevant in the context of the gender shifts occurring as a result of the processes of globalization and informationalization of the economy. Over the last two decades we have seen a worldwide increase in women's participation in the paid workforce. As Borja and Castells (1997: 49) put it: 'What has made women highly desirable workers in the new global information economy is their capacity to provide an equivalent service at a lower wage and under much more insecure working conditions than their male counterparts'. Part-time work, subcontracting, home-based work, fixed contract work and the processes of informationalization of the economy are fundamental mechanisms of the new model of flexible production. Frequently it is women who are available to take up these jobs, partly because in all countries they are still the ones to take by far the major share of childcare and other domestic responsibilities, while also being poorly unionized and hence easier to exploit. Thus in the UK women's economic activity rate has increased from 50 to 60 per cent between 1970 and 1994, with similar patterns in the USA (53 to 64 per cent), South Africa (47 to 54 per cent), Singapore (36 to 58 per cent) and Mexico (21 to 37 per cent) (UNDP 1995). Much of this work is part-time (see also Rees, this volume). In this context the argument for more flexible approaches to women's multiple activities and responsibilities are even more salient than they ever were.

If the shifts in employment patterns are taken together with social demographic shifts the argument for a more flexible city to accommodate difference becomes even stronger. In less than a quarter of a century we have witnessed the demise of the traditional nuclear family, again on a global scale. This dramatic shift has occurred as a result of a number of factors. At the level of the social, there is no doubt that the women's and gay liberation movements have shifted social attitudes such that less people are rushing into marriage (and if they do, at a later age) and more people are choosing to live alone or cohabit, with or without children, in heterosexual or gay relationships. At the same time, when relationships break down there is less and less stigma associated with divorce, with 1 in 2.8 marriages in Britain now ending in divorce. Many of these people repartner leading to the growing phenomenon of reconstituted families who have extended links with new and old relations and friends, or 'kith and kin', to use Rosemary Pringle's (1998) useful new formulation of how families could be reconceived.

Thus in the UK the traditional nuclear family now accounts for less than a third of all households. The growth in lone parent households (90 per cent of whom are headed by women) is the most striking demographic shift of the last two decades, increasing from 8 per cent in 1971 to 22 per cent in 1991. Single parents are very dependent on local authorities for their housing, especially women. One year after divorce, where this took place between 1991 and 1993, where the former matrimonial home was owner-occupied, 11 per cent of women were renting from the social sector. In 1994/5 in Great Britain more than a quarter of households consisted of one person living alone which is almost double the proportion in 1961 (Central Statistical Office 1996). This is in part the result of more older people living alone but also reflects the growing tendency of young people to live alone, particularly men. The number of men under pensionable age living alone is expected to be the largest group of one-person households by the year 2011.

The other major shift is in longevity with many people living into their eighties and nineties, particularly women. Currently women in the UK over pensionable age constitute the largest group of single people at 12 per cent. There are significant planning issues that result including housing, transport and community care provision. Older people, and older women particularly, form the largest group in local authority housing: 26 per cent of people over 65 and 27 per cent over 80 are public tenants. Cuts in local authority housing will thus have an immediate impact on this group whose other housing options are few. For the more than 60 per cent of older people who are homeowners there are different issues such as often poor quality stock which is in a state of disrepair and for which the owner may not have the money to fix or ameliorate. Thus, though there may be apparent housing security represented by statistical accounts of tenure, when these are cross-tabulated with age and gender, pockets of housing poverty may exist in localities of seemingly adequate housing.

These patterns are not unique to the UK, suggesting once again that many countries face similar challenges. Manuel Castells' (1997) chapter 'The End of Patriarchalism' in his book *The Power of Identity* presents a compelling case for related global shifts which he links not only with social movements but also with the rise of the informational global economy and technological changes in reproduction. Between 1970 and 1990 divorce rates per 100 marriages have increased from 18.6 to 38.3 in Canada, 11.0 to 28.1 in The Netherlands, 12.0 to 31.5 in France, to show some of the patterns in developed countries (Bruce *et al.* 1995). In less developed countries, Castells (1997: 142) draws on figures which show the percentage of first marriages which dissolved through separation, divorce or death among women aged 40–9 to illustrate similar trends: 37.3 per cent in Indonesia, 60.8 per cent in Ghana, 32.5 per cent in Colombia and 49.5 per cent in the Dominican Republic. These are striking figures indeed. As a result, lone parent families headed by women, as well as single households (the majority of whom are also women: two-thirds in the USA) are increasing as a proportion of households worldwide. According to the US Bureau of the Census (1994) the proportion of children living with their two biological parents was only 50.8 per cent in 1994, while according to Moser and Peake (1987): 'It is estimated that one third of the world's households are headed by women. In urban areas, particularly in Latin America and Africa, the figure exceeds 50 per cent . . . and globally the phenomenon is on the increase'.

The implications of these shifts are several. At the macro level is the shape of the city, or, to put it another way, urban form. Modernist planning which underpinned urban development in many cities of the world in the pre- and post-war periods rested on certain assumptions. Foremost was the notion of rationality reflected in Corbusier's urban designs and order. Central to this was the predicability of employment patterns and implicitly the stable patriarchal nuclear family. With different members of the household increasingly engaged in uneven patterns of work in differentiated spaces, urban policies need to address this complexity. The public transport system is crucial here. Traditionally women's diverse responsibilities – taking the kids to school, doing the shopping, taking an elderly parent to the doctor, engaging in part-time work, all in the space of one day – have meant that women are disadvantaged by a transport system organized around the regulated working day of traditional male employment. Women's lives, if you like, are marked by spatial and temporal diversity.

For households or individuals without access to a car, many of whom are women, older and younger people, there are severe constraints in carrying out the multiplicity of daily activities, particularly women who are responsible for dependants. A study of men and women's travelling patterns in Belo Horizonte, Brazil, found that the daily travelling time of women was three times longer than that of men (Schmink 1982). With the increasing fragmentation and diversification of employment the transport needs of women and the rest of the population are coinciding. New more flexible systems are being introduced in several countries where for example a range of vehicles from shared taxis to small buses are introduced into the public transport system. Light rail options and more bicycle-friendly cities are other such initiatives.

A similar flexibility is required from the housing system. The idea that a family buys a house that will last them for life is no longer appropriate. The dominance of home ownership, particularly suburban home ownership, in many countries is becoming increasingly inappropriate to meet housing needs particularly given the increasing numbers of women-headed households, many of whom are on low incomes or poor. Seventy per cent of the world's 1300m poor are women (UNDP 1995). Yet in many parts of the world subsidized housing is only available to those receiving a regular income from formal employment. For example the housing programme in Solanda, Ecuador initiated in 1982 with US government aid was aimed at 6000 low income families, yet the eligibility criteria meant that only 175 of the families who could opt for the programme were women (Borja and Castells 1997: 51). In the UK public housing is not delimited in this way but the problem is the shrunken size of the sector following the Conservative government's policies during the 1980s.

There has nevertheless been an increase in home ownership among women in Britain, including single and gay households. Interestingly there are now more women than men pairs gaining mortgages in Britain, for which there is no obvious explanation. Yet where studies have been done, evidence suggests that women own houses in poorer areas of lower quality and amenity value, reflecting their lower incomes. Home ownership however brings its hazards in the form of mortgage arrears and repossessions, and women who are in low paid or impermanent employment are particularly vulnerable here.

A flexible labour market requires a flexible housing market where the costs of mobility are not prohibitive as is generally the case with home ownership. Higher rates of divorce are also incompatible with home ownership, particularly where there are large mortgages involved. In many European cities there is a dominance of rental housing, both public and private, which is affordable, secure and not stigmatized. Different rental solutions from housing cooperatives, housing associations and the State need to be expanded to accommodate the diversity of households and life cycles. In Britain housing associations play an important role in housing non-traditional households, special needs groups such as the long-term homeless, as well as applicants through the housing waiting list.

In many countries there is a shift away from the zoning of residential areas as distinct from commercial and industrial areas, to more mixed-use development. Initiatives for more compact cities are in place to increase densities in inner-city areas enabling non-traditional households to afford smaller dwellings closer to the city centre and places of work. The Building Better Cities Programme initiated by the Labor government in Australia (1983–1995) was one such initiative. Although such policies are often contested by local residents protective of their own area (the 'not in my backyard' syndrome), attitudes are beginning to change as inner cities are revitalized. In the UK the advantages of mixed-use development are increasingly recognized as a route to the re-use of obsolete buildings, a greater diversity of households in one locality and the possible decrease in crime and pollution from car emissions. Where central business districts have shifted from predominantly commercial to mixed land uses women and older people and others who find the city-centre threatening have returned to city centres. This relates to Wilson's (1995) idea of seeing cities as potential spaces of freedom for women, challenging the relegation of women to the home.

For the foreseeable future women are likely to continue to take on domestic responsibilities in the home. There are some important policy issues that result from this. The design of dwellings impacts particularly on women's lives, yet they are often absent from the design process. This exclusion is even more acute when ethnic and racial differences are considered also. Different cultural practices require different housing forms. For example, many people require a space of worship in the house, or a particular alignment of the house in relation to light, Mecca or social customs. The health hazards associated with poor dwellings to which women, particularly older women, are vulnerable represent a further issue. In residential projects in developing countries the cooking and cleaning areas are frequently treated as a leftover space (Borja and Castells 1997). An estimated 70m women suffer respiratory and other health problems due to the high levels of household pollution from kitchen stoves (Shegal 1995).

The last area of strategic intervention into the city and its politics I want to consider is the terrain of discourse. Frameworks of meanings are produced in a whole range of contexts and specific sites (see Payne, this volume). In urban policy documents categories of individuals are constituted in the language used and the categories deployed, and these matter both in terms of how applicants see themselves and how they are seen by others. Perceptions in turn have effects in terms of how people are treated by others. Thus, homeless legislation as defined in the Housing Act 1985 part III and its successor, the Housing Act 1996 part VII is described by Holdsworth (1997) as encouraging a gatekeeper approach in that housing officers are required to exercise discretion as to who is 'intentionally homeless' and who is not. Under the 1985 Act applicants who can prove a local connection, non-intentional homelessness and priority need – which is conferred automatically on those caring for children – are eligible for accommodation. Women who are victims of domestic violence are exempted from being referred back to their former local authority for rehousing.

The discourse of local connection is however the most explicit in its underlying assumptions referring to residence, long residence of close family, employment or other special reasons. As Maxine Holdsworth (1997) points out, there is no acknowledgement of the need to be near friends, carers or healthcare, which is particularly important for those in non-traditional relationships or friendship structures like the people with HIV/AIDS in her study. The legislation is framed according to hetero-sexual norms and assumptions. Part VII of the Housing Act 1996 replaces the former legislation. As a result of a White Paper suggesting that lone parents were jumping the housing queue, the duty under the former Act to provide permanent accommodation to homeless applicants was weakened to an obligation to ensure suitable accommodation is available for a minimum of two years. The discourse underpinning these changes is that of homeless people as undeserving of permanent accommodation.

Postmodern urban policy foregrounds the idea of planning for differ-ence and recognizing diversity and complexity as well as inequality. It entails a recognition that there is no one solution that will suit all, and differences of age, gender, race, sexual orientation, physical ability and so on all have to be taken on board. This necessitates a greater involve-ment of different groups in planning their own cities which implies new forms of local democracy. Some cities are using the Internet as a way of opening discussions to the local citizenry through city home pages which display local plans for comment. Rather than the planners and policy makers deciding from above, this allows for planning from below chal-lenging the notion of the planner or gatekeeper as the expert exercising power through knowledge. Recent feminist work which lays significance on the symbolic meaning of home and place is relevant here (Thompson 1994). If it is recognized that people experience space and place differ-ently, and that different spaces/places open up different possibilities or constraints and a sense of safety or danger, then the planning system and urban policy will need to address more subjective experiences of cities if they are to become places of enablement and empowerment rather than disempowerment.

References

Borja, J. and Castells, M. (1997) *Local and Global: Management of Cities in the Informa-tion Age*. London: Earthscan.

Brion, M. and Tinker, A. (1980) *Women in Housing*. London: Housing Centre Trust.

Bruce, J., Lloyd, C.B. and Leonard, A. (1995) *Families in Focus: New Perspectives of Mothers, Fathers and Children*. New York: Populations Council.

Castells, M. (1977) *The Urban Question*. London: Edward Arnold.

Castells, M. (1997) *The Power of Identity*. Oxford: Blackwell.

Central Statistical Office (1996) *Social Trends*. London: HMSO.

Coles, L. (1980) Women and leisure: a critical perspective, in D. Mercer and E. Hamilton-Smith (eds) *Recreational Planning and Social Change in Australia*. Melbourne: Sorrett Publishing.

Council of Mortgage Lenders (1983) *CML Year Book*. London: CML.

Davidoff, L. (1979) The separation of home and work? Landladies and lodgers in nineteenth-century England, in S. Burman (ed.) *Fit Work for Women*. London: Croom Helm.

DHSS (1974) *Report of the Committee on One Parent Families* (The Finer Report), Cmnd. 4728. London: HMSO.

Duruz, J. (1994) Romancing the suburbs, in K. Gibson and S. Watson (eds) *Metropolis Now*. London: Pluto Press.

Gibson, K. and Watson, S. (eds) (1994) *Metropolis Now*. London: Pluto Press.

Gibson-Graham, J.K. (1996) *The End of Capitalism (as we knew it)*. Oxford: Blackwell.

Grosz, E. (1995) *Space Time and Perversion*. Sydney: Allen & Unwin.

Hamilton, K. and Jenkins, L. (1989) Why women and travel? in M. Grieco and L. Pickup (eds) *Gender, Transport and Employment: the Impact of Travel Constraints*. Aldershot: Avebury.

Hayden, D. (1981) *The Grand Domestic Revolution*. Boston: MIT Press.

Holdsworth, M. (1997) *HIV and Homelessness*. M.Sc. dissertation, School for Policy Studies, University of Bristol.

Huxley, M. (1994) Panoptica: Utilitarianism and land use control, in K. Gibson and S. Watson (eds) *Metropolis Now*. London: Pluto Press.

IJURR (1978) *The International Journal of Urban and Regional Research*, 2(3).

McDowell, L. (1983) Towards an understanding of the gender division of urban space. *Society and Space: Environment and Planning D*, 1(1): 59–72.

McDowell, L. and Massey, D. (1984) A woman's place, in D. Massey and J. Allen (eds) *Geography Matters*. Cambridge: Cambridge University Press.

Matrix (1984) *Making Space: Women and the Man Made Environment*. London: Pluto Press.

Mee, K. (1994) Dressing up the suburbs: representations of Western Sydney, in K. Gibson and S. Watson (eds) *Metropolis Now*. London: Pluto Press.

Moser, C. (1993) *Gender Planning and Development*. London: Routledge.

Moser, C. and Peake L. (1987) *Human Settlements and Housing*. London: Tavistock.

Murphy, P. and Watson, S. (1996) *Surface City: Sydney at the Millennium*. Sydney: Pluto Press.

Pringle, R. (1983) Women and consumer capital, in C. Baldock and B. Cass (eds) *Women, Social Welfare and the State*. Sydney: Allen & Unwin.

Pringle, R. (1998) Rethinking the family, in B. Caine, M. Gatens, J. Larbalestier, S. Watson and E. Webby (eds) *The Oxford Companion to Australian Feminism*. Sydney: Oxford University Press.

Pringle, R. and Watson S. (1992) Women's interests and the post-structural State, in M. Barrett and A. Phillips (eds) *Destabilising Theory*. Cambridge: Polity Press.

Probyn, E. (1996) *Outside Belongings*. Sydney: Allen & Unwin.

Rose, G. (1993) *Feminism and Geography*. Cambridge: Polity Press.

Schmink, M. (1982) *Women in the urban economy in Latin America*, in Low Income Households and Urban Services: University of Florida.

Shegal, N. (1995) *Women Housing and Human Settlements*. New Delhi: Ess Publications.

Thompson, S. (1994) Suburbs of opportunity: the power of home for migrant women, in K. Gibson and S. Watson (eds) *Metropolis Now*. London: Pluto Press.

United Nations Development Programme (UNDP) (1995) *Human Development Report 1995*. New York: Oxford University Press.

US Bureau of the Census (1994) *Diverse Living Arrangements of Children*. Washington DC: US Bureau of the Census.

Watson, S. (1986) *Housing and Homelessness: A Feminist Perspective*. London: Routledge & Kegan Paul.

Watson, S. (1988) *Accommodating Inequality*. Sydney: Allen & Unwin.

Watson, S. and Gibson, K. (eds) (1995) *Postmodern Cities and Spaces*. Oxford: Blackwell.

Wekerle, G., Peterson, R. and Morley, D. (eds) (1980) *New Space for Women*. Boulder CO: Westview Press.

Wilson, E. (1995) The invisible flaneur, in S. Watson and K. Gibson (eds) *Postmodern Cities and Spaces*. Oxford: Blackwell.

Woolf, V. (1929) *A Room of One's Own*. London: Hogarth Press.

4

'She's there for me': caring in a rural community

Imogen Taylor

'Carers are no longer the Cinderellas of social policy. One of the striking developments of the last decade has been the increased reference to carers in public policy documents . . . carers have moved out of the shadows into the policy arena' (Twigg and Atkin 1994: 1). But has their increased visibility resulted in real gains for carers? While male carers have been put on the agenda, have some women continued to be excluded? Have 'care in the community' and 'familism', or the ideology of family life (Hooyman and Gonyea 1995), simply served to reinforce the oppression of carers and keep them in the shadows? Although they are now beginning to appear, like the tip of an iceberg, policy for carers remains undeveloped and we do not yet have a good understanding of how their needs are met in relation to the mainstream service system (Twigg and Atkin 1994).

In this chapter, I explore issues of gender and caring which have taken on a heightened significance with the implementation of 'care in the community': 'The rhetoric hides the labour of women and by portraying it as both a service of choice for the consumer and the relationship of choice for the carer, the uncomfortable exploitation of carers can be glossed over' (Brown and Smith 1993: 188). I examine gender and caring in the light of findings from a small study of rural carers, a group who continue to remain particularly hidden. I then identify those features of a carer support service found to be responsive to the needs of carers, and from which lessons could be learnt for the wider service system. Finally, I highlight the paradox that a successful service for carers is dependent on women in the paid care-giving role.

This chapter encompasses care receivers who are adults, including older people, physically disabled people, people with learning disabilities and people with mental health problems. Although there are many differences within and between these populations and their concerns are not homogeneous, they share common quality of life concerns. Adult care receivers all have long-term disabilities which are likely to persist indefinitely. They are subject to interventions by health and social service systems which are increasingly focused on short-term interventions rather than long-term care. Finally, many such adults are poor and therefore lack choice and flexibility in their care (Hooyman and Gonyea 1995).

In this chapter, care-giving work is defined as 'maintenance help or services, rendered for the well being of individuals who cannot perform such activities themselves' (Hooyman and Gonyea 1995: 3). The distinction made between *caring for* and *caring about* (Dalley 1988) continues to be useful because it emphasizes that caring involves both services for people who cannot perform such activities themselves, and affection which may also include the work of managing feelings and sustaining relationships. However, there are also risks in linking caring for and caring about because the latter can be romanticized (Hooyman and Gonyea 1995). Carers who care about are expected to be self-sacrificing and caring tasks are not seen as real work because they do not resemble the structured, time regulated work of the marketplace.

Recognition that the needs of care givers and receivers are interactive and dynamic rather than mutually exclusive is fundamental. Morris (1991) drew our attention to the risk that a focus on carers excludes care receivers from analysis, and that viewing recipients of care as burdens marginalizes the needs of disabled people, who in older age groups are primarily women. Disabled people argue that the concept of care is inappropriately applied to their situation: they do not seek care but rather require personal assistance. Morris calls for care to be used only in the context of caring about, rather than caring for. While it is undoubtedly true that society disables people with impairments from functioning to their capacity by refusing to provide proper services, the right to determine types and standards of care should be extended to include both care receivers and care givers (Dalley 1996). In this chapter, the focus is on care givers, or carers.

Caring and gender

Caring for adults began to be addressed by feminists in the late 1970s when an increase in research focusing on older people shifted attention from younger women and children to an acknowledgement of women's responsibilities to care at each stage of the life cycle (Land 1978; Finch and Groves 1983; Graham 1983). There is now a substantial literature on women caring and increasing evidence that the requirement to care can have destructive effects on the mental and physical health of women, and be disastrous for their long-term economic independence as a result of lost salary and retirement benefits and lost potential for financial equity in relationships (Hooyman and Gonyea 1995). Nevertheless, socially constructed structural conditions and gender biased policies ensure that choices for women continue to be restricted.

The focus of attention on women carers has recently been challenged by evidence about the extent of caring for older people by their spouses, and in particular evidence of caring by men: 'The delivery of community care services can no longer function on simple expectations that women can, should and must care. Nor can it function any longer on assumptions that men cannot, do not and should not care' (Fisher 1994: 677). Rather it is important to understand the conditions under which caring by women and men is undertaken and how it can be supported by formal services.

It is also important to understand how the work of women and men is prescribed and proscribed by ideas from the New Right which emphasize traditional family values. In this world the family is viewed as the ideal source of care, and minimal backup or last resort services are justified on the basis of preserving the rights of the family to make their own decisions and be protected from state intervention: 'The onus of responsibility for caring is cloaked in the ideological sanctity of family values' (McDaniel 1993: 139). This perspective denies the existence of alternate family structures including single-parent families, or lesbian and gay families. It also assumes women are at home and free to provide care, and denies the reality that care in the family is frequently not loving and often abusive (Taylor 1991).

However, to argue that the caring role is always oppressive and a burden is too simplistic: 'the meaning of social caring is very different for white educated feminists, who are competing with men in the public sphere, than the private sphere of women with low incomes, black women and disabled women' (Bagilhole 1996: 41). In addition to gender, the caring experience is inevitably shaped by the social constructs of age, race, class and sexual orientation, factors I will discuss shortly.

Research into gender and care

Statistics provided by the Office of Population, Censuses and Surveys (1992) reveals that there are 6.8m carers in the UK, of whom 13 per cent are men and 17 per cent are women. This represents a wide range of caring experience – not all these individuals are involved in hands-on care, and many people designated as carers simply undertake paperwork and keep an eye on or keep the cared-for person company. A more recent analysis suggests it would be sensible to concentrate service development on carers who undertake physical and/or personal care, and that carers in these categories would number 1.29m over the UK as a whole (Parker and Lawton 1994).

In their analysis of the 1990 census data, Arber and Ginn (1995) found that 10 per cent of men compared to 13 per cent of women were undertaking some form of caring and they tended to be men in later life caring for spouses. (Regrettably, data about caring in the context of a lesbian or gay relationship is not available.) This data appears at first sight to challenge previous assumptions that the overwhelming majority of carers are women (Land 1978; Finch and Groves 1983; Walker 1983). However, three important distinctions between care provided by women and men remain. First, men's concerns focus most frequently on 'horizontal ties' to the spouse whereas women are concerned with 'vertical ties' to parents, in-laws, children and siblings as well as the spouse (Hooyman and Gonyea 1995: 22).

Second, in relation to spouse care, there is evidence that men have consciously *chosen* to adopt the caring role, even though marriage and co-residence constitute strong obligations (Bytheway 1987; Parker 1989; Braithwaite 1990; Fisher 1994). In contrast, women do not make a conscious choice but rather 'drift' into caring (Lewis and Meredith 1988; Aronson 1990). These differences are likely to have significant implications for the meaning of caring to carers and also to how services are viewed. There is evidence that women who perform caring work feel assistance is unnecessary or inappropriate, whereas men who perform such tasks feel entitled to help (Twigg and Atkin 1994). This may help to explain some findings that men carers experience less stress than women (Levin *et al.* 1988; Braithwaite 1990). Furthermore, it has been suggested that it is possible that women who have devoted much of their earlier life to caring for others may find the continuing role a disappointment, whereas 'men may find caring a welcome change and an opportunity to find a role after retirement from work' (Fisher 1994: 670).

Third, Arber and Ginn (1995) found that women carers are more likely to provide personal care and although cross-sex personal care is performed within the marital relationship, it is seldom provided by adult children caring for parents or in more distant caring relationships. This may reflect the preferences of care receivers for same-sex care.

> Cross-gender tending of an intimate character threatens conventional expectations concerning what a man should see and touch in relation to a woman and vice versa. These cross-gender rules have an asymmetrical character to them. What men may do for women in relation to bodily contact is more highly constrained than women for men.
>
> (Twigg and Atkin 1994: 32)

Based on their study of 90 carers, Twigg and Atkin concluded that 'men either found it more difficult to undertake cross-gender tending than women, or felt more justified in refusing to do it. Male carers were more likely to define specific boundaries around what they would or would not do' (1994: 32).

Data in relation to gender varies by class, although we do not know a great deal about this. There is evidence that co-resident care is more likely to be offered by working-class women and men than middle class (Arber and Ginn 1992). Carers with few material resources may be carrying the greatest burden of care. Carers are likely to find themselves in a situation of economic dependence because of the dependency of others, particularly women who lose employment income and associated pension rights (Glendinning 1990).

Race and caring is also under-researched. Evidence about African Caribbean and Asian carers is at best patchy. The caring of older Asian people is typically carried out by women (Gunaratnam 1993) but the assumption that Asian and African Caribbean families have extended family networks who provide caring is now being questioned. A significant proportion of Asian elders live alone (Fenton 1987; Blakemore 1993). In African Caribbean families, members may be isolated and relatively unsupported (Fenton 1987). The health of Asian and African Caribbean elders is worse than that of their white counterparts (Fenton 1987) yet inadequate housing and economic circumstances make it difficult for Asian kin to provide care (Atkin and Rollings 1993). There is also evidence of low take-up of services by ethnic minority carers (Social Services Inspectorate 1995). This has been attributed to lack of knowledge about service provision, inappropriate information giving, inappropriate service provision and racism (Gunaratnam 1993).

Carers in rural south west England

In 1995, Bristol University researchers undertook a study in rural south west England to examine the operation of a carer support scheme and make recommendations for its future (Fisher et al. 1995). In 1993, joint finance by health authority and social services staff had been agreed to support a two-year development project aimed at promoting services for carers and by 1995, five women carers' support workers (CSWs) had been placed in selected primary healthcare teams (PHCT) across the county. This was not intended to restrict the CSW to serving carers only known to that PHCT but rather to develop services across the geographical area in which she was located. Four areas were predominantly rural, the fifth comprised an area of small seaside towns favoured by retirees.

Our study drew on existing statistical data and policy documents, a survey of referrals to the service, interviews with health and personal social services staff and interviews with 15 carers in receipt of services. Most of the carers (85 per cent) referred to the service lived with the person they cared for. The service was clearly oriented towards the older carer, probably because the rate of attendance at PHCTs was likely to be higher among older people, and also three of the PHCTs were located in areas with a higher than average proportion of the population in the older age range.

The sample design prioritized the identification of key issues rather than gaining a representative sample of all carers, and CSWs were asked to select carers who exemplified people the service was designed to assist. Interviews were undertaken with nine women and six men carers, all of whom were white (less than one half of one percent of the population in the area concerned came from ethnic minority groups). Consistent with the national picture (Arber and Ginn 1995) the men tended to be caring for spouses in later life, whereas the women were concerned with vertical ties to parents, in-laws and children as well as the spouse. Included were three wives aged 60–70 caring for their husbands and one mother in her early forties caring for an adult son. There were four daughters and one son aged from early forties to 67 caring for parents. Six male carers whose ages ranged from mid-forties to early eighties were a husband/partner of the cared-for person.

Interviews lasted one to two hours and were taped and transcribed. Recognizing that the purpose of this study was to evaluate the operation of a carer support service rather than explore gender and caring, subsequent analysis of interview data provides the basis for the following discussion of selected aspects of gender and the caring experience: the level of care provided; caring as a choice; contact with formal services; and contact with informal networks.

Sophisticated and sometimes intensive care in the community

In all cases the carer was providing more than 20 hours care per week, including physical and personal care. The degree of 'sophisticated and sometimes intensive care' in the community (Brown and Smith 1993: 188) is graphically described by Vera and Jack. Vera, in her sixties, was caring for her husband of the same age who had a stroke three years earlier: recovered well and then had another which left him frail and incontinent,

'He couldn't walk. He couldn't sit up and he couldn't do much at all for himself . . . it's been hard work. A lot of exercises, making him do a little more each time . . . then he started getting very severe diarrhoea, going as much as twenty times a day . . . Over the course of the winter it's got me down rather a lot. I had to keep clearing up after him and the urgency of making sure he got into the toilet in time because his walking is still a bit slow . . . His left hand still does not work properly so there's the business of getting his clothes off quick enough.'

Jack, in his early eighties, was caring for his woman partner of some 50 years who had dementia, was losing her ability to walk and was incontinent:

'In the beginning when I was washing, I used to put five bath towels under her during the night. I'd put her to bed with two towels under her and then two hours afterwards, she'd be wet through so I'd take those towels away and put two more towels under her and then one under the sheet and every morning I had to wash two sheets and five towels apart from our washing.'

There was little discernible difference in the 'caring for' given by men or women spouses. However, the relative isolation experienced by each household and the absence of another member meant there were no obvious alternatives to cross-gender caring which research indicates men carers find more difficult (Wenger 1990; Twigg and Atkin 1994). The one exception was Tom, supported by his two daughters who lived nearby, in caring for his wife with Alzheimer's disease. He carried out the tasks of washing, dressing and toileting her and in addition his daughters came to bathe and wash her and see to her hair.

Harry looked after his parents in their nineties with a number of health problems. Harry left toileting his mother and care of her prolapse to his 90-year-old partially sighted father. As Harry's woman friend (seen by them both as crucial to his capacity to continue caring) commented, 'he draws the line there and I quite understand he has to be like that'.

Lack of alternative sources of same-gender personal care did not mean the men were at ease with this aspect of their role. Jack's comments highlight his ambivalence about cross-gender caring,

'It's not a man's work, is it? But it is, we're human beings and I know the body inside out . . . if you love a person you do a lot of things . . . I think a woman should look after a woman but I've learned that a woman relies on a man and all through my life I've always said that a woman is twice as good as a man.'

Interestingly, both Jack and Tom felt they had learnt in the Forces to be self-sufficient.

Caring as a 'choice'

'Choice' is a difficult concept in a society where women continue to be denied equal access to the public sphere and are more likely than men to be active in the private sphere of the family. Furthermore, the rhetoric of 'choice' associated with 'care in the community' masks an exploitation of both men and women carers (Brown and Smith 1993). However, there was some evidence that the men viewed caring as a job which they had a choice in taking on, providing a role following retirement even though it was clear that marriage and co-residence also constituted strong obligations (Bytheway 1987; Braithwaite 1990; Fisher 1994). Jack most strikingly conveyed this. On retirement from the Forces because he 'loved working' he had continued until he was 70 as a security guard:

'I've always been a Jack the lad then I realised that when [she] was poorly like she was, I'd have to calm down . . . [someone from social services] said that we would have to have help and [CSW] said to me "Would you like to become a carer?" and I said "I don't want nobody else to look after her while I'm alive" so I became a carer. Something I'm proud of.'

There was a strong element of pay-back in Jack's motivation to care and throughout the interview he referred to the reciprocity in their relationship: 'She's been a good friend to me . . . I've never done anything without her and she's never done anything without me. We worked together a long time'.

In contrast, there was an absence of a discourse of choice or even of pay-back in the interviews with women carers. In particular, daughters caring for parents reflected a 'drift' into the caring role (Lewis and Meredith 1988) and the explicit feeling that there was no other option (Aronson 1990, 1991). Ann's story described the progression from mum living independently round the corner to 'more or less' living with Ann and going home at night, to her moving in with them as her health deteriorated.

However, this drift was not exclusive to women carers. John, in his forties, caring for his wife with rheumatoid arthritis, also described the incremental nature of the caring role,

'When we first got married she could walk and do housework . . . It's only in the last few years that she hasn't been able to dress herself. I never really thought of it in the way that I was caring for her. It crept up on us so I carried on doing what was necessary.'

Contact with services

Carers are viewed ambiguously by formal services. They are 'on the margins of the social care system: in one sense within its remit, part of its concerns and responses; in another, beyond its remit, part of the taken-for-granted reality against which welfare services operate' (Twigg and Atkin 1994: 11). For carers in this study, a significant feature influencing access to services was undoubtedly geographic isolation. With one exception, all were living in rural areas, hamlets, villages or small towns, some distance from major centres of populations where services were provided. The experience of rural carers is under researched. The National Federation of Women's Institutes (1993) surveyed 7000 carers living in largely rural areas and found that as local services diminish and transport services are eroded, people are forced to rely on services further away. Certainly access to leisure facilities or support services was problematic for carers in this study. They were often not considered by transport providers to be entitled to transport in their own right to enable them to take a break from caring. Furthermore, the time required to make such a trip presented a difficult decision about leaving the cared-for person.

Bearing in mind it was contact with the CSW which resulted in the carers being included in this research, in common with other studies (Healy and Yarrow 1997) these carers shared a reluctance to seek help and to risk being a 'nuisance' to services which they knew were over-stretched. There is however, some indication of a gender difference in the stage that help was sought, with women carers appearing to continue coping without help for longer. The invisibility of these women was striking as they described only gaining attention as their health deteriorated. Ann had learnt that she only gained attention from the doctor when she (Ann) was ill:

'You've got to go in when you feel bad. I was going in all bright
and chirpy and cheerful and saying these things [about mother
needing help] and he would look at me and think "Well, you
can't be that bad because you look all right". I think the reason
the assessment was done so quickly was because last time I went
to the doctor, I was really down. That's something I've learnt, not
to wait until you feel strong enough to go to the doctor but go
when you are down, then they treat you more seriously.'

Services were offered to women based on 'their inability to cope rather than an analysis which focuses on the impossibility and unfairness of their situation' (Brown and Smith 1993: 186). Carers continue much longer without help than is reasonable for their health and that of their family. As Ann said:

'Because we've always been independent for a long time we've
never asked for any help and I now realize that if Mum was the
sort of person who went to the doctors, we could have got a lot
of help a long time ago. We've carried on further than some
people would without getting help. I now realize that you've got
to ask, people don't know what you need unless you ask for it.'

Jane, a widow, described her reluctance to accept a suggestion that she seek respite care for her 90-year-old mother who had said that going away would kill her. Ann could not imagine trusting a sitting service:

'The sitting service won't really work with mum as she is. In the
evenings she wants to go out and find *her* mum. Although they
tell me that people are experienced that come and do the sitting, I
don't know how they'd deal with that, because its not an easy
situation to deal with.'

Stories told by the men carers were characterized more by being offered help but turning it down, not because they did not feel entitled to it but for other reasons. John felt it cost too much, Jack was proud of being able to do the job himself and Harry's father would not allow his son to bring in extra help. Tom however, of all the carers in the interview sample, best exemplified a readiness to accept help, including a sitting service, respite care for one week in four, and membership of a carers group, in addition to regular contact with the CSW.

With the exception of Kath who travelled a daily 30 mile round trip to visit her parents, the carers were co-resident with the care receivers and lack of adequate accommodation was a common concern. Some had acquired elaborate equipment such as a stair lift and a mattress elevator, others used more prosaic aids such as incontinence pads and commodes. Homes were converted for caring purposes, giving new meaning to the term 'cottage hospital'. The only 'living room' of a small house lived in by Ann, her husband and their two teenage sons had been made into a bedroom for grandmother. However, lack of privacy and space was an issue and the family were in the process of moving to larger accommodation. Socio-economic status increased the accommodation options available (Arber and Ginn 1992; Healy and Yarrow 1997) and home ownership gave essential room for manoeuvre to some carers to enable needed privacy and space. However, for others, such as Mary and her husband in a cramped first floor council flat, this was out of the question.

Informal networks

Sir Roy Griffiths, architect of community care, proposed that formal agencies 'support and where possible strengthen' informal networks (Department of Health 1988: para. 3.2) and this was consolidated in the 1990 National Health Service and Community Care Act. It might be expected that informal networks are particularly important in more remote rural communities, distant from public services. Wenger (1984) in her study of rural networks and older people in North Wales emphasized the notion of support, and proposed that services work in cooperation with 'natural helpers'. However, in our study there was a compelling absence of informal networks, recognizing that in those situations where informal networks are working well, carers may not come to the attention of the CSWs.

With one exception, the carers were isolated from kin and carrying out their work largely single-handedly. In some cases, relatives were in other parts of the country, either because children had moved away or older people had moved to the south west to retire. In others, for example both Jane and Mary, there were conflicting relationships with adult children which inhibited sharing of the caring role. In contrast, Tom was well supported by his two daughters and son all of whom lived in the same town where they grew up. This town was the one centre of any size in the study which may have been a factor in enabling the adult children to live locally.

There was a degree of self-imposed isolation as, typically, both men and women carers protected their adult children from knowledge about the pressures they were under. As Ted, in his eighties, caring for his wife with Parkinson's disease said, 'We found that the family don't understand. Whether they don't or they don't want to I've never found out'. This isolation is compounded by the feeling of being different, as Ted said: 'There are times when I feel I'd like somebody to talk to but it's very difficult. It's almost the main thing. I do feel that. I can't relate to people about how my wife is. They don't understand'.

A reluctance to 'go public' with neighbours about the need for contact and support was a further isolating factor, possibly particularly for male carers. David was very clear about the risks of sharing information locally:

'If I said something to people in the flats it could get back to my wife. A lot of them are widowed and some of them have lost their partners while they've been here and they've got their own problems and it's not the kind of person you could talk to.'

Sustaining networks requires time and energy to make contact. One factor expressed particularly (but not only) by women carers was a reluctance to leave the cared-for person. Vera felt guilty enjoying herself and leaving behind her husband:

'I haven't been able to do much this winter and I don't like leaving him for two or three hours at a stretch, mainly because he's on his own and a bit fed up . . . I don't feel like going out and enjoying myself and leaving him sat here in his chair.'

Inviting friends into the family home may not be a solution to this problem. The presence of the care receiver may be difficult unless there is adequate space to allow for privacy. Mary found socializing with friends was prohibitive in the presence of her husband:

'He doesn't like visitors. He says "I'm a loner, I don't need people" and I say to him "Well, I'm not a loner, I'm a sociable body, but he just doesn't like me going anywhere . . . I like to be in company and I get very melancholy if I'm on my own too long. I have brought my friends in but that's his chair and he just sits there, hardly talks to them at all.'

Mary's husband had been physically and emotionally abusive towards her in earlier years and although he was now physically dependent, the emotional abuse continued as he exerted power from his silent position in the chair.

There is evidence that older men have smaller social networks than older women (Wenger 1984), but in our study there did not appear to be a significant difference. Retirement had negative implications for networks of both women and men. As Vera said:

'You find who your friends are and having moved down here eight years ago, I know quite a few people but not real friends. When my husband retired all our friends seemed to scatter to different parts of the country. They've been very supportive telephone-wise. It's not the same as having people more locally though I've got one good friend in the road who's been very supportive. People don't visit when you're a bit of a problem, you don't get asked out the same.'

Some carers had taken advantage of different kinds of support group. Ann for example felt she had benefited from contact with the Alzheimer's Society. Tom found a carers' group very helpful:

'[We] go and meet all different sorts of people and chat about problems. We have a cup of tea and a biscuit and if you've got any problems you can talk about it. We have stress meetings which is very helpful. It just gets you out of a rut. When you can go and talk to someone and have a laugh.'

However, John's experience had been painfully the reverse: 'I walked in and I was the odd one out by about twenty years. All the other carers were in their seventies. I felt out on a limb.'

If contact with relatives and friends does assist people to cope and avoid reaching breaking point (Levin *et al.* 1988; Wenger 1993), then, with the exception of Tom, men and women carers in this study were vulnerable to stress.

A carers' support service

Crucially, the effectiveness of the service offered by CSWs is that it enables carers to continue to cope, rather than focusing on the carer who breaks down or where services are already involved with the service user. Carers valued three key features of the CSW: 'psychological maintenance'; advocacy; and negotiating practical services (Fisher *et al.* 1995).

Psychological maintenance alleviated the isolation and gave the carer the sense that someone was available if required. Carers referred to the CSW as 'being there for me to turn to', 'somebody that cares', and 'she's there for me'. As Kath said, 'It's quite isolating looking after elderly people in their own home. It's very isolating so it's nice to have this person who you can think of as your on your side'.

Immediate and direct access was valued rather than having to convince reception staff of the need to make contact. This sense of security contributed to carers feeling they could risk trusting the CSW with the complexities of their situation without being adversely judged. This was most clearly expressed by the women carers, voiced in this instance by

Kath who was getting to the point where she could hardly bear to be in the same room with her father: 'I was feeling all the sort of guilt and all the things that people do feel. I was given permission to feel all the things that I felt without needing to feel guilt. That's a big help'.

The guilt was acute for women carers when their feelings of 'caring about' had been depleted, or when they were experiencing negative feelings towards the care receiver. Mary found that the CSW was the only person who supported her to give voice to the unthinkable:

'She [the CSW] didn't think I was abnormal. My husband was being absolutely bloody one day and I was almost reduced to tears and I put a cup of tea down in front of him and he never answered and as I walked away I thought "I wish you were dead" and I felt dreadful. I felt awful and it just wouldn't let me rest. I couldn't sleep and it was on a Friday night and I went to confession and I just stayed there for a good minute and I couldn't say it. In the end I said that I'd wished my husband dead and he said "Is that all?" Although I'd confessed it I felt I hadn't told anybody who would really understand until I told [the CSW].'

Interestingly, none of the six male carers expressed guilt of this kind and the focus of discussion in their interviews tended to be on more instrumental concerns. Even David who had initially contacted the CSW following an incident when 'I put my wife across my knee and gave her a spanking. Something I shall never forget', focused on his concern for the future ('I hope I never have to do it again') rather than remorse for the past.

The carers felt that the role of the CSW as advocate, independent of health and social services reinforced the sense of someone being 'on their side', in addition to the value of CSW's power to argue on their behalf: 'she negotiated very sensitively and very powerfully with social services'. Receiving support from independent CSWs was significant to gaining the trust of the carers:

'She [the CSW] doesn't come across as an official person, like the social worker has or the physio that I saw, all the other people . . . you've really got to be careful of what you say to them because you don't realize at the beginning that everything you say is noted . . . they all speak to each other, like a kind of case conference.'

Similarly, Bagilhole (1996) found in her study of mothers receiving care from volunteers that professionals were viewed as oppressive and powerful, not listening to the mothers or allowing them to feel they had anything to offer.

Finally, CSWs were also prepared to offer practical help such as delivering a commode, arranging for day care or sorting out a wrongly directed repeat prescription.

In these circumstances, the carefully negotiated offer of a practical service has the function not only of offering relief, but also of symbolically demonstrating that solutions can be found . . . Making the service available breaks a psychological log jam and carers begin to feel that life is bearable.

(Fisher *et al*. 1995: 37).

The carer support service was very highly valued by carers. 'It provides a lifeline to people who are often highly stressed, and whose continuing ability to care is vital to both the cared for person and to health and social services increasingly oriented towards care at home' (Fisher *et al*. 1995: 46). The initiative was relatively low cost, yet it was undoubtedly effective in achieving its purpose of developing services for carers and provides indicators of a direction services to carers could take nationally.

Gender and the CSWs

The five CSWs were all women who were or had been married and were employed for 20 hours per week. They were carrying out a complex role at the interface of health and social care and were to a large extent expected to operate independently, without supervision. Although some CSWs were professionally trained, a specific professional qualification was not required for the CSW role and they were paid at the level of community care assistants, lower on the salary scale than that of an unqualified social worker.

The CSWs exemplified 'maternal feminism' (Baines 1991: 37): women who transferred the values and caring functions they had learned and practised within the home to new fields of work. They were without exception women who were skilled in using their imagination and resourcefulness (Balbo 1987). However, there is a paradox: 'Although maternal feminism provided women with a rationale to work outside the home and served to unite women, it also reinforced the traditional role of women as caregivers' (Baines 1991: 37). In particular, given the low pay and status of the CSW, it reinforced the view that caring work is not of high value. This was particularly highlighted by the CSWs working alongside GPs, almost all of whom were highly paid men. Since completion of the evaluation, CSWs have been promoted to the level of community care assistants, their numbers have increased and they continue to all be women.

An agenda for carers

For community care to be non-sexist it is essential to understand the needs of women and men carers and for positive choices to be available for both, supported by social policy and public services (Fisher 1994). Efforts to reduce caring inequities must also encompass the diversities of race, ethnicity, class, age and sexuality as well as gender. To do this more effectively we must know more about these issues in relation to caring. In addition, we must know more about rural carers. Evidence in the study discussed in this chapter does much to dispel any notion of supportive rural networks and instead highlights the intense isolation of many rural carers.

Furthermore, it is important to acknowledge that the caring role is not inevitably oppressive. Feminists have been criticized for viewing caring as negative (Walker 1992). Caring is not necessarily a burden and it may be the outcome of positive choice. Caring is an area of women's expertise: 'Caring is socially important, essential to community, a rich necessity of life and can be emancipating for women' (Bagilhole 1996: 41). This may also be the case for some men.

Note

The Carers (Recognition and Services) Act 1995 was implemented after completion of the research discussed in this chapter. It was introduced 'to provide for the assessment of the ability of carers to provide care' (1995: 1). Although important in symbolizing recognition given to carers, its scope is limited. A carer is only entitled to request an assessment when a local authority is already carrying out an assessment of the person being cared for under the National Health Service and Community Care Act (1990), *and* where the carer 'provides or intends to provide a substantial amount of care on a regular basis' (s. 1b). The meaning of 'regular' and 'substantial' is for each local authority to interpret. It seems unlikely that it would have made a substantive difference to the experience of any of the carers in the study.

References

Arber, S. and Ginn, J. (1992) *Gender and Later Life: A Sociological Analysis of Resources and Constraints*. London: Sage.

Arber, S. and Ginn, J. (1995) Gender differences in informal caring. *Health and Social Care in the Community*, 3 (1): 19–31.

Aronson, J. (1990) Women's perspectives on the informal care of the elderly: public ideology and personal experience of giving and receiving care. *Ageing and Society*, 10: 61–84.

Aronson, J. (1991) Dutiful daughters and undemanding mothers: contrasting images of giving and receiving in middle and later life, in C. Baines, P. Evans and S. Neysmith (eds) *Women's Caring: Feminist Perspectives on Social Welfare*. Toronto: McLelland and Stewart.

Atkin, K. and Rollings, J. (1993) *Community Care in a Multi-Racial Britain*. London: HMSO.

Bagilhole, B. (1996) The effects on women as givers and receivers of voluntary care in Britain. *The European Journal of Women's Studies*, 3: 39–54.

Baines, C. (1991) The professions and an ethic of care, in C. Baines, P. Evans and S. Neysmith (eds) *Women's Caring: Feminist Perspectives on Social Welfare*. Toronto: McLelland and Stewart.

Balbo, L. (1987) Crazy quilts: rethinking the welfare state debate from a woman's point of view, in A. Showstack Sassoon (ed.) *Women and the Welfare State: The Shifting Boundaries of Public and Private*. London: Hutchinson.

Blakemore, K. (1993) Minority families and community care: the case for older people in Asian and Afro-Caribbean communities. Conference paper, December 1993, University of Bristol.

Braithwaite, V. (1990) *Bound to Care*. Sydney: Allen & Unwin.

Brown, H. and Smith, H. (1993) Women caring for people: the mismatch between rhetoric and women's reality? *Policy and Politics*, 21 (3): 185–93.

Bytheway, W.R. (1987) *Informal Care Systems: An Exploratory Study Within Families of Older Steel Workers in South Wales*, report to the Joseph Rowntree Foundation. York: Joseph Rowntree Foundation.

Dalley, G. (1988) *Ideologies of Caring*, 1st edn. London: Macmillan.

Dalley, G. (1996) *Ideologies of Caring*, 2nd edn. London: Macmillan.

Department of Health (1988) *Community Care: An Agenda for Action* (the Griffiths Report). London: HMSO.

Fenton, S. (1987) *Ageing Minorities: Black People as They Grow Up in Britain*. London: Commission for Racial Equality.

Finch, J. and Groves, D. (1983) *A Labour of Love*. London: Routledge.

Fisher, M. (1994) Man-made care: community care and older male carers. *British Journal of Social Work*, 24: 659–80.

Fisher, M., Taylor, I. and Phelps, K. (1995) *Now I've Got a Life: Evaluation of the Somerset Carer Support Project*. Bristol: Bristol University, School for Policy Studies.

Glendinning, C. (1990) Dependency and interdependency: the incomes of informal carers and the impact of social security. *Journal of Social Policy*, 19: 469–97.

Graham, H. (1983) Caring: a labour of love, in J. Finch and D. Groves (eds) *A Labour of Love*. London: Routledge & Kegan Paul.

Gunaratnam, Y. (1993) Breaking the silence: Asian carers in Britain, in J. Bornat, C. Pereira, D. Pilgrim and F. Williams (eds) *Community Care: A Reader*. Basingstoke: Macmillan.

Healy, J. and Yarrow, S. (1997) *Parents Living with Children in Old Age*. Bristol: The Policy Press.

Hooyman, N. and Gonyea, J. (1995) *Feminist Perspectives on Family Care: Policies for Gender Justice*. London: Sage.

Land, H. (1978) Who cares for the family? *Journal of Social Policy*, 7: 357–84.

Levin, E., Sinclair, I. and Gorbach P. (1988) *Families, Services and Confusion in Old Age*. Aldershot: Gower.

Lewis, J. and Meredith, B. (1988) *Daughters Who Care*. London: Routledge & Kegan Paul.

McDaniel, S. (1993) Caring and sharing: demographic ageing, family and the state, in J. Hendricks and C. Rosenthal (eds) *The Remainder of Their Days: Domestic Policy and Older Families in the United States and Canada*. New York: Garland.

Morris, J. (1991) *Pride Against Prejudice: Transforming Attitudes to Disability*. London: Women's Press.

National Federation of Women's Institutes (1993) *Caring for Rural Carers*. London: National Foundation for Women's Institutes.

Office of Population, Censuses and Surveys (1992) *General Household Survey: Carers in 1990*, OPCS Monitor SS 92/2. London: HMSO.

Parker, G. (1989) Unending work and care: a review article. *Work, Employment and Society*, 3: 541–53.

Parker, G. (1993) *With This Body: Caring and Disability in Marriage*. Buckingham: Open University Press.

Parker, G. and Lawton, D. (1994) *Different Types of Care, Different Types of Carer: Evidence from the General Household Survey*. London: HMSO.

Social Services Inspectorate (1995) *What Next for Carers*? London: Department of Health.

Taylor, I. (1991) For better or for worse. caring and the abused wife, in C. Baines, P. Evans and S. Neysmith (eds) *Women's Caring: Feminist Perspectives on Social Welfare*. Toronto: McLelland and Stewart.

Twigg, J. and Atkin, K. (1994) *Carers Perceived: Policy and Practice in Informal Care*. Buckingham: Open University Press.

Walker, A. (1983) Care for elderly people: a conflict between women and the state, in J. Finch and D. Groves (eds) *A Labour of Love*. London: Routledge and Kegan Paul.

Walker, A. (1992) Conceptual perspectives on family and gender caregiving, in J. Dwyer and R. Coward (eds) *Gender, Families and Elder Care*. Newbury Park, CA: Sage.

Wenger, C. (1984) *The Supportive Network: Coping With Old Age*. London: Allen & Unwin.

Wenger, C. (1990) Elderly carers: the need for appropriate intervention. *Ageing and Society*, 10: 197–219.

Wenger, C. (1993) The formation of social networks: self-help, mutual aid and old people in contemporary Britain. *Journal of Ageing Studies*, 7: 25–40.

5

Child protection policy and practice: women in the front line

Elaine Farmer and Margaret Boushel

Introduction

Some risk of harm is an inevitable part of growing up for children in all societies, as they experiment with newly-acquired skills and undertake unfamiliar activities. However, other risks, while common, are not inevitable, such as the risks to health and development which result from unsafe environments or from the harmful behaviour of particular adults.

In this chapter we will examine how risks to the well-being of children are defined and managed by the state in the UK and also by parents. We will argue that the management of risk by the state is, and always has been, a profoundly gendered activity, directed primarily at the mothers of the poorest and most disadvantaged families. We will also show that the very partial responsibility assumed by the state for the protection of children and the way in which that responsibility is carried out often leaves women trying to keep their children safe with inadequate support and with unrealistic expectations of their capacity to protect their children from other family members. It will be demonstrated that women's concerns about harm to their children and their strategies to protect them are wide-ranging and complex, albeit inadequately explored and acknowledged. When the state does intervene, not only are these strategies ignored, but the emphasis is on the regulation of mothering rather than on the provision of services and in contrast the risks posed by men to their children receive scant attention. It will be argued that effective social policies to protect children from abuse and harm need to take more account of the protective efforts actually made by mothers, while challenging these gendered constructions of risk.

In exploring these issues it is acknowledged that the rights and views of children about professional interventions and about the impact of abusive events are easily disregarded or marginalized by parents and the state. Although it is beyond the scope of this chapter to examine this area in any detail, it is recognized that children's rights and gender perspectives are often but not always congruent.

The state and child protection in the UK

The British state takes a very restrictive view of its role in child protection. Two themes about the relationship between the family and the state are reflected in policy in this area. The first is that legislation in the UK takes a residualist approach, rather than identifying overarching rights for children as, for example, occurs in Swedish legislation. Thus, the Children Act 1989, which provides the current legislative framework for child protection in England and Wales, gives local authorities a duty under Section 47 to investigate only where they have reason to believe that a child is suffering or is likely to suffer 'significant harm'. Section 17 of the Act gives local authorities the duty to provide a broader range of services to children 'in need', but it is the local authority itself which is empowered to identify 'need' and decide what if any services are appropriate. In practice, financial restrictions on local authorities have meant that services under this part of the Act are very poorly developed (Aldgate and Tunstill 1996). In addition, universal services to assist parents with child rearing, such as subsidized childcare facilities, are scarce.

The second theme is that state interference in parenting should be minimal (Parton 1991). As a result, power within families 'will lie where it falls' (Fox Harding 1991: 14). Thus there is a marked reluctance by the state to become involved in helping to solve disputes in families or to redress inequalities. As we shall see, this reluctance has a major effect on the acknowledgement of domestic violence in child protection investigations and on the support offered to mothers with violent partners.

This emphasis on the privacy of family life and the focus on specific harmful actions or omissions by parents not only ignores the much broader range of risks to children which mothers address but also encourages a professional approach to child protection which is narrowly investigative and judgemental rather than supportive. It also takes no account of the fact that the cirumstances which facilitate adequate parenting are unevenly distributed in our society. In the UK the poorest families are those with young children and particularly lone parents (see, for example, Middleton et al. 1997) and it is these families which are most likely to be drawn into the child protection system. This restrictive approach, which has been the central feature of British child protection policies for over a century, also encourages a situation where state concern shifts from one specific type of abuse to another, for reasons which are often more to do with prevailing concerns in the wider society than with the state of knowledge of children's welfare.

Since perceptions about risk to children alter over time, we will begin our examination of child protection policy with a brief historical analysis of child maltreatment in the UK.

The historical background: changing concerns about risks to children

Women have played a major part in many of the campaigns to force the state to take a more active role in the protection of children. In periods when the feminist movement has been strong it has been a major influence in drawing attention to physical and sexual violence by men within the home. When women's groups have been less active, societal concerns have come to rest on issues of neglect, which has been assumed to mean neglectful mothering. For example, the changes brought about by the 1889 Prevention of Cruelty to Children Act which for the first time gave courts the power to remove children from abusive parents and the 1885 Criminal Law Amendment Act, making 16 the age of consent for girls, were partly the result of major campaigns undertaken by the early feminist movement to increase the parental rights of women and to eradicate the double standards in sexual behaviour exemplified by the Contagious Diseases Acts of the 1860s (Jeffreys 1985). Both pieces of legislation, and the campaigns surrounding them, reflect a concern about men and *fathers* as perpetrators of both physical and sexual violence.

In the early twentieth century different concerns were fuelled by the evidence of the poor physical condition of Boer War volunteers and the links made by the eugenics movement between motherhood and the success of the Empire (Davin 1978). The health and child-rearing practices of working-class mothers became the focus of attention and the physical and sexual abuse of children all but disappeared from view as an issue of public concern. Issues of neglectful *mothers* were seen as the main concern, and the notion of the 'problem family' took a firm hold. Little if anything was said about fathers. This shift in emphasis coincided with the reduced prominence of the women's movement. The years between the First and Second World Wars were ones of complacency about child abuse.

The end of the Second World War heralded a renewed campaign to bring the issue of 'child suffering' back onto the public agenda. The driving force was the Women's Group on Public Welfare. Parker (1995) argues that the campaign foundered because of government fears about the resource implications, reluctance to increase state intervention in family life and resistance by the National Society for the Prevention of Cruelty to Children (NSPCC) to any encroachment onto its territory. Parker also makes the interesting point that the low level of referrals about physical abuse may have been in part because of the wartime mobilization of men. In the annual reports of the local children's committees and in the principal childcare publication of the early 1950s there are references only to neglect and deprivation. Poor *mothering* remained the focus of attention during this period.

In the UK the 'rediscovery' of child abuse, and specifically physical abuse, had to await the death of a 7-year-old child. Maria Colwell died in 1973 at the hands of her stepfather. Her death attracted enormous attention from the media, and the social workers who had returned her home at the request of her family were blamed for failing to protect her. This re-emergence of a recognition of physical abuse followed in the wake of the work of Henry Kempe and his colleagues in the United States. Drawing on evidence provided by new radiological techniques, which made it easier to detect injuries sustained by children, Kempe and his colleagues attributed such injuries to deliberate mistreatment on the part of parents (Kempe *et al.* 1962).

The result was a government circular in 1974, in which the framework for the current system of the management of child abuse in the UK was put in place. It devolved responsibility for child abuse investigations onto local authorities and had three dimensions. Local authorities were expected first to establish multi-disciplinary area review committees whose role was to oversee practice in their areas, second to ensure that multi-disciplinary case conferences were called to decide on action when a case of abuse came to light and third to establish a 'central record of information' (now called the Child Protection Register) of all children deemed to be at risk of abuse in order to facilitate interprofessional communication (Department of Health and Social Security 1974).

One of the broader trends which encouraged the re-emergence of physical abuse as a concern was that the women's movement had become more active and better organized. Its influence in the field of child and family welfare can be seen, for example, in the setting up of both the select committee on violence in marriage in 1974, and the select committee on violence in the family in 1976. A second factor in the renewed attention to child abuse was the availability of statistics provided by the NSPCC from 1974 onwards and the large numbers of referrals received by the newly-established generic social services departments (social work departments in Scotland). The notion that family problems and child abuse could be attributed to the inadequacy or delinquent characteristics of a small number of parents, rather than to poverty or other structural inequalities also suited the political philosophy of the Conservative government of the time.

The sexual abuse of children, often by a male family member, re-emerged as a major cause for concern in the 1980s after having disappeared from sight since the 1930s. The impetus was, once again, provided by the feminist movement, where the testimony of women seeking help from rape crisis centres in the United States and in Britain indicated that many had been sexually abused in childhood over prolonged periods and often by family members. Women working in the child protection arena campaigned to have these concerns addressed by their agencies (see, for example, Boushel and Noakes 1988). In the late 1980s, a government-funded public enquiry was set up to investigate the situation in one local area in Britain, Cleveland, where an unprecedented number of children had been diagnosed as having been sexually abused (again with the aid of the new medical diagnostic technique of anal dilation) and removed from the care of their parents (Secretary of State for Social Services 1988). Media and political attention focused on the activities of the female paediatrican and female local authority child abuse coordinator who were accused of over-hasty and inadequate assessments of risk. The refusal of the local male senior police staff to cooperate in investigations received far less attention (Campbell 1988).

Statistics show that the great majority of sexual abuse is committed by men and boys (Finkelhor 1984; Nash and West 1985; Baker and Duncan 1985; Kelly et al. 1991). They also show that although at first sight the responsibility for physical abuse is approximately equally distributed between women and men, when controlled for by household composition, birth fathers are implicated in 61 per cent of the injury cases where the child was living with them, and mothers in only 36 per cent of such cases (Creighton and Noyes 1989). Of course, the categories of maltreatment are not neutral and are themselves constructed around gendered definitions of proper parenting (Ferguson 1990). While in a two-parent family neglect could be considered to be the responsibility of either parent, in practice mothers are deemed to be responsible for childcare and therefore for any deficits in that care (Farmer and Owen 1995). As Gordon (1989: 166) puts it: 'the very concept of child neglect . . . arose from the establishment of [the] norm of male breadwinning and female domesticity'.

This brief historical analysis shows that the patterns of child maltreatment which concern society at any one time not only reflect the organization of child rearing in which mothers are assumed to play the major role, but have also been influenced by the extent to which the women's movement and child rescue organizations have been able to influence the political agenda. They are therefore profoundly gendered.

State intervention in families: a gendered activity

At the end of the 1980s, one result of public concern about professional interventions in Cleveland was that the Department of Health funded more than 15 research studies to explore what happened to children and families caught up in the child protection system and how effective it was in protecting children. The studies showed that the majority of children who were the subject of child protection investigations (about

180,000 children are referred each year) were being adequately protected from further abuse. However, the accumulated findings also forcefully suggested that too many children were being dealt with under formal child protection procedures who would have been better served by the deployment of family support services, and that when child protection procedures were enacted the welfare of the children and their parents received too little attention (Department of Health 1995). The publication of these studies heralded a prolonged debate on these issues.

However, other crucial messages from the research were not highlighted, in particular those concerning the impact of gender on the operation of the child protection system. This was despite the fact that an earlier Department of Health *Summary of Inquiry Reports* (1991) into child abuse deaths had concluded that these inquiries gave too little consideration to structural issues, in particular those relating to race and gender. There was less information in the studies about issues of race and child protection, although it was shown that cultural and linguistic misunderstandings and the fear of racism makes the impact of child protection procedures on black and minority ethnic family members particularly problematic (Owen and Farmer 1996).

Drawing on these studies and in particular on the study of decision-making, intervention and outcome in child protection work conducted by one of the authors (Farmer and Owen 1995), it will be shown that the child protection system shows a significant gender bias in the management of child abuse. The Farmer and Owen study uses data on a sample of 44 children whose names had been placed on the child protection register. This sample was drawn from 73 newly registered cases after attendance at 120 initial child protection case conferences in two local authorities. The parents, older children and key workers were interviewed after the initial case conference and again 20 months later. The children represented a fairly typical cross-section of cases registered by social services departments. Concerns centred on physical abuse in a third, on sexual abuse in another third, and the remainder were divided between cases of neglect and those deemed to constitute emotional abuse. Forty-four mothers were interviewed. In the third of families where there was a father or male partner he too was interviewed with two exceptions.

This research showed that mothers were under-included in offers of service but over-included in efforts to regulate their parenting. It also showed that rather than being treated as potential allies in the protection of their children, mothers were often treated with suspicion. At the same time father figures were left relatively untouched.

The under-inclusion of mothers in the provision of services

A study of 1825 referrals of suspected maltreatment by Gibbons *et al.* (1995) showed that among the referrals least likely to be pursued at both the initial referral and the subsequent investigation stage were those relating to lone mothers where the concerns were about neglect or emotional abuse. At neither stage were services provided for these mothers. This occurred even though lone mothers in the UK experience high rates of poverty and unemployment and are therefore likely to have less respite from childcare than other mothers (Bradshaw and Millar 1991). Such difficulties probably account for the fact that the children of lone mothers are eight times more likely than other children to enter substitute care (Bebbington and Miles 1989) and, as we shall see later, the range of strategies available for lone parents to cope with risks to their children are limited by the absence of a second adult in the household. In spite of these disadvantages lone mothers with parenting difficulties were systematically passed over in the allocation of services.

This lack of service has also been shown to be a particular feature of many cases of sexual abuse referred into the child protection system. Such cases were rapidly closed as soon as mothers were able to demonstrate that they had separated from their abusing partners and in this way keep their children safe. The two-year follow-up of cases in the Farmer and Owen (1995) study showed the flaws in this common practice. At follow-up many of the mothers were still traumatized by the revelation of their children's abuse and as a result they had not had the emotional resources to assist in the recovery of their abused children. They had also lacked management advice about how to deal with the behavioural consequences of the abuse of their children and many of the sexually abused children themselves had received no direct help or counselling about their abuse. At follow-up most of the untreated children were depressed and a number were suicidal.

The treatment of mothers as objects of suspicion rather than as allies

Despite the evidence on the gender of abusers, child protection professionals have been slow to disaggregate family members and to clarify the likely risks associated with each parenting figure. The notion of mothers who collude with the sexual abuse of their children has remained a dominant leitmotiv.

The enduring strength of this notion of mothers as collusive may help to explain why, even when mothers have themselves referred their children to the child protection agencies, they are often treated with suspicion. In the Farmer and Owen (1995) study some mothers who had talked openly to a professional such as a health visitor or their doctor about their concerns discovered later that the professional had made a subsequent child abuse referral to the social services department without informing them.

Until recently it was common practice to interview children suspected of having been sexually abused without informing or involving the non-abusing mothers. In the Farmer and Owen (1995) study this was the case in three-quarters of the sexual abuse cases. In this way the conduct of the investigation could marginalize non-abusing mothers and replicate their experience of discovering that their child had been abused without their knowledge (Farmer 1993). This practice appeared to be driven by police concerns that informing mothers would mean that information would be passed on by them to the alleged abusers. All mothers were seen as potential informers, since even when mothers had actually referred their children because of their concerns about sexual abuse, this practice was evident.

Once mothers had been brought into the investigation they themselves became the subject of professional scrutiny. In the Farmer and Owen (1995) study, in cases of alleged sexual abuse if mothers were uncertain whether they believed their children's allegations of abuse (a situation more likely to occur when the mother had not been present to hear the allegations in person) or were thought to have retained their attachment to the abuser, the possibility of removing the children was given active consideration.

Such mothers badly needed help in dealing with their feelings about what had happened. However, an exclusive focus on mothers as secondary perpetrators rather than as secondary victims of the abuse of their children often led social workers to judge them as 'non-protective' mothers and to withdraw support. Their need for feelings of shock, self-blame and loss to be understood and for support to be offered was rarely met and this in turn made it more difficult for mothers to provide the understanding needed by their abused children (Gomes-Schwartz et al. 1990). This is particularly worrying as research has shown that children have the best prognosis for recovery when they are believed and supported by a parent (Conte and Schuerman 1987; Wyatt and Mickey 1988; Berliner 1991).

The over-inclusion of mothers in the regulation of their parenting

The operation of the child protection system is characterized by an over-focus on the regulation of mothers and too little attention to fathers and male partners. The process starts early. Milner (1993) has drawn attention to the Department of Health's guidelines on comprehensive assessment (Department of Health 1988), in which most of the questions can only be addressed to the mother. Policies and procedures rarely caution workers about the need to explore the influence of male partners, their background, family history and role in the family which is crucial information if risks are to be well understood (O'Hagan and Dillenburger 1995), and attention is often diverted from the original allegation onto an examination of the quality of care provided by the mother.

Even if the abuse was committed by the father figure, responsibility for the abuse may be seen by professionals as shared by the mother based on the often unspoken assumption that she should not have allowed it to happen. Indeed, the expectation that mothers will protect their children from their male partners is one which is often made explicit at child protection conferences. In the Farmer and Owen (1995) study the issue of whether the mother could protect the child was considered at 60 per cent of the relevant conferences. In contrast the question of whether the father figure could protect the child was considered at only 19 per cent of the cases where there was a father figure in the family. Yet mothers may not be in a position to protect their children from their male partners, particularly when they are violent.

It was surprising to find that at initial child protection case conferences physical abuse by mothers was much more likely to lead to registration than was physical abuse by men. In the Farmer and Owen (1995) study, in over three-quarters (77 per cent) of cases where mothers were held responsible for physical abuse the child was registered, in contrast to less than half (48 per cent) where a father, stepfather or male cohabitee was held responsible. What might be the reason for this gender bias? All the mothers who had physically abused a child were lone mothers whereas all the father figures were in two-parent families. It may be therefore that lone parents of either gender will be vulnerable to registration and that mothers are disproportionately affected because they constitute the majority of lone parents. In addition, it might have been thought that the mothers in the two-parent families would be able to protect the child from the father figure. Another factor is that men who are violent or abusive pose real threats to front-line staff of social services departments, most of whom are women. It was clear that there were times when social services departments appeared unwilling to intervene where a man was seen as uncooperative and threatening (Miller and Fisher 1992).

Mothers are also affected by the prevailing ideology of motherhood. When children were registered mothers felt blamed and stigmatized, even when the abuse had been inflicted by their husbands or male partners. For some, registration was experienced as an additional pressure and this could actually lead to a deterioration in their circumstances.

This bias towards regulating women rather than men was also reflected in decisions to remove children. Lone mothers whose children were registered stood a greater chance of having children permanently removed from them than did couples (Farmer and Owen 1995). Indeed, studies from other countries highlight the same bias. Thorpe's study of child protection practice in Western Australia (1994) showed that the children of single female parents were more likely to enter care at the time of the investigation than children from other types of family. Gordon (1989) in her research also shows that this practice has long historical roots. At the turn of the century recommendations for removal of children in the United States were more often made in respect of single mother households than two-parent families.

The tendency for child protection work to focus on the regulation of women extends still further. In the Farmer and Owen (1995) study the children in the follow-up sample had been physically abused in equal proportions by men and women. After registration over half of them (56 per cent) remained living with the abusing parent. At the initial child protection case conferences in most cases professionals had been clear about the identity of the alleged abuser. However, after registration in all the cases of physical abuse by a father figure, interventions were directed at his female partner. Once professional attention had shifted in this way onto mothers, the work revolved around not the abuse itself but more general concerns about childcare. In only two cases was there a recommendation for an abusing man to undertake some work on managing their anger and both men refused treatment. A typical pattern of work in cases of physical abuse by a father figure was for emotional support to be offered to the *mother*, sometimes coupled with material help and occasional services to the children, such as activity groups. No work was conducted with the fathers. Indeed, there was no evidence of interventions to address physically abusing behaviour shown either by men or women.

This absence of a clear focus on the source of risk to children is not just a matter of academic interest. In a few cases it could be the difference between life and death for a child. If attention is not given to the parent who poses risks to the child then registration is unlikely to be effective. This has been the theme in a number of inquiries into child deaths, such as those concerning Jasmine Beckford and Tyra Henry (London Borough of Brent 1985; London Borough of Lambeth 1987). Indeed, in a child protection system developed and then driven by child deaths, most of which were committed by men, it is a paradox that attempts at regulation are unrelentingly directed at women.

This shift of focus away from men and onto women had an additional consequence. It allowed men's violence to women to disappear from professional sight. Research has shown the connection between violence by men to their female partners and their children. A study by Bowker *et al.* (1988) found that men who hit their wives also physically abused their children in 70 per cent of cases. Other studies reviewed by Hughes *et al.* (1989) found similar levels of association. In the Farmer and Owen (1995) study, where children had been sexually abused there was also domestic violence in two-fifths (40 per cent) of cases. Among the cases of physical abuse, neglect and emotional abuse, this rose to 59 per cent. In that study information about domestic violence in half of the relevant cases was not known by participants at the initial case conferences. Some had been concealed from the professionals by women who feared that their children might be removed if it was disclosed.

In the Farmer and Owen (1995) study, domestic violence when known about was treated by the professionals as if it had no bearing on children's safety. It was not taken into account in the management of cases even though it was a clear sign of a profound imbalance of power in the family. In addition, the fact that children were witnessing violence was noted as unsatisfactory in only two cases, where concerns were expressed about the impact on the child (Jaffe *et al.* 1990). Yet when women live with violent men who hit and damage them and are clearly unable to protect themselves, the chances of them being able to protect their children are remote (Kelly 1994; O'Hara 1994).

Before discussing the implications of these research studies for policy and practice, we will consider the extent to which the concerns and expectations embodied in official child protection policies match those of mothers trying to protect their children.

Strategies employed by mothers to keep their children safe

The broader range of concerns perceived and managed by mothers

Despite the onerous responsibilities placed on parents in the UK (and especially on mothers) to protect their children, very little research attention has been paid to the risks that mothers themselves identify in their children's lives and the protective strategies they use. Even less is known about fathers' views. A small number of studies provide glimpses of the everyday protective activities of mothers and the difficulties and choices they face (e.g. Graham 1980; Roberts *et al.* 1995). They include a pilot study of eight families undertaken by one of the authors to explore which risks to their young children mothers in disadvantaged circumstances perceive as most salient and the strategies they use to protect them (Boushel, forthcoming).

The range of immediate and longer-term risks to children's well-being which are identified by mothers relates closely to the economic and social circumstances of their families. They are very much broader than the concerns of child protection policy makers and professionals. A constant concern of mothers on low incomes is to ensure that their children are adequately fed. To achieve this their strategies include borrowing money from relatives and friends and going without food themselves (Graham 1993; Dowler and Calvert 1995; Middleton *et al.* 1997). They may also severely restrict the use of heating and hot water to reduce energy costs (Boushel, forthcoming).

The risk of child accidents is also a pervasive consideration, and with good reason. On a poor Glasgow housing estate, Roberts *et al.* (1995) found that in a one-year period, one-third of the 373 children in their survey suffered a 'serious' accident, (that is, an accident that was seen to require medical or dental attention), a figure that was twice the rate for Glasgow as a whole. The study demonstrated that this increased risk, which was caused by environmental deficits, was of great concern to mothers living on the estate. The risk to young children of accidentally swallowing medicines was also a considerable anxiety to the mothers in Boushel's (forthcoming) study. Most parents stored medicines out of their children's reach, but in the course of responding to the needs of several young children while trying to manage shopping, housework and cooking, accidents did happen.

Safeguarding their children's health makes considerable demands on the time and skills of mothers. In Boushel's (forthcoming) exploratory study, child asthma, which has been shown to be far more prevalent in deprived areas, needed constant vigilance both to safeguard the child's immediate health and to prevent mismanagement by professionals. The mothers spoke of confrontations with doctors in order to get timely treatment, the organization of complicated transport and childcare arrangements to deal with medical emergencies, and prolonged negotiation with school staff to ensure that a child's medicines were regularly administered.

Children's emotional health and development is also an area of concern and intervention. Women with black or mixed-parentage children who lived in mainly white areas worried about racism and developed strategies to deal with racist remarks from neighbours and at school. A frequent strategy was to send a child to an out-of-area multiracial school. In such cases, the additional transport costs were borne by mothers, not by the education authority (Boushel 1996; Boushel, forthcoming). The increased financial hardship and difficulties in monitoring the child's educational progress at a distance were seen as costs to be borne in order to reduce the risk to their children of exposure to racism. Mothers also spoke of their efforts to minimize the risks to their children's development caused by erratic contact by estranged fathers.

Where partners are present, even though they may take a limited role in the day-to-day child-rearing, their willingness to offer occasional respite from childcare responsibilities, back-up in setting boundaries for children's behaviour and access to transport means that they are often an important element of a mother's protective strategies. The support of others in the family and neighbourhood is also significant. For example, help with childcare from grandmothers is a crucial factor in determining whether a mother can get paid employment or an occasional break (Condy 1994; Boushel, forthcoming).

The responses of mothers to professionally acknowledged risks

The risks presented by the behaviour of family members which are a common trigger for state child protection interventions are also of concern to mothers. In several studies mothers have spoken of their concern about the risks which their own tiredness and frustration can present to their children and the strategies they use to deal with this. These include leaving a baby to cry and drowning out the noise by turning up the radio (Graham 1980). Seven of the eight mothers interviewed by Boushel were concerned about the damaging potential of their own anger and had developed strategies to help calm themselves and protect their young children. However, one impact of the experience of living in disadvantaged circumstances is that mothers need to take a relative view of risk and prioritize between risks. Thus, the immediate advantage of calming themselves with a cigarette or coffee on the doorstep (Graham 1987, 1993; Pearson 1992) are often seen to outweigh the long-term health risks of smoking or the risk of leaving a baby or toddler in the charge of a 5-year-old for a short period.

Several women in the Boushel study were also concerned about their partner's anger towards the children and tried to assist him to develop strategies to control it, with varying degrees of success. In situations of domestic violence, it is often the threat of violence to her young children, rather than the violence which she endures, which spurs a woman to leave her partner (see, for example, Mullender and Morley 1994). Some women will go to great lengths to protect their children while trying to maintain a relationship with their partner. After receiving notification about her partner's earlier conviction for violence towards a child, one woman ensured that for the first three years of his life her child was never left alone with this man. Her strategy of vigilance, and the strain of maintaining it after the birth of a second child, was never fully understood by the professionals involved, with tragic consequences for the new baby (Boushel and Lebacq 1992).

Gordon's (1989) research into 100 years of child abuse cases in Boston in the United States showed that women also often actively seek help from professional agencies in the hope of regulating the action of the men with whom they are living and thus redressing imbalances of power within families, despite the risk that their approaches will be treated with suspicion. This is still the case, as shown by the high proportion of referrals to child protection agencies by mothers (Farmer and Owen 1995; Sharland et al. 1996). However, the strategies that women are currently employing to protect their children and their views of the additional help they need are frequently neither acknowledged nor understood by professionals who are more likely to focus on the mother's own parenting. None the less, if they are drawn into the child protection system and their child's name is placed on the child protection register, some mothers try to make active use of this as a deterrent to their abusing partner by threatening to report any bruise on the child to the doctor.

As can be seen, the responsibility taken by mothers for keeping their children safe is considerable, varied and wide-ranging. Many of the perceived risks are caused by factors beyond their control and a range of circumstances, including cognitive skills, maternal mental state, social class and cultural factors will influence their ability to respond effectively. As Westlake and Pearson point out (1997), the evidence suggests that it is not lack of knowledge but lack of means which prevents most mothers from realizing their goals for their children's health and development.

Discussion and conclusion

The child protection system in the UK was set up in the wake of public anxiety about child deaths, most of which were inflicted by men. Yet in spite of a series of well-publicized child tragedies since then, child protection practice has continued to focus mainly on regulating the actions of mothers. How have the risks posed by men who have already physically injured their children escaped more sustained professional attention?

Feminist commentators have suggested that professionals have clung to the idea of mothers as collusive in the abuse of their children partly because it is a powerful defence against admitting the male abuse of power which would otherwise have to be faced (Nelson 1987) and partly because of the strength of the ideology of motherhood (Macleod and Saraga 1988) in which mothers are supposed to care for and protect their children and are therefore blamed when things go wrong. Feminist writers have also pointed out that men have 'assumed disproportionate control and influence' over the child protection industry (Hudson 1992: 130) and although most fieldworkers are women much local authority policy and practice is controlled by men, who fill the majority of senior management positions in social services departments (Hallett 1989).

We would suggest that there are also other reasons, which are illuminated by historical developments in child protection in the UK. The historical analysis given here shows that the ways in which children's welfare needs are interpreted is an outcome, in part, of the strength of the women's movement at any one time. While feminist analysis in the 1980s has had a strong influence on the major parameters which govern how professionals understand and deal with child sexual abuse (Macleod and Saraga 1988) and male domestic violence, it has had much less influence on practice in relation to physical abuse to children, partly because such abuse has not received sustained analysis from feminist researchers (Gordon 1989), nor been the subject of a sustained campaign to effect change. Moreover, despite wide-ranging theoretical contributions, feminist practice has traditionally concentrated on 'out-of-home' rescue services such as Women's Aid rather than on interventions within the family. This, and the (albeit understandable) focus on women, rather than children or men, as the target of support and intervention, has meant that feminist methods of practice that help support and protect women and children within their homes are relatively underdeveloped. This has now begun to be remedied both by an increased understanding of the link between violence to women and violence to children and by the development of feminist approaches to family therapy and attention to the needs of children in women's aid refuges.

However, the difficulties faced by women workers in engaging men should not be underestimated (O'Hagan 1997) and their fear of male violence is real. Appropriate professional skills to work with violent men have not been well developed and are not among the skills with which childcare social workers are generally equipped (Adams 1988; Hague and Malos 1993). It is also the case that men actively avoid social work visits or refuse to engage in any discussion of their children with the worker (Farmer and Owen 1995). More innovative methods need to be developed to motivate and work with men and in some cases legal sanctions may prove necessary to ensure that such work can be undertaken.

The major policy change to emerge from the Department of Health programme of research on child protection (Department of Health 1995) is a greater emphasis on family support services. This ought to benefit mothers who have lacked much needed services and whose situations have sometimes worsened when they have been unnecessarily brought into the child protection system. However, this will only happen if imbalances of power within families are addressed and women's own strategies to protect their children are built on, both at the wider level of family policy and by child protection professionals. Children's safety and well-being can only improve if their parents have sufficient resources to care for them and this entails improvements in income support, work opportunities and childcare. In addition, the gender bias underlying the operation of child protective services has until now received only fitful recognition and has proved remarkably resistant to change. This is the current challenge for the development of effective child protection policy in the UK.

References

Adams D. (1988) Treatment models of men who batter: a pro-feminist analysis, in Yllo, K. and Bograd, M. (eds) *Feminist Perspectives on Wife Abuse*. London: Sage.

Aldgate, J. and Tunstill, J. (1996) *Making Sense of Section 17*. London: HMSO.

Baker, A. and Duncan, S. (1985) Child sexual abuse: a study of prevalence in Great Britain. *Child Abuse and Neglect*, 9: 457–67.

Bebbington, A. and Miles, J. (1989) The background of children who enter local authority care. *British Journal of Social Work*, 19: 349–68.

Berliner, L. (1991) Interviewing families, in K. Murray and D.S. Gough (eds) *Intervening in Child Sexual Abuse*. Edinburgh: Scottish Academic Press.

Boushel, M. (1996) Vulnerable multi-racial families and early years services. *Children and Society*, 10 (4): 305–16.

Boushel, M. (forthcoming) *Parental Strategies to Protect Children*.

Boushel, M. and Lebacq, M. (1992) Towards empowerment in child protection work. *Children and Society*, 6 (1): 38–50.

Boushel, M. and Noakes, S. (1988) Islington Social Services: developing a policy on child sexual abuse. *Feminist Review*, 28: 150–57.

Bowker, L., Arbitell, M. and McFerron, J.R. (1988) On the relationship between wife beating and child abuse, in Yllo, K. and Bograd, M. (eds) *Feminist Perspectives on Wife Abuse*. London: Sage.

Bradshaw, J. and Millar, J. (1991) *Lone Parent Families in the UK*, Department of Social Security Research Report no. 6. London: HMSO.

Campbell, B. (1988) *Unofficial Secrets: Child Sexual Abuse – The Cleveland Case*. London: Virago Press.

Condy, A. (1994) Families and Caring, *Factsheet 4*, International Year of the Family 1994. London: Family Policy Studies Centre.

Conte, J. and Schuerman, J. (1987) Factors associated with an increased impact of child sexual abuse. *Child Abuse and Neglect*, 2: 201–11.

Creighton, S. and Noyes, P. (1989) *Child Abuse Trends in England and Wales 1983–1987*. London: NSPCC.

Davin, A. (1978) Imperialism and Motherhood. *History Workshop Journal*, 5: 9–65.

Department of Health (1988) *Protecting Children: A Guide for Social Workers Undertaking a Comprehensive Assessment*. London: HMSO.

Department of Health (1991) *Summary of Inquiry Reports*. London: HMSO.

Department of Health (1995) *Child Protection: Messages from Research*. London: HMSO.

Department of Health and Social Security (1974) *Memorandum on Non-Accidental Injury to Children*, LASSL (74)13.

Dowler, E. and Calvert, C. (1995) *Nutrition and Diet in Lone Parent Families in London*. London: Family Policy Studies Centre.

Farmer, E. (1993) The impact of child protection interventions: the experiences of parents and children, in L. Waterhouse (ed.) *Child Abuse and Child Abusers: Protection and Prevention*. London: Jessica Kingsley.

Farmer, E. and Owen, M. (1995) *Child Protection Practice: Private Risks and Public Remedies*. London: HMSO.

Ferguson, H. (1990) Rethinking child protection practices: a case for history, in the Violence against Children Study Group, *Taking Child Abuse Seriously*. London: Unwin Hyman.

Finkelhor, D. (1984) *Child Sexual Abuse: New Theory and Research*. New York: Free Press.

Fox Harding, L. (1991) *Perspectives in Child Care Policy*. London: Longman.

Gibbons, J., Conroy, S. and Bell, C. (1995) *Operating the Child Protection System*. London: HMSO.

Gomes-Schwartz, B., Horowitz, J. and Cardelli, A.P. (1990) *Child Sexual Abuse: the Initial Effects*. London: Sage.

Gordon, L. (1989) *Heroes of Their Own Lives*. London: Virago Press.

Graham, H. (1980) Mothers' accounts of anger and aggression towards their babies, in N. Frude (ed.) *Psychological Approaches to Child Abuse*. London: Batsford.

Graham, H. (1987) Being poor: perceptions and coping strategies of lone mothers, in J. Brannen and G. Wilson (eds) *Give and Take in Families*, Studies in Income Distribution. London: HMSO.

Graham, H. (1993) *Hardship and Health in Women's Lives*. London: Harvester Wheatsheaf.

Hague, G. and Malos, E. (1993) *Domestic Violence: Action for Change*. Cheltenham: New Clarion Press.

Hallett, C. (ed.) (1989) *Women and Social Services Departments*. London: Harvester Wheatsheaf.

Hudson, A. (1992) The child sexual abuse 'industry' and gender relations in social work, in M. Langan and L. Day (eds) *Women, Oppression and Social Work*. London: Routledge.

Hughes, M., Parkinson, D. and Vargo, M. (1989) Witnessing spouse abuse and experiencing physical abuse: a double whammy? *Journal of Family Violence*, 4 (2): 197–209.

Jaffe, P., Wolfe, D. and Kaye, S. (1990) *Children of Battered Women*. London: Sage.

Jeffreys, S. (1985) *The Spinster and her Enemies: Feminism and Sexuality 1880–1930*. London: Pandora Press.

Kelly, L. (1994) The interconnectedness of domestic violence and child abuse: challenges for research, policy and practice, in A. Mullender and R. Morley (eds) *Children Living with Domestic Violence: Putting Men's Abuse of Women on the Child Care Agenda*. London: Whiting and Birch.

Kelly, L., Regan, L. and Burton, S. (1991) *An Exploratory Study of the Prevalence of Sexual Abuse in a Sample of 16–21 Year Olds*. London: Child Abuse Studies Unit.

Kempe, C.H., Silverman, F.N., Steele, B.F., Droegmueller, W. and Silver, H.K. (1962) The battered child syndrome. *Journal of the American Medical Association*, 181: 17–22.

London Borough of Brent (1985) *A Child in Trust*. The report of the panel of inquiry into the circumstances surrounding the death of Jasmine Beckford. London: Borough of Brent.

London Borough of Lambeth (1987) *Whose Child?* The report of the panel appointed to inquire into the death of Tyra Henry. London: Borough of Lambeth.

Macleod, M. and Saraga, E. (1988) Challenging the orthodoxy: towards a feminist theory and practice. *Feminist Review*, 28: 16–55.

Middleton, S., Ashworth, K. and Braithwaite, I. (1997) *Small Fortunes: Spending on Children, Childhood Poverty and Parental Sacrifice*. York: Joseph Rowntree Foundation.

Miller, L.B. and Fisher, T. (1992) Some obstacles to the effective investigation and registration of children at risk: issues gleaned from a worker's perspective. *Journal of Social Work Practice*, 6 (2): 129–40.

Milner, J. (1993) A disappearing act: the differing career paths of fathers and mothers in child protection investigations. *Critical Social Policy*, 38 (13) 2: 48–63.

Mullender, A. and Morley, R. (eds) (1994) *Children Living with Domestic Violence: Putting Men's Abuse of Women on the Child Care Agenda*. London: Whiting and Birch.

Nash, C. and West, D. (1985) Sexual molestation of young girls, in D. West (ed.) *Sexual Victimisation*. Aldershot: Gower.

Nelson, S. (1987) *Incest: Fact and Myth*. Edinburgh: Stramullion.

Owen, M. and Farmer, E. (1996) Child protection in a multi-racial context. *Policy and Politics*, 24 (3): 299–313.

O'Hagan, K. (1997) The problem of engaging men in child protection work. *British Journal of Social Work*, 27 (1): 25–42.

O'Hagan, K. and Dillenburger, K. (1995) *The Abuse of Women within Childcare Work*. Buckingham: Open University Press.

O'Hara, M. (1994) Child deaths in contexts of domestic violence: implications for professional practice, in A. Mullender and R. Morley (eds) *Children Living with Domestic Violence: Putting Men's Abuse of Women on the Child Care Agenda*. London: Whiting and Birch.

Parker, R. (1995) A brief history of child protection, in E. Farmer and M. Owen (eds) (1995) *Child Protection Practice: Private Risks and Public Remedies*. London: HMSO.

Pearson, M., Dawson, C., Moore, H. and Spencer, S. (1992) Health on borrowed time? Prioritising and meeting needs in low-income households. *Health and Social Care in the Community*, 1: 45–54.

Roberts, H., Smith, S. and Bryce, C. (1995) *Children at Risk? Safety as a Social Value*. Buckingham: Open University Press.

Secretary of State for Social Services (1988) *Report of the Inquiry into Child Abuse in Cleveland 1987*, Cm. 412. London: HMSO.

Sharland, E., Jones, D., Aldgate, J., Seal, H. and Croucher, M. (1996) *Professional Intervention in Child Sexual Abuse*. London: HMSO.

Thorpe, D. (1994) *Evaluating Child Protection*. Buckingham: Open University Press.

Westlake, D. and Pearson, M. (1997) Child protection and health promotion: whose responsibility? *Journal of Social Welfare and Family Law*, 19 (2): 139–58.

Wyatt, G.E. and Mickey, M.R. (1988) The support by parents and others as it mediates the effects of child sexual abuse: an exploratory study, in G.E. Wyatt and G.J. Powell (eds) *Lasting Effects of Child Sexual Abuse*. London: Sage.

6

The criminalization of female poverty

Christina Pantazis

Traditionally the relatively small numbers of women in the statistics of offenders provided a justification for the absence of women in academic discussions of criminal behaviour (Smart 1977). When criminological studies did include women they were often stereotyped as sexual offenders (e.g. Pollak 1950; Cohen 1955). For example, women's involvement in prostitution was sexualized and not seen as a rational choice (Heidensohn 1968). Feminist criminology has made a significant contribution to ending the silence surrounding the whole area of female criminality. As well as recent feminist scholarship which has emphasized the centrality of linking notions of masculinity to criminological debates (Newburn and Stanko 1994; Walklate 1995), there now exists a large body of empirical and theoretical work which has specifically examined women offenders (Campbell 1981; McLeod 1982; Carlen 1988) and their treatment in the criminal justice system (Bowker 1978; Carlen 1983; Edwards 1984, 1989).

The increased visibility of the female offender has also been reflected in changes in the gender ratio of crime, as women now form a larger proportion of all known offenders. Feminist criminologists have suggested that this has led to a moral panic about the extent and nature of female criminality (Heidensohn 1985). Allegations abound about 'women's share of crime rising faster than that of men and rising particularly fast in unfeminine and untypical offences such as robbery and violence' (Heidensohn 1985: 6). Recent media concern and preoccupation with the supposed growth in violent girl gangs is evidence of this continuing moral panic (see, for example, BBC *Panorama*, November 1996; Pennington 1996).

Women's increased involvement in criminal activity has been identified with changing gender roles: women are catching up with men in committing acts of crime, matching similar shifts in drinking habits and sexual behaviour (Oliver James, BBC *Panorama*, November 1996). This current view appears to be rooted in an early 1970s explanation, which cited the women's movement as a cause of changes in female criminality (Adler 1975; Simon 1975). Simon (1975: 1–2) claimed that:

As women become more liberated from hearth and home and become more involved in full-time jobs, they are more likely to engage in the types of crimes for which their occupations provide them with the greatest opportunities. They are also likely to become partners and entrepreneurs in crime to a greater extent than they have in the past. [Furthermore] as a function of expanded consciousness, as well as occupational opportunities, women's participation, roles and involvement in crime are expected to change and increase.

However, this view is not universally shared within the discipline of criminology. Box and Hale (1983) have argued that methodological difficulties have plagued many of the studies connecting increases in female crime to women's emancipation. Furthermore, changes in female crime, rather than being associated with women's liberation, are argued to be more closely linked to women becoming poorer and increasingly economically marginalized (Box 1983; Box and Hale 1983; Carlen 1988; Cook 1997). As Box (1983: 197) has argued:

although some upper middle-class women have made inroads into formerly male professions, the vast bulk of women have become increasingly economically marginalized – that is, more likely to be unemployed, or unemployable, or if employed, then more likely to be in insecure, lower paid, unskilled, part-time jobs, where career prospects are minimal. [Furthermore] the welfare state, on which proportionately more women than men depend, has tightened its definition of who deserves financial assistance and at the same time has become increasingly unable to index these payments in line with inflation.

In an examination of indictable offences committed in England and Wales over the period 1951–80, Box and Hale (1984) showed that increases in the rate of female unemployment were linked to increases in the rate of conviction for violent crime (assault and wounding), theft, handling stolen goods, and fraud. This was followed by a review of 50 North American and British studies of unemployment and crime, which led Box (1987) to conclude that the most convincing explanation for increases in female crime was that women had become economically marginalized during the recession.

Other criminologists have specifically referred to the 'feminization of poverty' to explain changes in female criminality (Edwards 1987; Carlen 1988; O'Neil 1997). Pat Carlen, in her study of the criminal careers of

39 women, has argued that the policies on employment, taxation, tax allowances, social security and social services introduced under the Thatcher governments resulted in this 'feminization of poverty' which had the effect of criminalizing a larger number of women:

> The effects of such policies are that more young women are to be seen begging on the streets of the capital; that more young women either coming out of residential care or leaving families too poverty-stricken themselves to keep unemployed teenagers are turning to a street life of begging, prostitution or drug abuse; and that more women on social security are making themselves vulnerable to pro-secution either by putting forward fraudulent claims to benefits or by engaging in the hidden economy.
>
> (Carlen 1988: 8)

The 'feminization of poverty'

The feminization of poverty thesis evolved in the United States and holds that as a result of recession and cuts in public spending, women are increasingly represented among the world's poor (Scott 1984; Rein and Erie 1988). Lone parent families and elderly single person house-holds which are often female-headed have been particularly affected. While traditionally women have helped keep two-earner families out of poverty, they have become the sole earner in an increasing number of families with dependent children. Furthermore, the income earned by lone parents is often insufficient to support their families and the benefits paid to them have declined in real terms in recent years.

The idea that poverty has only recently become feminized has been contested in Britain on the grounds that it ignores the extent to which women have traditionally been much poorer than men (Payne 1991; Lewis and Piachaud 1992). For example, it has been shown that British women constitute a roughly similar proportion of the poor today as in 1900 (Lewis and Piachaud 1992): at the start of the century, 61 per cent of adults in receipt of poor relief were women, and in 1983 women formed 60 per cent of those on supplementary benefit.

Critics of the thesis argue that it is the composition of female poverty which has changed, resulting in a greater visibility in women's poverty. Nowadays, women are less often poor within large poor households, because demographic changes have resulted in female poverty being concentrated among lone women, especially women with dependent children, and elderly women (Payne 1991). The change in the composition of poverty means that poor women can be more easily counted in surveys, although the extent of poverty suffered by women within large households still remains hidden just as it did in the last century (Pahl 1989).

The thesis may also be criticized for ignoring the extent to which the numbers of both men and women living in poverty have grown over the last 20 years as a response to two recessions. Numerous studies conducted in the 1980s and 1990s established that poverty had increased among many types of household (Walker and Walker 1987; Joseph Rowntree Foundation 1995a, 1995b; Oppenheim and Harker 1996). One study found that the proportion of people who could be objectively defined as living in poverty in Britain increased by 30 per cent between 1983 and 1990 (Gordon and Pantazis 1997). By 1990, 20 per cent of households (approximately 11m people) were living in poverty. Thus, both more men and more women were likely to be living in poverty by the 1990s. However, women were more likely to be experiencing poverty alone, or as lone parents rather than as wives and mothers in traditional couple households.

This chapter explores the connections between the growth in female poverty and changes in female criminality over the 1980s and 1990s. The first part of the chapter provides evidence from *Criminal Statistics* to illustrate trends in the criminalization of both men and women in England and Wales. The second part offers a more detailed analysis of trends in the criminalization of offenders committing 'crimes of poverty' such as television licence evasion, prostitution, and social security fraud. These offences may be considered as 'crimes of poverty' because past studies have found that poverty and poverty-related factors are often the main reasons given by the majority of offenders to justify their criminal behaviour.

British criminology and the study of the female offender

With the advent of feminism, the study of women and girls has been a significant development within criminology. Much more in now known about the female offender mainly due to feminist efforts in making women more visible in the study of crime and in challenging stereo-typical perceptions of the female offender (Heidensohn 1985).

We know for instance that the female offender commits the same types of crime as the male offender, except that the female offender commits fewer of them (Hedderman 1995). We also know that the nature of female crime is disproportionately non-serious. This pattern between gender and offending is the same across the world (Harvey *et al.* 1992). Most British studies examining the gender differences in rates of crime rely on the criminal statistics of 'indictable offences' (see, for example, Heidensohn 1985; Morris 1987; Walklate 1995). These are offences which may be tried by judge and jury at a Crown Court, and include the more serious types of crime such as burglary, robbery, and violence. One problem with many of the studies examining the gender bias of offending behaviour is that they fail to analyse statistics relating to summary offences, which are offences tried in magistrates' courts (for exceptions, see Hedderman 1995; Coleman and Moynihan 1996).

Summary offences are those relating to mostly trivial crimes such as motoring offences, and include other crimes such as obstructing the pavement with a dustbin, and cycling on a pavement. The classification does, however, include a number of serious offences relating to public order, firearms, and health and safety. It also includes those offences such as prostitution, social security fraud and television licence evasion which will be considered shortly. Summary defendants should be invited to plead guilty by the magistrates' court and therefore avoid a court appearance. Most of the defendants appearing in court will be relying on the court's duty solicitor, who will have most probably been given the case file only on the day of the trial, and whose 'speech in mitigation' will tend to be brief (Allen 1989). Criminologists often overlook the summary criminal statistics as a result of 'the trivial nature of many of these offences, the routine pattern of their processing, the scantiness of any formal deliberation, and in most cases the absence of much significant sexual bias' (Allen 1989: 71).

Yet, analysing summary offences is important for at least two reasons. First, summary offences form the bulk of cases passing through the criminal justice system: more than 80 per cent of all criminal trials relate to summary offences (Allen 1989). Second, a strong gender bias exists when looking at the overall figures for summary offences: figures for 1994 show that 79 per cent of all female offenders had been found guilty of summary offences, compared with only 53 per cent of men[1] (Home Office 1995).

Counting criminals

Before considering gender trends in criminalization over the 1980s and 1990s the difficulties involved in understanding and interpreting the *Criminal Statistics* need to be highlighted. They contain a range of data which have been provided by the police and the courts, including offences recorded by the police, offenders found guilty or cautioned, court proceedings, and sentencing. In order to examine trends in criminalization, this chapter makes use of offender-based data which contains limited information on the characteristics of those who are processed (e.g. age and gender) and their offences.

Walker (1995: 34) has pointed out a major limitation with the offender-based data in the *Criminal Statistics*:

> the number of suspects and offenders dealt with by the criminal justice system, the offences listed in relation to them, and the outcome of court proceedings, represent only a partial picture of the

offender population. These are, of course, 'known offenders', the ones that got caught and were dealt with. [Furthermore] there is no reason to suppose that these offenders are representative of all offenders in the community, in respect of gender, age, or race.

The issue of 'known offenders' is related to the 'dark figure' of crime, which can 'refer to that vast number of unrecorded crimes and criminals [the conventional usage], or it can refer to our picture or imagery of the undetected offender and his/her offences'[2] (Coleman and Moynihan 1996: 3). Victimization surveys have estimated the extent of the dark figure of conventional crime by establishing that the real amount of crime is far greater than 'crimes known' to the police (see Mirrlees-Black *et al.* 1996). However, less is known about white-collar crime and white collar criminals because although white-collar crimes are widespread they rarely appear in police statistics (Sutherland 1949) and they generally lie outside the scope of victimization surveys (for exceptions, see Pearce 1990). Some criminologists have drawn a parallel here to female crime and female criminals.

Pollak (1950) has argued that women's crime is less likely to be reported than crime committed by men. He further claimed that even if reported, female crime was less likely to be detected, and once detected would be treated more leniently by the courts. Pollak is thus suggesting that the gender bias in criminal statistics for offending is mythical. Unsurprisingly, his work has come under fierce criticism, particularly since self-report studies on criminal behaviour have shown that despite the narrowing of the sex ratio in relation to criminal activity, crime is still predominantly male defined (see Morris 1987). Nevertheless, traces of Pollak's ideas can be found in contemporary debates on the treatment of female offenders in the criminal justice system (see Farrington and Morris 1983).

There are a number of technical limitations that we need also to be aware of (see Coleman and Moynihan 1996). First, offenders may be processed for more than one offence on each occasion. However, the statistics show only the offence for which the most serious penalty has been, or can be, given. This has the effect of underestimating convictions of summary offences, since if there were a conviction for an indictable offence at the same time as a summary offence the summary offence would not be included in the statistics. Second, the statistics for persons proceeded against show the number of persons dealt with during the year, not the number of different persons. Thus, repeat offenders will appear more than once if dealt with on more than one occasion during the year (Walker 1995). This affects the ratio of male to female offenders, since men are more likely to be repeat offenders (Phillpotts and Lancucki 1979).

Finally, we need to be aware of the likely impact of new legislation on counts of offenders through the creation or abolition of offences. The introduction of some legislation may result in changes in the definition of offences, and new offences may also be created such as those under the Sexual Offences Act 1985 which established kerb crawling as a criminal offence, while others may be abolished. For example, recent amendments to the Sexual Offences Act 1967 decriminalized homosexual acts in private between consenting males over the age of 21. With these qualifications in mind, we may now turn to criminal statistics data to examine changes in criminalization over the 1980s and 1990s.

Criminalization in the 1980s and 1990s

Despite increases in recorded crime over this period, the total number of people criminalized dropped significantly (Hillyard and Gordon 1985). The number of people convicted and sentenced for all offences fell from approximately 918,000 in 1980 to 788,000 in 1996.[3] However, these figures conceal huge gender discrepancies. Figure 6.1 shows that whereas the number of men sentenced for offences dropped from 785,000 in 1980 to 597,000 in 1996, the number of women sentenced rose by 30 per cent, from 133,000 to 191,000 over the same period.

When these figures are broken down to show the number of men and women sentenced for indictable and summary offences, we find that there has been a decline in the number of defendants sentenced for the former offence type. Figure 6.2 illustrates that there was a 32 per cent drop in the number of men sentenced for indictable crimes, from 388,000 in 1980 to 262,000 in 1996. There was an even more significant decline in the number of women sentenced for similar offences, a drop from 68,000 to 38,000 in the same years. This would suggest that the expansion in female criminalization over the 1980s and 1990s must have occurred in the area of summary offences.

Indeed, while the numbers of men sentenced for summary offences fell by approximately one-fifth over these years, criminalization among women grew substantially. Figure 6.3 illustrates that summary offences more than doubled for women from 65,000 in 1980 to 153,000 in 1996. A striking change to occur as result of this increased criminalization is the closing gap between women and men in the sentencing of summary offences between 1980 and 1996. Whereas in 1980 there were six times the number of men sentenced for summary offences, by 1996 only twice as many men as women were sentenced for this offence category.

Although analysis of indictable and summary statistics is significant in illustrating gender distinctions, it is useful to break this down further into offence categories to illuminate variations in offending. This chapter does not include an analysis of indictable offences as they are regularly included in most studies examining differing patterns of offending among the sexes (see above). Instead the focus is on changes in selected summary offences between 1980 and 1996 only.

Figure 6.1 Total number of offenders sentenced in England and Wales by gender, 1980–1996*

Thousands

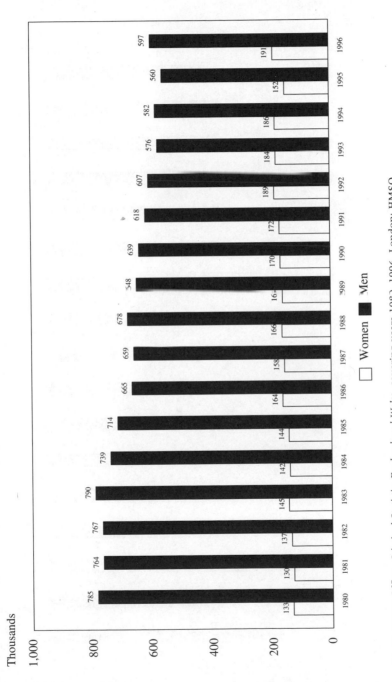

Source: Home Office, *Criminal Statistics England and Wales,* covering years 1980–1996. London: HMSO
Note: *Excludes all summary motoring offences.

Figure 6.2 Total number of offenders sentenced for indictable offences in England and Wales by gender, 1980–1996

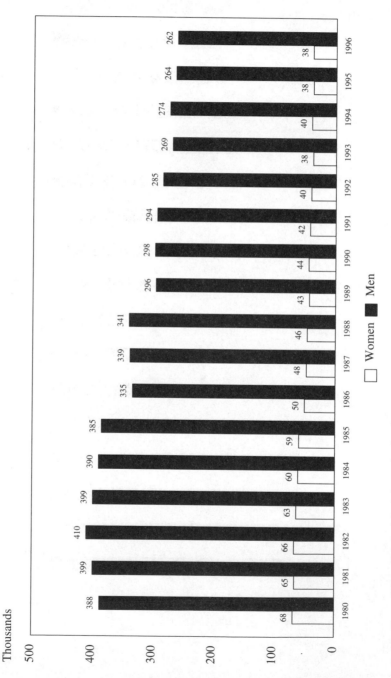

Thousands

Source: Home Office, *Criminal Statistics England and Wales*, covering years 1980–1996. London: HMSO.

Figure 6.3 Number of offenders sentenced for summary offences in England and Wales by gender, 1980–1996*

Thousands

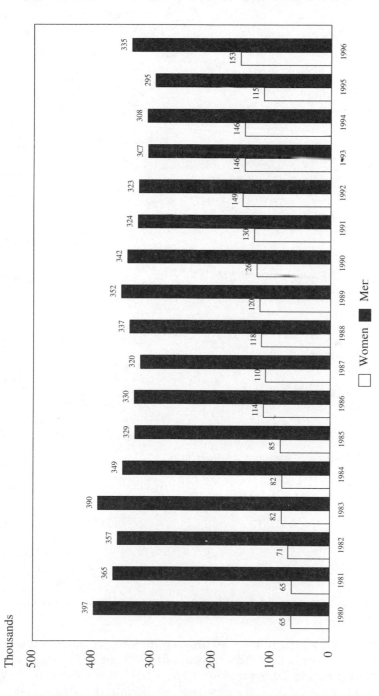

Source: Home Office, *Criminal Statistics England and Wales*, covering years 1980–1996. London: HMSO.
Note: *Excludes motoring offences.

Table 6.1 Number of defendants proceeded against in England and Wales for selected summary offences by gender, 1980 and 1996

Offence	Number of defendants proceeded against	
	1980	1996
Assault		
Women	2,428	6,574
Men	13,120	41,019
Criminal damage		
Women	3,099	2,647
Men	40,589	33,529
Drunkenness		
Women	9,178	2,368
Men	103,932	28,602
Public Order Act 1986		
Women		3,622
Men		39,005
Social security offence		
Women	5,285	4,403
Men	11,295	6,805
Prostitution		
Women	3,482	5,667
Motor licence evasion		
Women	4,225	21,103
Men	76,774	127,103
Television licence evasion		
Women	23,470	118,422
Men	22,636	69,686
Unauthorized taking of motor vehicle		
Women		573
Men		12,346
Vagrancy		
Women	116	463
Men	1,983	2,155
Other (excluding motoring)		
Women	19,394	12,998
Men	153,380	64,115

Source: Home Office 1982, 1998a.

Table 6.1 shows the number of prosecutions across gender for selected summary offences in England and Wales in 1980 and 1996. There are two important points to be made with respect to changes. First, there were more men prosecuted for every type of summary offence, with the exception of television licence evasion. Second, changes in prosecutions for men and women between 1980 and 1996 were similar. The number of prosecutions fell for both sexes in relation to criminal damage, drunkenness, and social security fraud, while prosecutions increased for offences relating to assault, motor licence evasion, vagrancy, television licence evasion and prostitution in the case of women. A major observation is the huge growth in the numbers prosecuted for offences relating to television licence evasion over this period.

At least four of the selected summary offences in Table 6.1 may be regarded as 'crimes of poverty': television licence evasion, prostitution, social security fraud and vagrancy. The next part of the chapter gives detailed consideration to these 'crimes of poverty' through an examination of trends in the prosecution of defendants. The factors accounting for those trends are also explored. Vagrancy offences have been left out due to the small number of offenders involved.

Television licence evasion

Television licence evasion was traditionally a neglected area of criminological interest. In response to the substantial growth in prosecutions and the consequential growth in the numbers imprisoned for defaulting on fines originally imposed on television licence offences, academic interest in this area of criminology has expanded in recent years (Wall and Bradshaw 1987; Gordon and Pantazis 1994; Wall and Bradshaw 1994; Pantazis and Gordon 1997). Like many other summary offences, television licence evasion was ignored because it was considered as 'not really a crime'.

The purpose of the licence fee is to provide income for the BBC radio and television services. Under the wireless telegraphy acts anyone using or owning 'with intent to use' a television to watch any channel (including satellite or cable) or to record and watch video tapes needs a licence which at the time of writing costs £97.50. In comparison to the price of second-hand televisions, the cost of the licence is relatively expensive, compounded by being an annual expense. Each year a substantial minority of householders risk prosecution through evasion.

Figure 6.4 illustrates that between 1980 and 1996 there was a substantial growth in the number of prosecutions for television licence offences, an increase from 46,100 to 187,500.[4] Gender distinctions began to emerge in the early 1980s. While in 1980, approximately equal numbers of women and men were prosecuted for licence evasion (22,600 and 23,500 respectively), by 1996 prosecutions had increased to 69,000 for men and to 118,000 for women. By 1996, 63 per cent of total prosecutions for television licence offences involved women.

Prosecutions for television licence evasion grew to such an extent over the 1980s and 1990s that by 1996 these offences formed the largest single component of all female crime. Figure 6.5 shows that between

Figure 6.4 Number of defendants proceeded against for television licence evasion in England and Wales by gender, 1980–1996

Thousands

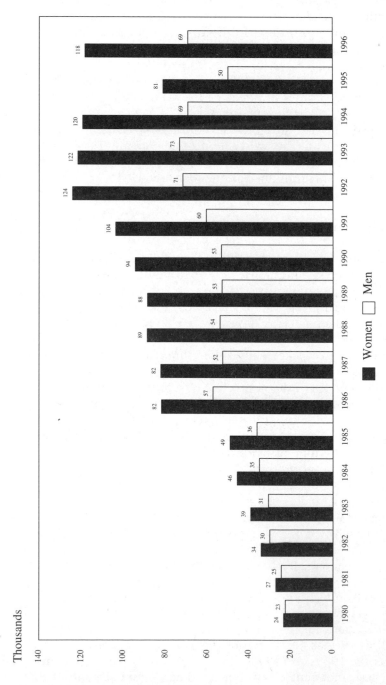

■ Women ☐ Men

Source: Home Office, *Criminal Statistics England and Wales: Supplementary Tables*, covering years 1980–1996. London: HMSO.

Figure 6.5 Convictions for television licence evasion as % of all convictions* in England and Wales, 1980–1996

Per cent

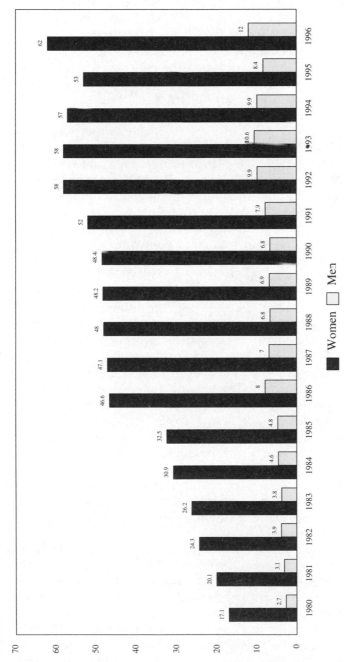

Source: Home Office, *Criminal Statistics England and Wales*, covering years 1980–1996. London: HMSO. Home Office, *Criminal Statistics England and Wales: Supplementary Tables*, covering years 1980–1996.
Note: *Excludes summary motoring offences.

1980 and 1996 the proportion of female convictions for television licence evasion offences grew from 17 per cent to 62 per cent, while male
convictions grew from 2.7 per cent to 12 per cent. Thus, convictions for
television licence offences as a proportion of all other offences increased
across the board between 1980 and 1996 but was more marked for women.

There are a number of inter-connecting factors which explain the
disproportionately high presence of women in the statistics for television
licence offending. Women due to their caring responsibilities are more
likely to be at home during the day when enquiry officers make their
calls at suspected unlicensed households.[5] While in the early 1980s it
was the man as the head of household who was liable to prosecution,
recent prosecution policy is targeted at the partner who is prepared to
be interviewed (Walker and Wall 1997). Thus, a prosecution policy
introduced in the 1980s designed to treat men and women equally has
resulted in the disproportionate criminalization of women. Furthermore,
we can speculate that the partner prepared to be interviewed in poor
couple households will more likely be the woman. This is because they
tend to have greater knowledge about the household finances, as previous
studies have shown that women of poor couple households often have
the responsibility of managing the budget, including payment of bills
such as the television licence (Land 1977; Wilson 1977; Pahl 1989; Payne
1991).

Demographic factors have also been important in increasing the number
of women who are potentially liable for prosecution. This period has
witnessed a significant expansion in the proportion of female-headed
households. While the proportion of married/cohabiting couple households has fallen from 66 per cent in 1981 to 59 per cent in 1996, lone
parent households with dependent children have increased from 4 to 7
per cent and single person households have risen from 22 to 27 per cent
over the same period (Thomas *et al.* 1998). Lone parent and single
person households are more likely to be headed by women. However,
not only did the number of these households increase over this period,
but their chances of living in poverty was greater than most other types
(Bradshaw and Millar 1991; Walker 1992; Dowler and Calvert 1995).
For instance, one survey found that 55 per cent of female lone parent
households were living in circumstances of multiple deprivation in 1990
(Payne and Pantazis 1997).

The economically disadvantaged position of many television licence
evasion offenders has been confirmed by several studies (Central Office
of Information 1985; Wall and Bradshaw 1987). In a Home Office study,
the main reason given by offenders for not having a licence when ap-
proached by the television licence officer was financial (Softley 1984).
Furthermore, where financial details were available, one-third claimed
that the head of the defendant's household was unemployed at the time
of their hearing. Twenty-eight per cent of evaders were lone parents,
separated or divorced.

The expansion in the number of households living in poverty, and the consequential increase in the numbers unable to afford the television licence is the main reason why prosecutions for licence evasion grew to such an extent over the 1980s and 1990s (Wall and Bradshaw 1987; Gordon and Pantazis 1994). Other reasons, such as increases in the real level of the licence fee, more effective policing by the television licence authorities, and an increase in criminality and wickedness have been discounted by previous studies (Wall and Bradshaw 1987; Pantazis and Gordon 1997).

It has further been suggested that prosecution practices serve to disfavour the poor by giving householders with financial means, under some circumstances, the opportunity to avoid prosecution (Walker and Wall 1997). The possibilities for this include:

> where in circumstances of non-renewal the licence is purchased and short-dated to cover the period of unlicensed use (unless there is a previous warning or conviction within three years); where a licence is purchased on the same day as the visit and the only provable use is for that day; and where there has been 'short term' evasion, provided a licence is purchased immediately and (if evasion of six weeks or more is established) the period of unlicensed use is also covered. Those who fail to escape the system by these paths may be further condemned for this very failure; the court is frequently advised . . . that [offenders] were told they would not be prosecuted if they obtained a licence, though official TVL policy is that inquiry officers should not make such comments. Not surprisingly, the people who do eventually make the transition from notice to prosecute to an appearance in the magistrates' court are disproportionately poor, unemployed, single parents – and females predominate in that social group.
>
> (Walker and Wall 1997: 179)

Furthermore, it appears that prosecution policies also serve to highlight the traditional distinction made between the 'deserving' and the 'undeserving' poor. This can clearly be seen in the prosecution policy document which states that it would not be in the public interest to prosecute certain groups, i.e. persons under 18 years, persons over 65 years, and the infirm.[6] On the other hand, it appears that the prosecution of the unemployed and lone parent mothers, groups traditionally seen as the 'undeserving poor', is acceptable.

Prostitution

Prostitution itself is not a crime in England and Wales, although soliciting for trade is. Under the Street Offences Act 1959, only women are defined as prostitutes and prosecuted for the offences of loitering and soliciting for the purposes of prostitution. Men are not liable to prosecution for loitering or soliciting, though those who offer a sexual service to other men are liable to arrest for 'importuning' in the pursuit of an 'immoral' activity under the Sexual Offences Act 1967, where 'immoral purpose' has been taken to imply homosexuality (Edwards 1996).

Prostitution has been referred to as a classic 'crime of poverty' (Cook 1997), though various feminists and prostitutes have also argued that it can represent an autonomous choice for women, which may be preferable to other work options available. While there are often complicated reasons why women engage in prostitution including drug addiction, peer-group pressure, low self-esteem and vulnerability, several studies have established that prostitution is often seen as a solution to living in poverty (McLeod 1982; Edwards 1984; Pheonix 1997). As O'Neil (1997: 12) states:

> As a response to poverty, selling sex is often a last resort, the body's last commodity. We cannot look at prostitution without looking at the social and economic contexts which give rise to it. The majority of women's work is part time, low status, and low paid. There is an absence of good quality child care facilities. There is an increasing number of young people, disenfranchised, disaffected and homeless.

The economic powerlessness which many women find themselves in prior to prostitution was reflected in a study which examined a sample of women who became caught up in the criminal justice system (Edwards 1984). Of the 108 women whose primary motive was financial, only 5 were employed, either as cleaners or in similar part-time employment. Many women were unemployed and some were in receipt of neither unemployment nor supplementary benefit. For example, one woman felt she was unable to 'sign on' because she thought the DHSS would make enquiries as to why she had been able to survive without claiming benefit. Other women who claimed benefit talked of the need to supplement it with prostitution.

Pheonix's (1997) in-depth study of the lives of 21 women revealed that the huge financial costs involved in working as a prostitute, served to further impoverish women. The women interviewed spoke about the initial costs involved in 'starting up' including money spent on make-up, clothes, and accommodation; the inability to raise money from loans based on their (undeclared) earnings; and the fines they incurred as a result of prosecution. Thus, rather being a solution to poverty, prostitution helped keep women trapped to a life of continuing poverty.

Although the reasons for women's entry into prostitution are now well established, the number of women known to be working as prostitutes is unknown. While the *Criminal Statistics* mainly involve the 'street' prostitute, an increasing number of women are resorting to working in 'off street' prostitution. In particular, since the Sexual Offences Act 1985, which provided for the prosecution of the kerb crawler, more women are now seeking alternative methods of contacting clients, such as sauna and massage parlours, strip joints, bars, clubs and escort agencies. However, the *Criminal Statistics* do provide us with information on trends in the criminalization of the women who engage in the trade of prostitution, particularly those who work on the streets. Figure 6.6 shows the number of women defendants prosecuted for prostitution. The most dramatic change in prosecutions occurred in the early 1980s when there was a threefold increase in criminalization. Prosecutions rose from 3482 in 1980 to 10,674 in 1983. Thereafter until 1991 prosecutions fluctuated between approximately 8300 and 10,500. Since then there has been a steady decline: by 1996 there were only 5667 women prosecuted for prostitution, reflecting a return to pre-1983 levels.

Several factors contributed to the dramatic growth in the prosecution of prostitutes in the early 1980s. It almost definitely reflected the adoption by the Metropolitan Police of a 'get tough' policy towards 'off street' prostitutes which followed the abolition of imprisonment for soliciting by the Criminal Justice Act 1982 (Edwards 1987). Even without this change in policing procedures and practices, Edwards maintains that the figures for soliciting had been rising throughout the 1980s as a response to the deterioration of women's economic position. An increasing number of women fell into the poverty trap as a result of weakening employment opportunities and the erosion of welfare benefits. Thus, an analysis of trends in prosecutions for prostitution 'must look beyond the operational response of the police and courts. It must examine factors contributing to women's poverty as being primary conditions for prostitution' (Edwards 1987: 43).

Social security fraud

The high political and media profile of social security scroungers since the 1970s has made benefit fraud a more emotive issue than the other types of offending behaviour so far considered. Responses to benefit fraud should be seen in an ideological context which perceives 'most welfare benefit claimants as wilfully idle, "undeserving" and lacking in moral fibre. By contrast, taxpayers are represented as victims: victims of the idle poor (who are financed by the taxpayer) and victims of the state bureaucracy itself' (Cook 1989: 11). This was clearly an outlook which underpinned the tax and social security policies of Conservative governments over the 1980s and 1990s.

Traditionally, all governments have chosen to target some types of benefit fraud more than others. Large-scale fraud involving a high degree of organization, such as multiple identity fraud, forgery of order books, and housing benefit fraud by landlords is seen as less problematic than fraud committed by people who claim benefit while working ('doing the double') or female claimants who are cohabiting (Cook 1997). Benefit

Figure 6.6 Number of women defendants proceeded against for prostitution in England and Wales, 1980–1996

Source: Home Office, *Criminal Statistics England and Wales: Supplementary Tables*, covering years 1980–1996. London: HMSO.

fraud by claimants is committed by people who are, by definition, living in poverty (Cook 1989).

Numerous studies have found that financial imperatives often dictate in motivations for benefit fraud (Evason and Woods 1995; Cook 1989; Dean and Melrose 1996, 1997). As Cook (1997: 38–9) has argued: 'social security fraud can be regarded as another illegitimate response to living in poverty. If welfare benefits are not adequate to meet needs, then fiddling the system may, for some, present a way of making ends meet'. In another study, economic necessity or inability to live on benefits was the principal reason for fraud in 27 out of 35 cases (Dean and Melrose 1997). However the same study revealed that there were often complex justifications offered by those committing benefit fraud. Some perceived fraud as a reaction to their dependency and disempowered status, while others saw it as a form of justified disobedience, particularly in a context of being 'messed about' by the system.

Gender considerations are also an important feature of benefit fraud. According to Cook (1987: 42):

> those who refuse to remain in poverty have only two legitimate courses open to them: they can either work (an option not open to many in times of recession) or they can be pushed back into a relationship where they are once more financially dependent upon a male. A third option is social security fraud or other crime.

Cook's (1987) study of female lone parent claimants shows that they are subject to a higher degree of suspicion of benefit fraud involvement because of the assumptions underpinning the welfare principles provided by Beveridge. These principles assume the universality of the patriarchal family, and therefore fail to take into account the position of lone parent families, the female heads of which are seen as being 'between men' rather than as alternative heads of households (Wilson 1977; Barrett and McIntosh 1982; Squires 1990). The State assumes that when a couple live together there exists an economic relationship in which the man is the provider and the woman the dependant. Lone parent claimants challenge this assumption because their economic dependence is on the State (Land 1995). Suspicion of lone mothers reached significant levels in the early 1980s with the setting up of special claims control units (SCCUs) to detect fraud among high-risk groups. In questioning mothers about their relationships with men, these units soon acquired the status of 'sex snoopers', and their controversial methods of surveillance led to their demise in 1986.

Most social security fraud offenders are dealt with summarily under the Social Security Administration Act 1992 which allows for the prosecution of claimants knowingly making false statements. There is no requirement to prove deliberate dishonesty or intention to defraud the department (as in tax fraud or more serious social security offences which are dealt with under the Theft Act 1968).

Figure 6.7 Number of defendants proceeded against for social security offences in England and Wales by gender, 1980–1996

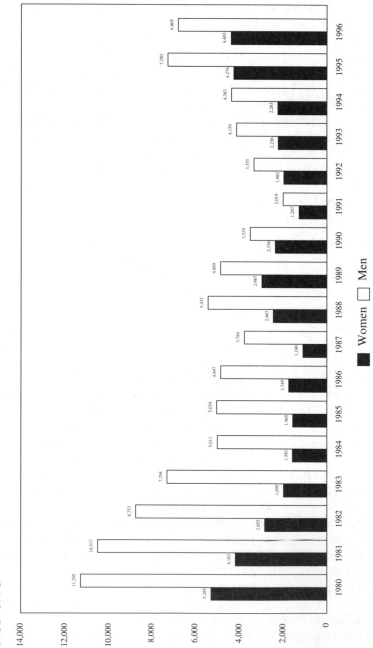

Source: Home Office, *Criminal Statistics England and Wales: Supplementary Tables*, covering years 1980–1996. London: HMSO.

Turning now to the *Criminal Statistics* we find that prosecutions for benefit fraud actually fell throughout the 1980s and 1990s. Figure 6.7 shows that while in 1980 there were a total of 16,580 prosecutions for social security offences, by 1996 prosecutions fell to 11,208. Women constituted nearly one-third of all social security fraud offenders in 1996. Despite the drop in prosecutions over this period, it would be misleading to assume that either the scale of benefit fraud had shrunk or that benefit fraudsters were not paying for their crimes in other ways. This is because the prosecution-based policies of the 1970s were abandoned in 1983 in favour of a cost-savings policy which 'encouraged' the withdrawal of suspect claims, repayment of money, and warnings against future abuse (Loveland 1989). Critics have voiced a number of complaints concerning the aggressive style of investigators, and particularly the possibility that the withdrawal of claims has often been achieved where a formal prosecution would have failed: for example, due to lack of evidence (NACRO 1986; Cook 1989).

While the fall in prosecutions can be explained in terms of a change in policy, some academics have suggested that there may have been an expansion in benefit fraud throughout this period (Jordan and Redley 1994). The strategy of depressing benefits and deregulation of the labour market resulted in increasing the attractiveness of benefit fraud, particularly fraud involving undeclared earnings (Evason and Woods 1995). Thus, the increase in poverty over this period probably resulted in more benefit fraud being committed, but this remains undetected in the figures for prosecutions.

Punishing the poor

The fine is the most frequently used punishment in the criminal justice system, regardless of whether the offence is tried summarily or tried on indictment. This is still the case of the 'crimes of poverty' considered in this chapter. Table 6.2 shows the range of punishments received by offenders of television licence evasion, prostitution and social security offences by gender in 1996.

An important observation to be made is that the fine is imposed on almost all television licence evasion offenders, regardless of their gender. Ninety-eight per cent of television licence offenders were fined in 1996. Offences relating to prostitution were also likely to attract fines (87 per cent). However, the fine was less likely to be imposed on defendants of social security offences (only 27 per cent of females, and 38 per cent of males) and this may reflect the counts. Forty-four per cent of female social security offenders were discharged either absolutely or conditionally, and 26 per cent were dealt with by higher tariff offences such as probation, community service, supervision or unsuspended prison sentences. In comparison with females, a lower proportion of male social

Table 6.2 Type of sentence imposed on defendants for television licence evasion, prostitution and social security fraud in England and Wales by gender, 1996

| Offence | Total for sentence | Discharge | Fine | Number of defendants receiving type of sentence | | | | |
				Probation order	Supervision order	Community service order	Unsuspended sentence of imprisonment	Other
Television licence evasion								
Women	105,432	1,682	103,661	1	–	–	–	88
Men	59,412	1,019	58,322	–	1	2	2	66
Prostitution								
Women	5,319	657	4,601	30	4	1	–	26
Social security fraud								
Women	4,183	1,833	1,146	528	–	546	25	105
Men	6,402	1,762	2,451	388	1	1,510	112	178

Source: Home Office 1998a.

security offenders were discharged (28 per cent), while a marginally higher proportion were dealt with by probation, community service or supervision or unsuspended prison sentences (31 per cent).

While the fine is recovered in most cases, some individuals will default by not paying the fine within the period of time specified by the court. At this stage, the court may sentence them to a term of imprisonment depending on the amount of fine still outstanding. The court may do this if it is satisfied that the default is due to the offender's wilful refusal or culpable neglect, or if it has considered or tried all other methods of enforcing payment of the sum and it appears to the court that they are inappropriate or unsuccessful. A report on the imprisonment of fine defaulters claimed that:

> defaulters on low incomes are often imprisoned on the grounds of 'culpable neglect', as the court judges that they have spent money on other priorities than the fine. Many such defaulters are in practice imprisoned because of an inability to manage on a low income.
>   (Penal Affairs Consortium 1995: 3)

Several studies have pointed to the material difficulties faced by defaulters of fines. One study based on a dossier of 35 case studies of defaulters (including television licence evaders) showed most of the defaulters to be out of work, often for more than 12 months (National Association of Probation Officers 1994), and that most were living a life on State benefits and had multiple debts. The majority of offenders end up defaulting on their fines because they need the money for things such as shoes and clothing, food and housekeeping, rent, rates, unspecified bills, light and heating, and public transport (Softley 1978). The crucial problem appears to be that offenders are given fines that they simply cannot afford to pay. This is despite the fact that courts are required to take into account the offender's means in the setting of fines.

The injustice of the imposition of fines on 'crimes of poverty' offenders can most clearly be seen in relation to prostitution where it has been argued that in setting fines the criminal justice system acts a 'revolving door' in processing prostitutes (Cook 1997). Large sums of money can be accrued by some prostitutes, who may then make the rational economic decision to go to prison for fine default rather than pay (Edwards 1987). Thus, in sentencing the prostitute to a financial penalty, courts are reinforcing a vicious circle which forces these women back into prostitution to pay their fines, or forces them into prison.

Table 6.3 shows the number imprisoned for defaulting on fines for television licence evasion and for offences relating to prostitution by gender between 1991 and 1996.[7] Between 1991 and 1995 there was a sharp increase in the number of persons imprisoned for defaulting on fines for television licence evasion, from 394 in 1991 to 728 in 1995. In 1996, however, there was a dramatic fall in the number of men and

Table 6.3 Number of offenders imprisoned for defaulting on fines for television licence evasion and prostitution in England and Wales by gender, 1991–6

Offence	Number of offenders imprisoned for fine default					
	1991	*1992*	*1993*	*1994*	*1995*	*1996*
Television licence evasion						
Women	136	163	278	243	235	89
Men	258	405	547	487	493	238
Prostitution						
Women	96	95	82	103	77	27

Source: Home Office Research and Statistics Directorate.
Note: No information on social security fraud fine defaulters is available.

women imprisoned for defaulting on fines for television licence evasion – there were only 238 males and 89 females imprisoned in 1996. There has been a similarly significant decline in the use of imprisonment for females defaulting on fines for prostitution offences, from 96 in 1991 to 27 in 1996. Two major developments affected fine enforcement practice to fall in 1996 (Home Office 1998b). Both of these developments took place within a context of extensive media coverage focusing on the plight of imprisoned fine defaulters, particularly lone parent mothers.[8]

Conclusions

This chapter has examined the *Criminal Statistics for England and Wales* between 1980 and 1996 to explore the criminalization of female poverty. Despite the difficulties involved in interpreting trends in prosecution and sentencing, it has been suggested that there have been real increases in 'crimes of poverty' over this period. It has further been suggested that 'crimes of poverty' offenders are doubly punished through the imposition of fines which they often cannot afford to pay within the time specified by the court, and which may consequently lead to their imprisonment for fine default. The clearest example has been in relation of television licence evasion, which now constitutes the largest single component of female crime, and after motoring offences accounts for the largest number of imprisoned fine defaulters.

Arguments in favour of scrapping the licence fee and raising the level of general taxation as an alternative method of funding the BBC have been put forward elsewhere (Pantazis and Gordon 1997). More imaginative solutions need to be thought of in relation to the criminalization of prostitutes and social security offenders. While debates on the decriminalization of prostitution have been popular among some academics and women campaign groups, such solutions to benefit fraud have not been so forthcoming. A policy designed to encourage non-prosecution is to be welcomed, so long as claimants can be assured that investigations will be carried out in a fair manner. However, it is difficult to envisage a decline in benefit fraud without adequate increases in the level of benefits.

Notes

1 Excluding summary motoring offences.
2 By conventional usage, I presume Coleman and Moynihan (1996) are referring to conventional crimes such as burglary, robbery, and assault, etc.
3 Excluding all summary motoring offences.
4 The figures for 1995 are low as a result of an error in data processing procedures which led to a shortfall in the recording four summary offence classifications, including Wireless Telegraphy Acts offences.
5 Enquiry officers visit suspected households between Monday and Saturday from 9 a.m. to 9 p.m. Personal correspondence with TV Licensing.
6 TVL Prosecution Policy document, paragraphs 7.1 and 7.2.
7 Separate information on television licence evasion was unavailable prior to 1991.
8 A Queens Bench Judgement in Crawley which clarified the legislative position concerning the need to consider all enforcement procedures led to a judicial review in a number of cases and the immediate release of prisoners. The issue of the good practice guidance for the courts in July 1996 by the Government's Working Group on the Enforcement of Financial Penalties and the extension of the power to impose an attachment of earnings order in the Criminal Procedure and Investigations Act 1996 have also contributed to the fall in the use of imprisonment for fine defaulters.

References

Adler, F. (1975) *Sisters in Crime*. New York: McGraw-Hill.
Allen, H. (1989) Fines for women: paradoxes and paradigms, in P. Carlen and D. Cook (eds) *Paying for Crime*. Milton Keynes: Open University Press.
Barrett, M. and McIntosh, M. (1982) *The Anti-Social Family*. London: Verso.
Bowker, L. (1978) *Women and the Criminal Justice System*. Lexington, MA: Lexington Books.
Box, S. (1983) *Power, Crime and Mystification*. London: Routledge.
Box, S. (1987) *Recession, Crime and Punishment*. London: Macmillan.
Box, S. and Hale, C. (1983) Liberation and female criminality in England and Wales revisited. *British Journal of Criminology*, 22: 35–49.
Box, S. and Hale, C. (1984) Liberation/emancipation, economic marginalization or less chivalry? *Criminology*, 22: 473–97.
Bradshaw, J. and Millar, J. (1991) *Lone Parent Families in the UK*, (Department of Social Security Research Report no. 6). London: HMSO.

Campbell, A. (1981) *Delinquent Girls*. Oxford: Basil Blackwell.

Carlen, P. (1983) *Women's Imprisonment*. London: Routledge & Kegan Paul.

Carlen, P. (1988) *Women, Crime and Poverty*. Milton Keynes: Open University Press.

Central Office of Information (1985) *TV Licence Anti-Evasion Campaign*. London: COI.

Cohen, A. (1955) *Delinquent Boys*. London: Free Press.

Coleman, C. and Moynihan, J. (1996) *Understanding Crime Data*. Buckingham: Open University Press.

Cook, D. (1987) Women on welfare: in crime or injustice, in P. Carlen and A. Worrall (eds) *Gender, Crime and Justice*. Milton Keynes: Open University Press.

Cook, D. (1989) *Rich Law, Poor Law: A Differential Response to Tax and Benefit Fraud*. Milton Keynes: Open University Press.

Cook, D. (1997) *Poverty, Crime and Criminal Justice*. London: Child Poverty Action Group.

Dean, H. and Melrose, M. (1996) Unravelling citizenship: The significance of social security fraud. *Critical Social Policy*, 48 (3): 3–31.

Dean, H. and Melrose, M. (1997) Manageable discord: fraud and resistance in the social security system. *Social Policy and Administration*, 31 (2): 103–18.

Dowler, E. and Calvert, C. (1995) *Nutrition and Diet in Lone-Parent Families in London*. London: Family Policy Studies Centre.

Edwards, S. (1984) *Women on Trial*. Manchester: Manchester University Press.

Edwards, S. (1987) Prostitutes: victims of law, social policy and organised crime, in P. Carlen, and A. Worrall (eds) *Gender, Crime and Justice*. Milton Keynes: Open University Press.

Edwards, S. (1989) *Policing Domestic Violence*. London: Sage.

Edwards, S. (1996) *Sex and Gender in the Legal Process*. London: Blackstone.

Evason, E. and Woods, R. (1995) Poverty, deregulation of the labour market and benefit fraud. *Social Policy and Administration*, 29 (1): 40–54.

Farrington, D. and Morris, A. (1983) Sex, sentencing and reconviction. *British Journal of Criminology*, 23 (3): 229–58.

Gordon, D. and Pantazis, C. (1994) Television, crime and poverty. *Radical Statistics*, 57: 3–8.

Gordon, D. and Pantazis, C. (1997) *Breadline Britain in the 1990s*. Aldershot: Ashgate.

Jordan, B. and Redley, P. (1994) Polarisation, underclass and the welfare state. *Work, Employment and Society*, 8 (2): 153–76.

Joseph Rowntree Foundation (1995a) *Inquiry into Income and Wealth*, vol. 1. York: Joseph Rowntree Foundation.

Joseph Rowntree Foundation (1995b) *Inquiry into Income and Wealth*, vol. 2. York: Joseph Rowntree Foundation.

Harvey, L., Burnham, R., Kendall, K. and Pease, K. (1992) Gender differences in criminal justice: an international comparison. *British Journal of Criminology*, 32: 208–17.

Hedderman, C. (1995) Gender, crime and the criminal justice system, in M. Walker (ed.) *Interpreting Crime Statistics*. Oxford: Clarendon Press.

Heidensohn, F. (1968) The deviance of women: A critique and an enquiry. *British Journal of Sociology*, 19 (2): 160–75.

Heidensohn, F. (1985) *Women and Crime*. London: Macmillan.

Hillyard, P. and Gordon, D. (1995) Arresting statistics: the trend towards informality in the criminal justice system. Unpublished.

Home Office (1982) *Criminal Statistics England and Wales: Supplementary tables*. London: Home Office.

Home Office (1995) *1994 Criminal Statistics England and Wales*. London: HMSO.

Home Office (1998a) *Criminal Statistics England and Wales: Supplementary tables*. London: Home Office.

Home Office (1998b) *Prison Statistics for England and Wales*. London: HMSO.

Land, H. (1977) Parity begins at home: women's and men's work in the home and its effects on their paid employment. London: Equal Opportunities Commission/Social Science Research Council.

Land, H. (1995) Families and the law, in J. Muncie, M. Wetherell, R. Dallos and A. Cochrane (eds) *Understanding the Family*. London: Sage.

Lewis, J. and Piachaud, D. (1992) Women and poverty in the twentieth century, in C. Glendinning, and J. Millar (eds) *Women and Poverty in the 1990s*. London: Harvester Wheatsheaf.

Loveland, I. (1989) Policing welfare: local authority responses to claimant fraud in the housing benefit scheme. *Journal of Law and Society*, 16 (2): 187–209.

McLeod, E. (1982) *Women Working: Prostitution Now*. London: Croom Helm.

Mirrlees-Black, C., Mayhew, P. and Percy, A. (1996) *The 1996 British Crime Survey*, Home Office Statistical Bulletin, issue 19/96. London: Home Office Research and Statistics Directorate.

Morris, A. (1987) *Women, Crime and Criminal Justice*. Oxford: Basil Blackwell.

NACRO (National Association for the Case and Resettlement of Offenders) (1986) *Enforcement of the Law Relating to Social Security*, report of a NACRO working party. London: NACRO.

NAPO (National Association of Probation Officers) (1994) *Fines, Defaulters and Debtors Gaol*. London: NAPO.

Newburn, T. and Stanko, E. (1994) *Just Boys Doing Business*. London: Routledge.

O'Neil, M. (1997) Prostitute women now, in A. Schambler and G. Schambler (eds) *Re-Thinking Prostitution: Purchasing Sex in the 1990s*. London: Routledge.

Oppenheim, C. and Harker, L. (1996) *Poverty: The Facts*. London: CPAG Ltd.

Pahl, J. (1989) *Money and Marriage*. London: Harvester Wheatsheaf.

Pantazis, C. and Gordon, D. (1997) Television licence evasion and the criminalisation of female poverty. *Howard Journal*, 36 (2): 179–86.

Payne, S. (1991) *Women, Health and Poverty*. London: Harvester Wheatsheaf.

Payne, S. and Pantazis, C. (1997) Poverty and gender, in D. Gordon and C. Pantazis (eds) *Breadline Britain in the 1990s*. Aldershot: Ashgate.

Pearce, F. (1990) *Second Islington Crime Survey: Commercial and Conventional Crime in Islington*. Centre for Criminology: Middlesex University.

Penal Affairs Consortium (1995) *The Imprisonment of Fine Defaulters*. London: Penal Affairs Consortium.

Pennington, S. (1996) Women: this woman hits her husband. *The Guardian*, 11 November, G2T, page 6.

Pheonix, J. (1997) *'Making sense of prostitution today'*, unpublished Ph.D. thesis, University of Bath.

Phillpotts, G. and Lancucki, L. (1979) *Previous Convictions, Sentence and Reconviction*, Home Office Research Study 53. London: HMSO.

Pollak, O. (1950) *The Criminality of Women*. New York: A. S. Barnes.

Rein, M. and Erie, S. (1988) Women and welfare state, in C. Mueller (ed.) *The Politics of the Gender Gap*. London: Sage.

Scott, H. (1984) *Working Your Way to the Bottom: the Feminization of Poverty*. London: Pandora.

Simon, R. (1975) *Women and Crime*. Lexington, MA: Lexington Books.

Smart, C. (1977) *Women, Crime and Criminology: A Feminist Critique*. London: Routledge & Kegan Paul.

Softley, P. (1978) *Fines in Magistrates' Courts*, Home Office Research Study 46. London: HMSO.

Squires, P. (1990) *Anti-Social Policy*. New York: Harvester Wheatsheaf.

Sutherland, E. (1949) *White Collar Crime*. New York: Dryden.

Thomas, M., Walker, A., Wilmot, A. and Bennett, N. (1998) *Living in Britain – Results from the 1996 General Household Survey*. London: OPCS.

Walker, A. (1992) The poor relation: poverty among older women, in C. Glendinning and J. Millar (eds). *Women and Poverty in Britain*. London: Harvester Wheatsheaf.

Walker, A. and Walker, C. (eds) (1987) *The Growing Divide: A Social Audit 1979–1987*. London: CPAG Ltd.

Walker, C. and Wall, D. (1997) Imprisoning the poor: television licence evaders and the criminal justice system. *Criminal Law Review*, March, 173–86.

Walker, M. (1995) Criminal justice and offenders, in M. Walker (ed.) *Interpreting Crime Statistics*. Oxford: Clarendon Press.

Walklate, S. (1995) *Gender and Crime*. London: Prentice Hall/Harvester Wheatsheaf.

Wall, D. and Bradshaw, J. (1987) The television licence: prosecution and poor households. *Howard Journal*, 26 (1): 47–56.

Wall, D. and Bradshaw, J. (1994) The message of the medium. *New Law Journal*, 9 September: 1198–9.

Wilson, E. (1977) *Women and the Welfare State*. London: Tavistock.

7

Domestic violence policy in the 1990s

Gill Hague

Domestic violence exists in almost all known societies. Defined here to mean violence against women by men with whom they have (or have previously had) an intimate or sexual relationship, violence of this type has blighted women's lives throughout the millenia. At the same time there is evidence that such violence has always been resisted, either individually or collectively in a wide variety of ways in different time periods, places, countries and cultures globally (see, for example, Pleck 1987; Davies 1994). There has been an organized international movement of women against domestic violence for very many years which has been markedly active in recent times in various parts of the world, with resultant increases in awareness of and attention to the issue. Combatting domestic violence was a major topic, for example, at the 1995 Beijing Fourth World Conference on Women, and was highlighted in the comprehensive, global *Platform for Action* which the conference produced (United Nations 1996). Considerable international effort has also gone into the adoption and implementation of the historic 1993 *United Nations Declaration on the Elimination of Violence against Women* (which amplifies the 1979 *Convention on the Elimination of all Forms of Discrimination against Women)*. Within the UK, the domestic violence movement has been particularly evident since the early 1970s, developing out of the larger women's liberation movement.

Until the end of the 1960s in the UK, little public attention was paid to the issue of domestic violence against women (although the struggle against it had formed part of the women's rights movement of the nineteenth and early twentieth century). There were few services in existence, very little publicity or public awareness, and, importantly, no emergency accommodation whatsoever for women and children attempting to escape violence in the home (see Hague and Wilson 1996 for a discussion of domestic violence in the immediate post-war period up until 1970). With the dramatic advent of women's liberation, however, the refuge movement, organized through Women's Aid and other grass-roots feminist campaigning groups, sprang into life. Very rapidly throughout the 1970s, refuges and other services for women experiencing domestic violence and their children were set up throughout the country, leading to the development of national coordinating bodies, the Women's Aid federations (in England, Scotland, Wales and Northern Ireland) and a whole variety of other organizations. It is largely as a result of this movement, and its vibrant struggle over the last 25 years, that domestic violence is now on the public and political agenda. Policy, practice and awareness-raising initiatives have developed as a result, which have both grown out of, and in turn fed back into, the Women's Aid movement. The effectiveness of these developments is currently patchy and services remain inadequate, but they do nevertheless represent a real transformation. Activists who remember the situation 25 years ago, and the struggles since, sometimes express disbelief that things have changed so much.

So what has changed and why? Are the recent developments situated within a wider framework of supportive policy and practice? How serious is government interest in domestic violence and how enduring are the changes as a feature of social policy? This chapter will briefly discuss these issues. More detailed accounts are available elsewhere (see, for example, Dobash and Dobash 1992; Hague and Malos 1993; Mullender 1996).

A brief overview of current provision relating to domestic violence

In Britain the 1990s has been a period when the elaboration of good policy and practice guidelines, the embracing of domestic violence training and the promotion of multi-agency initiatives have become areas of growing interest. In recent years there have been many domestic violence conferences, seminars and training courses and scarcely a week goes by without a conference on the subject. There are now occasional publicity campaigns and at least the beginnings of public education. The first public awareness programme on a national level, operating mainly through BBC radio, was held in 1995 with input from the Women's Aid federations. The last few years has also seen the growth of local zero tolerance campaigns in many areas, following the initial ground-breaking zero tolerance public awareness campaign developed by Edinburgh District Council women's unit. Domestic violence has been addressed on *Brookside, Eastenders, Coronation Street* and *The Archers*, and as a result has provoked national discussion.

Over the last few years various general grass-roots campaigns on domestic violence have highlighted the plight of abused women and their children. Within this current campaigning and networking activity, the position of women who have suffered extensive and prolonged domestic abuse, and who are finally driven to kill their partners, has begun to receive attention, with several well-publicized campaigns and actions coordinated through groups such as Justice for Women, Southall Black Sisters, Women's Aid, Rights of Women and others.

There are now more than 300 refuges throughout the country, including a variety of specialist refuges for black women and women from minority communities. These include specific projects, most commonly for Asian women, but also for African and Caribbean women, and Latin American, Turkish, Irish and Chinese women in various areas. The first Jewish women's refuge was opened in London in 1997. However, many of these specialist projects are in a shaky financial position. Most refuges are affiliated to the Women's Aid federations in either England, Scotland, Wales or Northern Ireland which coordinate the provision of refuge, support and advocacy services and work to promote the interests of abused women and their children nationally. Some refuges remain independent of the federations, usually those associated with church groups, or increasingly in the mid-1990s with housing associations (which frequently provide housing services only, with little attention to support, care and advocacy issues). Independent refuges also include some black women's organizations and *Refuge*, the successor to Chiswick Women's Aid (and Chiswick Family Rescue) which maintains a high profile.

However, refuges are still unable to cope with the demand. Many cannot accommodate half or more of the women and children who approach them, although most will offer advice and support and will refer women on to other projects in the refuge network. In 1975, the Parliamentary Select Committee on *Violence in Marriage* recommended in its *Report* the provision of one refuge place per 10,000 of the population in order to meet the need, but this estimate has been less than one-third realized today, more than 20 years later. Refuges for black women and children are even more severely under-resourced (see Mama 1996), and outreach and development work is often unfunded. A 1996 study of children's workers in refuges highlighted both the innovative work undertaken and also the constant resource shortage and lack of funding which jeopardizes this work (Hague *et al.* 1996b). While the facilities offered by refuges have improved in recent years, and some are now purpose-built or purpose-designed and offer training and support to staff (through the Women's Aid federations), many still depend on volunteer labour and almost all paid employees work long hours for poor financial rewards.

At least until the mid-1980s, the refuge movement was alone in taking on domestic violence, attempting to raise the voices of abused women and children in an empowering way and developing an analysis of domestic violence based on gendered understandings of the unequal position of women throughout society. Women in the movement were the first to elaborate explanations of domestic abuse which looked at power and control issues in relationships between men and women. They developed new understandings of the way in which violence is often used as a strategy of dominance in which men attempt to get their own way by using physical, sexual or emotional assault (see, for example, Schechter 1982). At the same time, research during the 1970s and 1980s stressed time and time again the inadequacies of services, and documented the ways in which agencies failed to respond well to women and children experiencing domestic violence (Dobash and Dobash 1980; Borkowski *et al.* 1983; Dobash *et al.* 1985; Pahl 1985; Hague and Malos 1993). By the mid-1990s, however, policy and practice changes had occurred in many agencies, and current research studies record substantial but uneven improvements (as well as remaining inadequacies) (see Hague *et al.* 1996b; Mullender 1996). A gendered analysis of power in relationships is also now adopted to a greater or lesser extent by a wide range of agencies.

Policy development in agencies

The police and probation

After years of inattention to domestic violence during which the police acted as if a man's home was indisputably his private castle (Edwards 1989; Hague *et al.* 1989), gradual improvements in the police response began towards the end of the 1980s. An influential Home Office research paper by Lorna Smith (1989), together with developments in a few police forces (including the Metropolitan Police in London), led to various Home Office Circulars including Circular 60/90 (Home Office 1990). This Circular recommended that the police adopt pro-arrest, pro-prosecution policies regarding perpetrators, accompanied by the setting up of domestic violence units and domestic violence liaison officer posts to support abused women and children and to assist in policing domestic violence. The Circular also recommended that the police engage in multi-agency initiatives on domestic violence. While these recommendations were initially viewed with ambivalence, not only by the police but also by the refuge movement, they have begun to pay dividends over the years and are now widely regarded more favourably. Women using domestic violence units speak highly of the services offered in many areas (Mullender 1996). However, implementation of the reforms has been patchy, as documented in a Home Office research study (Grace 1995).

Some specialist, experimental projects have been set up with initial funding from the Programme Development Unit of the Home Office (for example, the *Domestic Violence Matters* project in London which until recently provided civilian support from within a police station for women experiencing violence), and police domestic violence units have developed a variety of approaches to the problem and ways of supporting abused women. These initiatives by the police and the Home Office in the UK have learned much from developments in Canada and the USA. Difficulties in policing domestic violence persist, however, not least due to ambivalence from some abused women about a response which may criminalize their own partner, despite a widespread belief that the criminalization of domestic violence itself is a social policy response long overdue and to be much welcomed (see Hague and Malos 1993; Morley and Mullender 1994; Cretney and Davis 1996).

The probation service has also attempted to address domestic violence in recent years. The Association of Chief Officers of Probation produced a useful statement on domestic violence in 1992, updated in 1996, with guidelines for good practice (Association of Chief Officers of Probation 1996). Some individual probation services have produced their own policies for both criminal and family court work, and have taken a key role in inter-agency domestic violence initiatives. In addition, probation officers are now becoming involved in programmes for perpetrators of domestic violence, sometimes in partnership with voluntary sector groups, although there is much contention as to the effectivness and usefulness of such programmes.

Unresolved questions include whether men completing such pro grammes change their violent behaviour reliably and in the long term, and what to do about the characteristically high drop-out rate. Concerns also exist about the dangers of short-term group programmes (meeting perhaps once a week for a limited period) replacing a potentially more comprehensive response by the criminal justice service. However, abusers' programmes are becoming more and more popular (see Hague and Malos 1993; Mullender 1996).

Evaluations of individual projects are now emerging (see, for example, Dobash *et al.* 1996). Best practice examples are currently based on the model developed by the Duluth Domestic Abuse Intervention Project in Minnesota, USA, (see Pence 1989; Pence, forthcoming). Such programmes operate a curriculum based on a gendered analysis of power and control in relationships and avoid a therapeutic or 'colluding' approach. Further best practice developments include the operation of some management input into the programme by local women's services, and the prioritizing of women's and children's safety as one of the first principles of the project, often involving the provision of a 'sister' support project for women partners. Overall, there is evidence that perpetrators' programmes work most effectively if they are embedded in a wider network of services and justice responses (see, for example, Mullender 1996).

Social services and health

Traditionally, social services did not address domestic violence issues, partly because of the lack of statutory responsibility with respect to the abuse of women. Social workers have frequently adopted a conciliatory role, sometimes operating practices which blame or stigmatize the abused woman (see, for example, Maynard 1985). This has changed in recent years. Both community care and children's service plans now frequently feature domestic violence, and some departments have good practice guidelines and policies in place on working both with abused women and with abusing men. Some participate actively in inter-agency work on domestic violence, and liaison is beginning to be built between local area child protection committees and inter-agency domestic violence forums.

The impact on children of living with or witnessing domestic violence against their mothers is now also being addressed in policy and practice (Mullender and Morley 1994; Hague *et al.* 1996a), as is the interconnectedness of child abuse and domestic violence. While exact figures are impossible to work out, somewhere between 20 per cent and 70 per cent of cases involves both kinds of abuse (Bowker *et al.* 1988; Kelly 1994). The striking disregard of domestic violence in child protection work which certainly characterized such work in the past (see Farmer and Owen 1995) is now changing, with social services sometimes instituting innovative new policies. However, it is still the case that child protection specialists may neither work closely with domestic violence practitioners locally nor adopt an understanding attitude to mothers experiencing violence. The new interest within child protection also means that, in some instances, there has been a swing from overlooking the issue completely to adopting overly bureaucratic or harsh responses to women for failing to protect their children from experiencing either domestic violence or child abuse.

Health services have a vital role to play in treating the effects of domestic violence and in building a coordinated response to combat it. Small-scale research on health responses is now being conducted in various areas, and some accident and emergency departments and primary healthcare practitioners are developing specific policies and protocols (for example, the Camden Domestic Violence Forum has produced comprehensive practice guidance for healthcare workers). However, many health services continue to fail to take violence against women very seriously. One example of this is the marked absence of health services from many multi-agency domestic violence responses. Further government guidance on health issues in relation to domestic violence would be much welcomed (Hague *et al.* 1996b).

Legal protection

The introduction of civil law remedies to domestic abuse within specific domestic violence legislation was a key moment in the mid-1970s. Two Acts were enacted at that time: the 1976 Domestic Violence and Matrimonial Proceedings Act and the 1978 Domestic Proceedings and

Magistrates' Courts Act. However, the effectiveness of civil law injunctions under these Acts against a violent partner has always been doubtful especially since the legislation had little force, and was, in any case, interpreted with a large measure of discretion by judges and magistrates (see Barron 1990). In 1992, the Law Commission produced a useful report recommending substantial improvements in the legislation and these have been incorporated in the 1996 Family Law Act, albeit in a somewhat reduced form. This Act increases the legal protection available to abused women, extending the time period of injunctions and strengthening the policing of them. It also amends the 1989 Children Act to introduce a new measure to exclude the abusing partner from the home in cases of child abuse.

Domestic violence training and development of policy guidelines

Domestic violence inter-agency initiatives have sprung up all over Britain. These initiatives often take the form of domestic violence forums bringing together relevant statutory and voluntary sector organizations in order to build joint responses to domestic violence, to conduct educative and awareness-raising work and to attempt to improve policy and practice in local agencies (see Hague *et al.* 1995, 1996b). Widespread initiatives on domestic violence training for agencies now exist, although many are underfunded or run by volunteers. Some are provided by local refuges or inter-agency initiatives, and are delivered on either a single agency or a multi-agency basis. Specific domestic violence training manuals have been produced (see London Borough of Hammersmith and Fulham Community Safety Unit 1991; Leeds Inter-agency Project 1993), and many statutory and voluntary sector workers have now undertaken initial training. The need for local training of agency staff on domestic violence is widely recognized by bodies ranging from the United Nations to small voluntary groups, although such training cannot be regarded as a panacea and makes little difference if it is not accompanied by service provision and delivery.

Training often goes hand in hand with the implementation of domestic violence policies. Many agencies throughout the UK are now developing good policy and practice guidelines, as well as information packs and guides for staff and for the public, frequently with input from local inter-agency initiatives and refuge groups. Within education, for example, education packs have been produced in various local authorities for use by schools and youth services (see, for example, London Borough of Islington 1995). These packs provide guidelines and exercises for work with children and also material for teacher education. Their aim is to raise awareness about domestic violence, to assist children living in violent home situations, and, by educating the young on the issue, to contribute to building a society intolerant of violence against women.

Together with such training initiatives, public education campaigns (e.g. zero tolerance), awareness-raising strategies and the provision of wide-ranging information and advice on domestic violence are all issues which have been taken up by local authorities and other agencies, often with attention to equality issues (e.g. disability awareness, anti-racist strategies, translation into community languages and onto audiotape etc., and, less often, lesbian and heterosexism issues). Some local authorities have been particularly active in this work, especially where they have an equalities, community safety or crime prevention unit in operation, and a few have developed a corporate authority-wide response to domestic violence in recent years.

Contradictory government policy: will this change?

The Labour government, elected in the UK in 1997, has made clear its commitment to improving domestic violence services. Domestic violence featured in both the election manifesto of the Labour Party and in their *Peace at Home* policy document (Labour Party 1995). Possible improvements which have been mooted include funding for the national refuge network, the consolidation of inter-agency initiatives and the issuing of improved guidance to agencies. The Women's Aid federations and other domestic violence activists have cautiously welcomed these possibilities, and consultation and liaison are in progress. One development has been the issuing of a new Circular on domestic violence in September 1997 (Department of Health 1997). The Circular covers the Family Law Act Part iv but also contains some wider guidance. However, at the time of writing, it is not clear if, how or when further new policies and government initiatives will be put into place, although the government is currently preparing a new general strategy on violence against women.

At central government level, at least in the past, there have been very contradictory attitudes to domestic violence and, in general, government departments sideline the issue despite expressing interest. The refuge movement has struggled for many years for legislative protection, rehousing polices, economic and social support, effective law enforcement and refuge services. In her book on the social work and probation response to domestic violence *Rethinking Domestic Violence*, Audrey Mullender (1996: 4) suggests that: 'none of these battles has yet been fully won. It has always been an uphill struggle to get women's danger and distress taken seriously. In particular, Government has lacked or resisted a comprehensive understanding of the problem that could underpin action across a range of fronts'. She points out that in the mid-1990s Britain did seem at last to be in the midst of a wave of serious attention to the issue on a national level. Until recently, however, contradictions and lack of consistency in government policy on domestic violence could be clearly surmised from the way that responsibility for dealing with it has constantly fallen between various ministerial stools – the Home Office, the Department of the Environment and the Department of Health.

Encouragingly, in the early 1990s, the Home Office was accepted as the lead government agency in domestic violence work, and both an inter-ministerial group and an inter-departmental group of officers to deal with domestic violence have been established across the departments. The Home Office itself has initiated a variety of improvements in policy and practice within the police service, as discussed, and one of the main projects conducted so far by the interdepartmental groups has been the encouragement of multi-agency initiatives on domestic violence and the commissioning of the 1995 Inter-agency Circular (Home Office 1995) on inter-agency coordination. So far, so good. But it is difficult to guess how far government commitment to combat violence in the home will go in the face of continuing cut-backs in public services, healthcare, benefit levels and the provision of public-sector housing.

Apart from these initiatives, little change has occurred so far as a result of government action: for example, there are no coordinated funding policies for services. The emphasis on individual criminal justice solutions (as indicated by the Home Office as the lead ministry) can sometimes appear to be at the expense of more collectivist solutions and social and welfare measures. The current lack of services coupled with cutbacks and underfunding in those which do exist has led to fears among some domestic violence activists that central government's preference for individual solutions to domestic violence through the police and the criminal justice system may be being viewed as an alternative to more comprehensive government action (Hague and Malos 1993). Such action would include funding both adequate temporary and permanent housing options for women and children escaping violence, and also other welfare, health and social services which would begin to meet their needs. While this issue has been discussed here in terms of the former Conservative government, (Hague and Malos 1993) things may be similar in this respect with the present Labour one.

The background to government policy

From 1979 to 1997, the Conservative governments of Thatcher and Major adopted a particularly strong line in favour of the traditional, nuclear family, initiating in its support a range of social policies (see, for example, Every 1991). However, the endemic nature of violence in the home by men against women runs counter to the myth that the heterosexual nuclear family is necessarily the best social environment for us all. Domestic violence presents a contradiction to policies bolstering the traditional family. Such policies can conflict with government desires (developed in recent years partly as a result of pressure from Women's Aid, the refuge movement and a variety of other organizations) to be seen to be both strongly opposed to violence and abuse, and protective of abused women and children. Thus, the recent Conservative and present Labour governments have been quite open in their condemnation of domestic violence in a way that governments have not been in the past. In fact, long-term activists point out how such condemnations would previously have been unthinkable.

Central government now clearly regards violence against women in the home as on a par, in theory at least, with other violent crime. Such proclamations are broadly to be welcomed. But the policy to accompany them is often either contradictory or non-existent. Whether the present Labour government's policies on domestic violence will be translated into reality is not yet clear. However, both the Labour and the Conservative party frequently express 'pro-family' sentiments and favour two-parent situations as ideal for successful child-rearing. Frighteningly judgemental attitudes towards single parent families which, for some years now, have featured strongly in Conservative Party ideology began in 1997 to find their way into the rhetoric of the Labour government, not least in the words of the prime minister himself who, for example, made it clear in a June 1997 speech that New Labour regards lone mothers as part of a 'dependency culture'.

Policy ambivalences

The Children Act: forgetting domestic violence?

An example of the contradiction and ambivalence within government approaches to domestic violence is the way in which the far-reaching 1989 Children Act, the centre-piece of government family policy, more or less 'forgot' about domestic violence, at exactly the same time that some other government departments were starting to take it on. In line with government pro-family ideology, the Act assumes that children are best brought up in family units involving both biological parents, and that statutory intervention should be kept to a minimum. But what then happens in cases of domestic violence?

The private provisions of the Children Act, including residence and contact arrangements for children, have proved particularly problematic in cases where the mother has experienced violence. In a piece of research published in 1996, abuse of either mothers or children as a result of contact visits with fathers after separation was found to occur in all but 7 of 53 such cases investigated (Hester and Radford 1996). This research has led to a general questioning by Women's Aid and a variety of other organizations of the current legal presumption in favour of contact for children with fathers until it is found to be unsafe. Recommendations have been made that the opposite arrangement should prevail. This is not to suggest that children should not have contact with their fathers, but rather to say that there should be a presumption that contact should only occur *if* it can be surmised to be safe. Problems can also be experienced where mediation is attempted in cases of domestic violence (see Hester *et al.* 1997), although family court welfare officers and mediators are currently attempting to improve practice in various localities, and training programmes on these issues are being developed, both locally and nationally.

The provisions in the Children Act for unmarried fathers to increase their rights by applying for parental responsibility, together with the conditions of many residence and contact orders for fathers, can cause considerable problems for women and children escaping domestic violence and attempting to establish violence-free lives. If contact with abusive partners is enforced by law, almost as a matter of course, it can be virtually impossible for women to escape from violent men (Morley 1993: 192).

The Child Support Act

The 1991 Child Support Act which came into force in April 1993 obliges mothers claiming benefit to reveal the name of the father of their children so that he may be pursued for maintenance payments. In its original draftings, the Act ignored domestic violence completely, a telling omission by a government publicly committed to protecting abused women. Due to the efforts of Women's Aid and others, a clause was inserted which allows women to be exempted from this potentially dangerous requirement if they have 'good cause' to fear that they will experience 'harm or distress' as a result. How this provision is being carried out in practice by the Child Support Agency, and what sort of evidence of 'harm or distress' is being requested seems to vary widely. Women's Aid nationally reports that some officers and offices take the issue very seriously, but some show little sensitivity or understanding, placing women and children in renewed danger. In general, child support payments, even where the woman is willing for the action to occur, can lead ex-partners to seek renewed contact with women and children which they would not have done prior to the Act, and there is evidence that this has led to further abuse or harassment.

The Home Affairs Committee 1993

Advocates and activists on behalf of abused women and children, disillusioned by government forgetfulness or indifference about the subject during the 1970s and 1980s, were greatly encouraged in March 1993 when the House of Commons Home Affairs Committee *Inquiry into Domestic Violence* (1993) made a series of forward-looking recommendations in its inquiry report. It endorsed many of the proposals of the Women's Aid federations (see WAFE 1992) and recommended, for example, that a national funding strategy be adopted to improve the provision of refuges nationally. However, in response to the Home Affairs Committee report the government hedged its bets and in general failed to commit itself to any of the proposals and recommendations (Government Reply 1993). We have yet to see what the present Labour government will make of this.

Contradictions in the police response

While Home Office initiatives to develop a more positive police response are most welcome in contrast to previous police inaction, as discussed, concerns have been expressed from some quarters about the civil liberties issues involved, particularly in relation to the potential for increased police surveillance of black and other communities (Southall Black Sisters 1989; Morley and Mullender 1994; Mama 1996). Thus, women who are themselves immigrants (or whose partners are), or who come from minority ethnic communities, may be particularly reluctant to involve the police in their affairs. Women experiencing violence whose immigration status is dependent on that of their husbands can be in a particularly dangerous and difficult position. On a more general level, there are fears about building inter-agency collaboration with the police while aggressive and potentially racist police practices continue to exist and the dominant police culture remains authoritarian and masculine (Hague *et al.* 1996b; Mama 1996).

Overall, contradictions in domestic violence policy are revealed by the fact that pro-arrest, pro-prosecution practices can only succeed as one part of an overall multi-faceted community response against domestic violence, including the provision of coordinated support services for the women and children involved (Pence 1989). To date, at least, recent governments have encouraged pro-prosecution policing policies without facilitating the necessary support framework of services and policy, so that they are almost certainly being set up to fail.

Ambivalences in inter-agency work

In theory, central government encouragement of multi-agency work on domestic violence can be perceived as an adequate response to this difficulty (and forms part of a general trend towards viewing inter-agency collaboration as the panacea for all evils). Multi-agency initiatives have, indeed, led to innovations in domestic violence responses in many localities. However, a 1996 national study of inter-agency initiatives (Hague *et al.* 1996b), conducted by the Domestic Violence Research Group (of which the present author is a member) both acknowledged the creative potential of such initiatives, but also revealed how this potential is currently being held back by lack of resources and by the sheer difficulty of getting agencies to work together successfully. Getting all relevant organizations to take on domestic violence and to work together to combat it can be viewed as the obvious next step after the provision of basic emergency and support services. However, the 1996 study concluded that this strategy will only work effectively and lead to constructive change if it is resourced and if Women's Aid, domestic violence survivors and the refuge movement are centrally involved. Without these factors, the innovative potential of multi-agency initiatives to move domestic violence work forward to a new stage can be easily lost, and they can become talking shops, time-wasters or smokescreens disguising inaction and lack of meaningful policy (Hague *et al.* 1995, 1996b; Department of Health 1997; Harwin *et al.*, forthcoming).

Thus, official encouragement of unfunded inter-agency coordination is an example of central and local government giving with one hand and taking away with the other by encouraging the approach but not then providing the tools and resources to do the job effectively. Some sceptics have viewed government support for inter-agency projects as a cheap option in any case, and one which could be seen to be taking the initiative away from the Women's Aid network. While Women's Aid supports the establishment of inter-agency work, there are dangers that the refuge network could become marginalized if domestic violence work continues to inch towards the mainstream, and government money, limited as it is, is funnelled into multi-agency projects, often fronted by the local authority or the police. The thorny but engaging issue then becomes how a social movement of women can connect with, or be organically part of, a mainstream agency response. At the moment, the refuge network is part of a feminist-inspired movement of women against male violence, which has been fairly successful (compared with the situation in some similar countries) in maintaining its autonomy and independence of both state and church organizations.

Social security and housing: cutbacks in resources

Social security benefits provide a crucial example of resource shortage. Their availability is a vital source of economic independence for women and children fleeing abuse. But these benefits have been substantially cut back in recent years. When viewed against lack of benefits, underfunded services, and cuts in health and social services, government policies on domestic violence presently look somewhat fragile and inadequate, despite encouraging messages from New Labour politicians and their officials.

The availability of safe, permanent housing options for women and children who have been forced to leave home because of abuse is of key importance in meeting their needs. However, government housing policy throughout the 1980s and early 1990s has been deliberately designed to reduce the provision of council housing in favour of owner-occupation, housing associations and private rented accommodation (Greve 1991; Shelter 1991). These policies have led to a substantial shortage of public-sector housing in the UK (with housing associations unable to fill the gap), which has led in turn to a huge increase in homelessness, with direct and often tragic effects on the lives of women and children homeless due to violence (Malos and Hague 1993).

The 1996 Housing Act amended homelessness legislation to remove the previously-existing right of those defined as 'statutorily homeless' under the Act to be permanently rehoused. People so defined are now entitled only to temporary housing and must then compete on one unified housing list with all other applicants for permanent accommodation, although such lists can now be 'weighted' in favour of the homeless. While domestic violence is identified and defined within the legislation more clearly as a cause of homelessness than in the previous legislation, which is of some assistance, the Act removes provisions for so-called 'persons from abroad' and encourages, for both temporary and permanent rehousing, the use of insecure private provision, a housing tenure which is often unsuitable for abused women and children.

Many local authorities are currently doing whatever they can to get around the provisions of the Act so that they can still permanently rehouse women and children experiencing domestic violence fairly quickly, but the legislation, if it remains on the statute book under Labour, is a licence for less liberally-minded authorities to adopt harsher measures. Encouragingly, some local authorities and housing associations have implemented formal, written domestic violence good policy and practice guidelines and provide training on domestic violence and housing issues for housing officers (Malos and Hague 1993).

Conclusion

Domestic violence policy remains ambivalent. Attitudes and ideas about domestic violence are undoubtedly changing and the issue is very much on the public agenda, with developments in policy and practice almost inconceivable 25 years ago. Refuges are now an established feature of social provision, yet funding for many individual refuges and for the refuge federations remains so shaky that the future of these organizations is thrown into crisis on a recurring basis. Some refuges close and disappear from view; many struggle along from one funding crisis to the next; some find themselves in competition with new refuge projects established by housing associations which characteristically have little provision for staffing or for the social care issues involved.

Local and central government commitments to take a stand against domestic violence, frequently ambivalent in themselves, are often further undermined by funding cutbacks. For example, lack of resources is currently holding back both the specialist work of the police in domestic violence units and the development of multi-agency intiatives with their creative potential for a coordinated approach to domestic violence. Individual criminal justice responses continue to be encouraged without accompanying them with wider, more collective social and welfare measures. Considerable evidence exists that such criminal justice responses are only successful if they are embedded in a wider service framework.

There is some inspiration from the Duluth model and from other examples (mainly in the USA, Canada, Australia and New Zealand) of integrated, multi-faceted community and agency coordinating projects to tackle domestic violence, which have often developed in tandem with the refuge movement. These projects usually include a strong criminal justice response with comprehensive pro-arrest, pro-prosecution policies for perpetrators, plus carefully monitored abusers' programmes, all of which are positioned within a wide-ranging frame of policies, community development and services for abused women and children (which are broadly speaking accountable to them). The objective is that agencies, domestic violence survivors, the local state and community members can move forward in concert towards a society where domestic violence is no longer tolerated. The vision is both positive and also innovative as agencies come together in multi-agency groupings and in other ways to exchange ideas and to build new policies and practices previously quite unprecedented.

While such inspiring examples of comprehensive domestic violence intervention projects are presently rare, moves in this direction have been made in various areas of the UK (for example, by the pioneering Leeds Inter-agency Project and the Derby Domestic Violence Action Group, among others, working together with local women's projects). Despite funding difficulties and cut-backs, women's grass-roots organizations throughout the country continue to campaign, to apply pressure on the government and to provide support, resources and ideas as domestic violence work inches towards the mainstream. Thus there is, perhaps, a hopeful future in which activists, domestic violence workers and domestic violence survivors can take their place alongside central and local government, the public, and key agencies and organizations in both the statutory and the voluntary sectors, creating historically new forms of resistance to domestic violence.

References

Association of Chief Officers of Probation (1996) *Position Statement on Domestic Violence*. London: ACOP.

Barron, J. (1990) *Not Worth the Paper: The Effectiveness of Legal Protection for Women and Children Experiencing Domestic Violence*. Bristol: WAFE.

Borkowski, M., Murch, M. and Walker, V. (1983) *Marital Violence: The Community Response*. London: Tavistock.

Bowker, L., Arbitell, M. and McFerron, R. (1988) On the relationship between wife beating and child abuse, in K. Yllo and M. Bograd (eds) *Feminist Perspectives on Wife Abuse*. Newbury Park, CA: Sage.

Cretney, A. and Davis, G. (1996) Prosecuting domestic assault. *Criminal Law Review*, March: 162–73.

Davies, M. (1994) *Women and Violence: Realities and Responses Worldwide*. London: Zed Books.

Department of Health (1997) *Family Law Act 1996, Part iv Family Homes and Domestic Violence*. Local Authority Circular 15/97. London: Department of Health.

Dobash, R. and Dobash, R. (1980) *Violence Against Wives*. London: Open Books.

Dobash, R. and Dobash, R. (1992) *Women, Violence and Social Change*. London: Routledge.

Dobash, R., Dobash, R. and Cavanagh, K. (1985) The contact between battered women and social and medical agencies, in J. Pahl (ed.) *Private Violence and Public Policy*. London: Routledge.

Dobash, R., Dobash, R., Cavanagh, K. and Lewis, R. (1996) *A Research Evaluation of Programmes for Violent Men*. Edinburgh: Scottish Office Central Research Unit.

Dunhill, C. (ed.) (1989) *The Boys in Blue*. London: Virago.

Edwards, S. (1989) *Policing Domestic Violence*. London: Sage.

Every, J. (1991) Who is 'the family'? The assumptions of British social policy. *Critical Social Policy*, 33 (Winter): 62–75.

Farmer, E. and Owen, M. (1995) *Child Protection Practice: Private Risks and Public Remedies*. London: HMSO.

Government Reply to the Third Report from the Home Affairs Committee Session 1992–3, HC245 (1993) (Domestic Violence). London: HMSO.

Grace, S. (1995) *Policing Domestic Violence in the 90s*, Home Office Research Study no. 139. London: HMSO.

Greve, J. (1991) *Homelessness in Britain*. York: Joseph Rowntree Foundation.

Hague G. and Malos E. (1993) *Domestic Violence: Action for Change*. Cheltenham: New Clarion Press.

Hague, G. and Wilson, C. (1996) *The Silenced Pain*. Bristol: The Policy Press.

Hague, G., Harwin, N., Meminn, K., Rubens, J. and Taylor, M. (1989) Policing male violence in the home, in C. Dunhill (ed.) *The Boys in Blue*. London: Virago.

Hague, G., Malos, E. and Dear, W. (1995) *Against Domestic Violence: Inter-agency Initiatives, SAUS Working Papers*. Bristol: The Policy Press.

Hague, G., Kelly, L., Malos, E. and Mullender, A. (1996a), *Children, Refuges and Domestic Violence*. Bristol: WAFE.

Hague, G., Malos, E. and Dear, W. (1996b) *Multi-agency Work and Domestic Violence*. Bristol: The Policy Press.

Harwin, N., Malos, E. and Hague, G. (forthcoming) *Inter-agency Work and Domestic Violence*. London: Whiting and Birch.

Hester, M. and Radford, L. (1996) *Domestic Violence and Child Contact Arrangements in England and Denmark*. Bristol: The Policy Press.

Hester, M., Pearson, C. and Radford, L. (1997) *Domestic Violence: A National Survey of Court Welfare and Voluntary Sector Mediation Practice*. Bristol: The Policy Press.

Home Office (1990) *Domestic Violence Circular 60/90*. London: HMSO.

Home Office (1995) *Inter-agency Co-ordination to Tackle Domestic Violence*, Inter-agency Circular. London: Home Office.

House of Commons Home Affairs Committee (1993) *Inquiry into Domestic Violence*. London: HMSO.

Kelly, L. (1994) The Interconnectedness of domestic violence and child abuse, in A. Mullender and R. Morley (eds) *Children Living with Domestic Violence*. London: Whiting and Birch.

Labour Party (1995) *Peace at Home*. London: Labour Party.

Leeds Inter-Agency Project (1993) *Violence against Women by known Men: Training Pack*. Leeds: Leeds Inter-Agency project, Sahara Black Women's Refuge and Leeds Women's Aid.

London Borough of Hammersmith and Fulham Community Safety Unit (1991) *Challenging Domestic Violence: Training and Resource Pack*. London: London Borough of Hammersmith and Fulham.

London Borough of Islington (1995) *STOP: Schools Take on Preventing Domestic Violence*. London: London Borough of Islington Women's Equality Unit.

Malos E. and Hague G. (1993) *Domestic Violence and Housing*. Bristol: WAFE and School of Applied Social Studies.

Mama, A. (1996) *The Hidden Struggle: Statutory and Voluntary Sector Responses to Violence against Black Women in the Home*. London: Whiting and Birch.

Maynard, M. (1985) The response of social workers to domestic violence, in J. Pahl (ed.) *Private Violence and Public Policy*. London: Routledge.

Morley, R. (1993) Recent responses to domestic violence against women: a feminist critique. *Social Policy Review*, 5: 177–206.

Morley R. and Mullender A. (1994) *Preventing Domestic Violence*, Home Office Police Research Group Crime Prevention Series, 48. London: HMSO.

Mullender, A. (1996) *Rethinking Domestic Violence*. London: Routledge.

Mullender, A. and Morley, R. (eds) (1994) *Children Living with Domestic Violence*. London: Whiting and Birch.

Pahl, J. (1985) *Private Violence and Public Policy*. London: Routledge.

Parliamentary Select Committee on Violence in Marriage (1975) *Report from the Select Committee on Violence in Marriage*. London: HMSO.

Pence, E. (1989) *The Justice System's Responses to Domestic Assault Cases: A Guide for Policy Development*. Duluth, MN: Duluth Domestic Abuse Intervention Project.

Pence, E. (forthcoming) The Duluth Domestic Abuse Intervention Project, in N. Harwin, E. Malos, and G. Hague (eds) *Inter-agency Work and Domestic Violence*. London: Whiting and Birch.

Pleck, E. (1987) *Domestic Tyranny: The Making of Social Policy against Family Violence from Colonial Times until the Present*. Oxford: Oxford University Press.

Schechter, S. (1982) *Women and Male Violence: The Visions and Struggles of the Battered Women's Movement*. London: Pluto Press.

Shelter (1991) *Urgent Need for Homes*. London: Shelter.

Smith, L. (1989) *Domestic Violence: An Overview of the Literature*, Home Office Research Study no. 107. London: HMSO.

Southall Black Sisters (1989) Two struggles: challenging male violence and the police, in C. Dunhill (ed.) *The Boys in Blue*. London: Virago.

United Nations (1979) *Convention on the Elimination of all Forms of Discrimination Against Women*. New York: United Nations.

United Nations (1993) *Declaration on the Elimination of Violence against Women*. New York: United Nations.

United Nations (1996) *The Beijing Declaration and the Platform for Action*. New York: United Nations Department of Public Information.

WAFE (1992) *Written Evidence to the House of Commons Home Affairs Committee Inquiry into Domestic Violence*. Bristol: WAFE.

8

Fatherhood, children and violence: placing the UK in an international context

Marianne Hester and Lynne Harne

Changing ideologies of fatherhood – from authority figure to caring parent – have had a considerable impact on the direction of social policy in the UK and many other European countries, North America and Australasia, with increasing emphasis on the presence of fathers as necessary for the well-being of children. These developments have influenced family policy and law reform in a number of ways, for instance, in the assessment of the best interests of children in the case of separation and divorce and in the stigmatization of lone mothers. This chapter examines these developments, looking at the changing construction of fatherhood, changes in policy and legal discourse, and the contradictory implications for the parenting of children. We argue that, while the attempt to incorporate fathers into the lives of children has been presented as a means of bettering children's lives and of equalizing women's and men's position in the family, in some circumstances it has also done the opposite by providing a vehicle for abusive fathers, in particular, to extend their power over both children and their mothers.

Changing constructions of fatherhood

Until the 1970s it was commonly assumed in UK family law that all parental rights and authority were invested in the father, although looking after children was seen as the mother's responsibility. The Guardianship of Minors Act 1973 represented a major departure in giving mothers equal decision-making powers over children within marriage (Cretney 1979). Similarly, divorce reform made it much easier and less costly to obtain a divorce thus enabling far more women than previously to escape from violent and oppressive marriages, and changes in attitude brought about largely by the Women's Liberation Movement diminished the stigma of single parenthood (Hoggett and Pearl 1987; Harne and Rights of Women 1997).

Following divorce, the courts usually allowed women to retain custody of their children on the legal presumption that young children needed their mothers (the so-called 'maternal presumption'), although this practice depended on a particular construction of 'good' motherhood. While adultery committed by women was no longer considered a bar to retaining custody, lesbian mothers were frequently denied custody on the grounds that they would not provide a 'normal' family with a father and a mother for their children (Rights of Women 1984; Harne 1997). These trends, with an apparent shift from father right to maternal preference, were echoed elsewhere in Europe and in North America (see Nordenfors 1996; Fuszara 1997).

Feminists were challenging women's position in the family and at work, placing issues such as male violence against women and labour market reforms on the UK policy agenda. New legislation on domestic violence provided emergency protection and made it easier for women to obtain injunctions against violent partners (Barron 1990; Hague and Malos 1993; Chapter 7, this volume), and the Equal Pay and Sex Discrimination Acts were enacted at this time (see Chapter 9, this volume). However, the reforms were resisted by some men, especially those fathers who saw easier access to divorce and perceived maternal preference in custody arrangements as having negative consequences for themselves.

Fathers' rights movements developed at this time in the UK as well as in North America and other European countries. Parenting was set to become a major arena of contestation in male-female relations in the UK and elsewhere. In 1974 the pressure group Families Need Fathers emerged in the UK, presenting as its main argument that fathers were being deprived of their decision making and access rights when sole custody was awarded to mothers on divorce, although at this time most fathers did not contest the custody of their children (Maidment 1976; Eekelaar and Clive 1977). Unmarried fathers, it was also argued, should be given the same rights to children within law as married fathers. These arguments began to influence socio-legal discourse in the direction of joint custody for both parents.

While the idea of joint custody appeared to suggest an equality of parenting, Families Need Fathers were originally arguing for a reinstatement of fathers' 'natural' and traditional rights of authority and decision-making powers, with the day-to-day care of children continuing to be women's responsibility (Brophy 1989; Harne and Radford 1994). By the early 1980s other discourses were also beginning to influence the debate. Two issues in particular were highlighted: the right of fathers to equal participation in parenting, and the necessity of fathers to children's well-being. These issues highlight the complexity and ongoing tensions regarding male-female relations in the parenting debates and policy changes in the UK, and also elsewhere, in North America and Europe.

Equal parenting

In the UK, research inspired by the new men's movements claimed that fathers were increasingly becoming involved in childcare, and that father 'deprivation' had not been taken into account in assessing children's emotional and cognitive development (McKee and O'Brien 1982; Richards 1982). Some of this research, often on very small samples, was initiated as a response to feminist demands that men should become more involved with childcare, but the concept of the 'new father' was also used to promote the idea that fathers and mothers were now equal carers of children (Beail and McGuire 1982; McKee and O'Brien 1982).[1] Moreover, it was argued that fathers were being prevented from participating equally as parents by social policies that gave preference to women, or by the actions of the women themselves.

Despite these claims, research does not provide a clear indication of greatly increasing involvement by fathers in childcare in the 1980s or beyond. On the contrary, feminist research and studies on fatherhood and masculinity have demonstrated that in the UK there has been little real movement in men sharing childcaring tasks equally with women (Cacace and d'Andrea 1996; Burghes *et al.* 1997). In their reassessment of the fatherhood research, Lewis and O'Brien (1987) state that 'the evidence for the existence of [the new caring and nurturant father] is less than convincing' (p. 2). While there had been a small shift in fathers taking some responsibility for childcare (where both partners worked full-time) a number of surveys in the 1980s showed that it was still women who shouldered the major responsibility for looking after the children. In a more recent analysis of 1990 census data, fathers were still found to have limited involvement in childcare in the UK, with systematic involvement in the care of their children in only 14.5 per cent of families where both parents were working (Gilbert 1993). The analysis revealed that washing and ironing, house cleaning, preparing dinner and nursing sick children continued to be tasks carried out by women in at least 75 per cent of families (Social Trends 1990).

A European Commission survey has indicated that at an attitudinal level fathers' interest in children is increasing, with 87 per cent of the 13,000 interviewees across Europe believing that a father should 'participate fully in the upbringing of his children starting at an early age' (Cacace and d'Andrea 1993). However if we look more closely at fathers' involvement in the care of their children across European countries it becomes apparent that the UK figures are not untypical. The Scandinavian countries, and Denmark and Sweden in particular, are usually considered to have the greatest 'equality' in parenting. That there is a greater involvement in childcare by fathers in these countries is borne out by a study of men's and women's labour market and family involvement (Nordic Council 1990). However, there are still discernable differences in the extent and nature of this involvement.[2] Moreover, women in Scandinavia are perhaps even more likely to be carrying the burden of the 'double shift' – that is, both paid work outside the home and the domestic labour associated with children – than women elsewhere (see Aunbirk 1993).

There is further evidence from a number of countries, including Denmark, Canada and the UK, that the fathers do not want sole responsibility for children, or an equal share of childcaring responsibilities, either within the family or post-divorce (Bertoia and Drakich 1995; Simpson et al 1995; Aunbirk 1993). In Bertoia and Drakich's research with Families Need Fathers in Canada, the fathers said they: 'do not want sole responsibility for children, nor do they want an equal division of childcare and responsibility' (1995: 252). Bertoia and Drakich conclude in relation to post-divorce parenting that fathers want to play a role in their children's lives, but for many that role appears merely a continuation of their pre-divorce role of the traditional father who exercises his power and control (1995: 252–3).

Clearly, 'equal' parenting does not currently appear to be a reality and the notion of 'caring' needs to be examined more closely to make sense of the seemingly contradictory material regarding fathers' involvement in childcare. The gendering of parenting is an important consideration in this respect. It may seem strange that men have increasingly perceived themselves as caring fathers, given that the care of children has long been seen in Western cultures as having a low (feminized) value. However, if we place the notion of 'caring' in the context of the empirical evidence above, we see a gendered division in childcare where the tasks men carry out tend to be less to do with the necessary servicing activities of preparing food, feeding, washing or clothing the child etc. Smart (1995) calls the latter activities, which continue to be mainly carried out by women, 'caring for'. The caring that many men see themselves as doing involves a more distanced caring *about* children. Smart explains these distinctions as follows:

> Caring about such things as famines in Ethiopia, civil war in Rwanda, torture in South Africa is traditionally seen as an ethical stance. Caring for, however, is the actual act of caring which might be to nurse the sick child, tend to the daily needs of the frail and so on.
> (1995: 176–7)

These assumptions concerning 'caring for' (by women) and 'caring about' (by men) enable a construction where relatively greater credence is given to men's involvement in childcare: 'The caring about of fathers for children is generally lauded. The caring for of mothers for children is ignored or denigrated' (Smart 1995: 174).

It may be argued that most fathers are not, nor for the most part in practice do they want to be, equal carers with mothers in the sense of 'caring for' their children. Instead, claims about fatherhood and involvement in childcare may be seen in the context of men's wider concerns about threats to their position *vis-à-vis* women and ownership of children, and their attempts to forge new identities in this context. Moreover, paternal involvement in childcare is not unproblematic. Research in the UK has shown that fathers' involvement in childcare may reinforce gendered inequalities between boys and girls, and ideologies of paternal authority (McGuire 1982; Sharpe 1994; Mann 1996). Demands for equal parental responsibility are often concerned with control and power over women's and children's lives post-divorce and separation. As Lewis and O'Brien (1987: 2) suggest: 'recent accounts of fatherhood should be replaced by an understanding of paternal involvement in the context of the continuing domination of women by men in the public sphere, and in certain respects within the family itself'.

Father deprivation

Since the early 1980s, policy debates in Europe and North America concerning outcomes for children where parents separate or divorce have increasingly emphasized that the presence of fathers is crucial to the well-being of such children. The notion of father deprivation was largely derived from a number of small-scale studies in the USA into children and divorcing parents (Wallerstein and Kelly 1980). It has been argued that father 'deprivation' has not been taken into account in assessing children's emotional and cognitive development (Beail and McGuire 1982; McKee and O'Brien 1982). Research has also highlighted that separated fathers may lose contact with their children in the longer term (Bradshaw and Millar 1991), and has examined the problems the non-residential father might have in his parenting role with the mother as the other parent (Lund 1987; Simpson *et al.* 1995; Bradshaw and Stimson 1996). In both the European and North American contexts the 'father deprivation' discourse has been central to an increasing emphasis on contact or access with absent parents (meaning fathers), which has appeared alongside the development of joint custody or shared parental responsibility policies.

Drawing on the idea of 'father deprivation', New Right theorists in the UK such as Murray (1990) and those from the ethical and Christian socialist movements (Dennis and Erdos 1992) have also argued that it is only through fatherhood responsibilities that men are made to behave in a civilized way. Lone mothers, and specifically never married and black mothers, have been targeted within this discourse as being responsible for the creation of an underclass where young men do not see the necessity of taking paid employment because they do not have fatherhood responsibilities. In effect, onus is placed on both children and women for the social integration and 'civilized' behaviour of men: 'As many have commented through the centuries, young males are essentially barbarians for whom marriage – meaning not just the wedding vows, but the act of taking responsibility for a wife and children – is an indispensable civilising force' (Murray 1990: 39).

However, the conflation of children's welfare with father presence has been challenged by various reassessments of the psychological research (Mott 1993; Hooper 1994; Marsiglio 1995; Richards 1997).[3] Both Mott and Hooper, for example, have stressed that it is not the presence of fathers *per se* in families that enhances children's emotional and cognitive development, but the quality of children's contact with caring individuals: 'the presence or absence of the father matters less for cognitive development for black and white children than does the quality of the child's environment – the presence of caring individuals, and the extent to which they are willing to work and stimulate their children' (Mott 1993: 123). Research on the children of lesbian mothers who have been brought up without any father presence similarly indicates that there is no connection between father presence and children's well-being (Donovan *et al.* 1997).

Moreover, as Amato and Keith (1991) point out from their analysis of 92 American and British studies on the effect of family breakdown on children, children are most likely to be affected negatively in circumstances of 'parental conflict' (see, for example, Cockett and Tripp 1994). This has led Richards (1997), for instance, to conclude that children may be better served by not seeing the non-residential parent (usually the father) if the conflict is likely to continue. Thus, mere father presence does not automatically lead to positive outcomes for children. Moreover, such an approach tends not to take individual children's needs into account, but merely subsumes them to the needs of their fathers: 'Children's needs must be detached from their current conflation with ongoing relationships with their fathers; they must be addressed in their own right. At the moment, contact too often provides a means of children meeting father's needs rather than vice versa' (Hooper 1994: 98).

Policy

As indicated, the past 25 years have seen a conceptual shift in the way the social status of fathers is regarded within social policy and family law. Simpson *et al.* (1995), echoing New Right discourse, suggest that fathers are no longer perceived as powerful figures who exert control and authority within families. Rather they are seen as caring parents who have been denied equal rights to parent and pushed to the margins of families, where they are 'in danger of becoming socially, economically and emotionally obsolete' (Simpson *et al.* 1995: 3). Reflecting these concerns, by the end of the 1980s there were a number of changes in social policy which resulted in what Collier (1995a, b) argues was a reconstitution and modernization of paternal claims to authority and power within families. The new ideology of fatherhood, involving father presence and 'equal' participation in parenting, is now embedded in family and social welfare legislation in many Western and Australasian countries. In the UK there have been three pieces of legislation which may be seen to incorporate these discourses. These were originally implemented by the last Conservative government, but have also been broadly supported by New Labour.

The first of these, the Children Act 1989, changed the notions of custody and access, (which carried with them an apparent 'ownership' of children), to an emphasis on 'parental responsibility' where both married parents continue to share 'responsibility' for children after separation and divorce. It was also made easier for unmarried fathers and other carers to apply for parental responsibility of children. The Children Act has as a central tenet that decisions should be made according to the welfare principle, that is 'in the best interests of the child'. Echoing international debates about children's rights, enshrined in the United Nations' Convention on Children's Rights 1989, it has put more emphasis on the needs and wishes of children than previously. Since its implementation the courts have increasingly interpreted the welfare principle to mean that children should always have contact with the non-residential parent (nearly always fathers) on divorce and separation, whatever the circumstances (Hester and Radford 1996; Smart and Neale 1997). Underlying the Children Act, but not actually mentioned in the legislation, was the presumption that parents could, and should, negotiate outcomes for their children.

The Child Support Act 1991 was enacted to ensure that biological parents pay and share maintenance for their children, both post-separation and even if the parents have neither lived together nor had a relationship. An underlying aim was to reduce state benefit payments by making mothers claim child support and their own maintenance from biological fathers rather than from the State. Somewhat ironically, given the emphasis in fatherhood discourses on equal parenting, this legislation met with most resistance from fathers' rights movements who claimed that the amount of maintenance they were being forced to pay was far too high. As a consequence the legislation was modified so that no father would have to pay more than 30 per cent of his aggregate income, and significantly further concessions were made where fathers had staying contact with the children.

The Family Law Act 1996 has made it harder for those with children to divorce, by increasing the time it takes to 18 months and by legislating that arrangements for the children and family finances must be agreed before a divorce will be allowed. The legal presumption from the Children Act, where the welfare of a child is equated with contact, has been further reinforced in the Family Law Act, which states that 'the welfare of the child is best served by . . . his [sic] having regular contact with those who have parental responsibility for him' (Section 11). The Family Law Act has also placed further emphasis on mediation as the primary means of settling post-divorce arrangements. Those applying for legal aid must consider attending mediation, unless there is demonstrable evidence of domestic violence. A further aspect of the Family Law Act aims to increase women and children's protection from abuse through strengthening the power of civil injunctions. It has also made it possible for third parties such as social services and the police to remove an abuser from the family home. Yet, in practice, the greater emphasis on children's contact with the non-residential parent (usually the father) in one part of the Act is likely to be counter to the protective measures regarding domestic violence in another part (see Hester and Radford 1996).

A major thread running through these different policy changes has been to sustain the familial relations of the heterosexual nuclear family, even after separation and divorce. Despite the emphasis in the Children Act on the possibility of non-biological parenting, the different pieces of legislation together place an increasing emphasis on biological parenting and thus greater involvement by fathers. The consequent impact and limits on women's autonomy within families have been felt in particular by women and children escaping domestic violence.

In many European countries similar trends can be discerned, and the particular problems that result for women and children have been highlighted by a number of researchers. In some countries, including Denmark and Poland, the idea that mothers and fathers should be able to parent jointly and preferably without interference from the state has led to obvious difficulties. In Poland what Fuszara (1997: 167) calls 'joint parental rights' means that both parents have to participate in all official decisions concerning the child 'regardless of whether the second parent has any contact with the child whatsoever and whether the child's fate concerns him [sic]'. This may result not only in detrimental consequences for the child but it also may allow an abusive parent to control outcomes for the child. Fuszara cites the example of a child denied a holiday abroad because passport officials could not issue a passport for the child without the consent of both parents (1997: 167–8). In Denmark 'joint parental authority' has created particular difficulties for women who have left violent male partners. For instance, if any problems arise concerning access such that the child is kidnapped or not returned by the father after a visit, the authorities are unlikely to intervene as both parents are deemed to have equal authority with regard to the child (Hester and Radford 1996).

In Sweden, emphasis on both father deprivation and equal participation in parenting has led to the inclusion of a clause regarding 'sabotage' in the custody legislation. Sabotage is seen as involving the impeding of access between a child and her or his non-resident parent, and is a more extreme version of the legal concept of 'implacable hostility' as applied in the UK. In cases where the Swedish courts consider sabotage to have occurred, sole custody may be awarded or transferred to the 'non-sabotaging' parent. There have been a number of instances where mothers, in an attempt to protect their children from sexual abuse from fathers, have denied these fathers access. Consequently the fathers have sought and been awarded custody (Nordenfors 1996). The underlying assumption in the Swedish legislation that women deliberately set out to prevent fathers from caring for children has also been voiced in some of the contributions to the fatherhood debate in the UK (Simpson *et al.* 1995; Burgess 1997). However, research which has been undertaken with mothers who have left due to domestic violence has found that the majority of women wish their children to continue to have involvement with their fathers (Hester and Radford 1992, 1996; Anderson 1997; Women's Aid Federation of England 1997). Women's concerns are with the *quality* of contact and childcare that divorced and separated fathers offer, and with protecting themselves and their children from further violence and abuse.

Fathers, children and violence

Feminist research has shown that violence or threats of violence are used as a means to assert male power and to intimidate and control women within heterosexual relationships and those attempting to escape such relationships. In Dobash and Dobash's ground-breaking research during 1979, interviews with women revealed that men used violence to assert their ownership of women as a consequence of their own possessiveness and jealousy, to reinforce their own 'expectations of women's domestic work', to 'punish women for perceived wrong doing' and to 'maintain or exercise their position of authority' (Dobash and Dobash 1992: 4). Subsequent studies with men using research of this kind on the construction of violent masculinities has confirmed the findings that such reasons are used by men to excuse violence against their female partners (Mooney 1993; Hearn 1996; Dobash *et al.* 1996).

Feminist and child welfare research concerned with child protection has also begun to reveal the connections between domestic violence and child abuse. In 1985 Stark and Flitcraft in the USA, in a review of hospital records, found a correlation between physical abuse of children and women who had received treatment for physical injury as a result of domestic violence. The violence to both woman and child was nearly always from the same man: that is, the husband/partner and father/father figure. Since then, research in the UK has shown that there are links between domestic violence and the physical, sexual and emotional abuse and neglect of children by male partners (Abrahams 1994; Farmer and Owen 1995; Hester and Radford 1996; Hester *et al.* 1998; Hester and Pearson 1998). Moreover, abuse of both mothers and their children by the male partner/father not only takes place while they are all living together but is also likely to continue after separation (Hester and Radford 1996; Hester *et al.* 1998; Hester and Pearson 1998). Inquiries into child deaths have also highlighted the connections between children killed by fathers and stepfathers and domestic violence perpetrated by the same men against the children's mothers (Bridge Child Care Consultancy 1991; National Children's Bureau 1993; James 1994; O'Hara 1994).

Yet within the fatherhood research and related policy discourses outlined earlier, male violence against women and children has generally
been ignored or minimized. There has been little or no examination of
the impact of male violence on the roles and responsibilities of fathers,
either within families or post-separation and divorce (see Burgess and
Ruxton 1996). Research on fatherhood has instead emphasized, and
contributed to, the notion of the generally 'good father', whose mere
presence is enough to contribute to the well-being of children.

There has been some increased recognition that women need protection from male violence within social policy reforms (e.g. Part 4 of the
Family Law Act 1996; see also Chapter 7, this volume). However, despite
the existence of research in the UK and elsewhere which indicates that
post-separation violence needs to be an important consideration in relation to family law and policy, policy makers and practitioners have tended
to assume that once partners separate and divorce the violence automatically comes to end (Hester and Radford 1996; Hester et al. 1997). As
a result it has been difficult for the violence to women post-separation
to be acknowledged within policy and legal practice, with consequent
lack of safety for women and their children. Research by the Home Office
found that over one-third of domestic violence incidents happened post-
separation (Mirrlees-Black 1995), while other research found that women's
experience of domestic violence from partners post-separation was more
frequent than before (Mooney 1993). The research by Hester and Radford
(1996) on domestic violence and child contact found that ex-male partners
typically used arrangements or negotiations concerning child contact as
a means to continue their harassment and initimidation of the mother,
with detrimental consequences for the children concerned. Such abuse
took place in a number of different situations, including any situation
where women were expected to meet face to face with their ex-partner –
such as in-court mediation meetings where couples were expected to reach
agreement about the arrangements for the children, and particularly at
contact handover times (Hester and Radford 1996). These findings have
been confirmed by other studies (Smart 1995; Anderson 1997; Women's
Aid Federation of England 1997). In the research by Hester and Radford
(1996) only 7 out of 53 families in England where child contact was set
up suffered no subsequent violence and abuse from ex-partners.

In Hester and Radford's (1996) study, mothers reported that children
had been physically and/or sexually abused or neglected on contact visits
with fathers, and children were also being used to collude in ongoing
abuse of the mother. Children were used by ex-partners to convey threats
and abusive messages to women and were pressurized into carrying
out acts of violence against mothers as well as being involved in plans to
kill mothers.

A further study involving all court welfare services in England and
Wales found that the vast majority of court welfare officers (97 per cent)
recognized that children were at risk of harm in circumstances of domestic violence, which could also lead to risk of harm to children when

contact was awarded to perpetrators of domestic violence. However, these views tended not to be presented, or were minimized, in the court setting due to the predominance of the legal presumption regarding children's contact with non-resident fathers (Hester and Pearson 1997; Hester *et al.* 1997).

There has been little recognition by the courts that father-child contact may facilitate violence and abuse of women, or that children's safety may be put at risk. Women's fears tend to be perceived as exaggerated (or worse, ignored) and it is often women themselves who are viewed as being in the wrong if they try to protect themselves or their children. While men have tended to be construed as 'good fathers', women have tended to be construed in legal and in wider child welfare and popular discourses as 'bad mothers' (Collier 1995a; Humphries 1997). As Humphries has pointed out, the mother who strives to protect her young child from sexual abuse in custody cases with fathers is now demonized within the discourse of the 'falsely accusing mother'. Humphries demonstrates that mothers who allege child sexual abuse within the context of divorce are regarded as being 'malicious' by the courts, and that there is a disregard for the empirical evidence which shows that the majority of cases arising in this context are in fact found to be true (Humphries 1997: 538). In her own research into child protection practice Humphries also found that social workers 'came with a profound cynicism about sexual abuse disclosures which occurred in the context of divorce', and that social work practitioners regarded as 'common knowledge' that mothers 'maliciously' or 'misguidedly' brought 'false allegations of child sexual abuse into the context of divorce proceedings' (1997: 537).

The assumptions concerning 'bad mothers' can be seen in a number of reported appeal decisions where women have been constructed as 'selfish and implacably hostile' by the courts if they have opposed contact on the grounds of protecting their own or their children's safety (*Re O Contact: Imposition of Conditions*: 24 (hereafter, *Re O*); Smart and Neale 1997). It should be noted that most cases of implacable hostility probably involve domestic violence (Jolly 1995). A double standard can also be discerned regarding 'implacable hostility' in the decisions of the courts. Smart (1997) has pointed out that there is evidence, in her own research on post-divorce families, first that fathers with residence orders who deny contact to mothers are not constructed as 'implacably hostile' and second that the courts and legal practitioners do not regard it as practicable to force fathers to have contact given that it is usually fathers who fail to keep to contact arrangements.

A closer look at judicial decisions reveals an overt prejudice towards mothers and a bias towards viewing favourably even the most unsuitable fathers in contact disputes. In the case of *Re O* (1995), a case which has been cited as a precedent in a number of subsequent appeal decisions, the father had a suspended prison sentence for repeated molestation and pestering of the mother. The child, aged 2, who had had little involvement with the father since birth was clearly distressed by direct contact with the father at a contact centre. This was acknowledged by the court welfare officer who questioned the benefit for the child of direct contact between the father and child.

In 1994 a court decision ordered the mother to accept indirect contact, with a number of conditions which included ordering her to read out the father's letters to the child and to send the father school progress and medical reports. The mother appealed against this order, her appeal was disallowed, and the appeal judgment does not cite the reasons for her objections to indirect contact. Instead the judgment cites the lower court Judge's 'favourable impression of the father' over a number of hearings, and defines the mother's objections as 'irrational repugnance' (*Re O*: 126). It also cited a previous judgment where Lord Justice Balfour had stated that 'implacable hostility' by the mother should not impede contact: 'the danger of allowing the implacable hostility of the residential parent (usually the mother) to frustrate the court's decisions is too obvious to require repetition on my part' (*Re J (A Minor) (Contact)*).

As Smart has argued, the case of *Re O* (1995) 'made it clear that the courts should not hesitate to use their powers of enforcement', in ensuring that contact happened. Following the judgment in *Re O* there have consequently been a number of cases where women have been threatened with imprisonment or loss of residence in refusing contact in the context of domestic violence. (*A v N [1997] (Committal: Refusal of Contact)* (hereafter, *A v N*); Smart and Neale 1997).

In *A v N* (1997), which was an appeal against a mother's commitment to prison, the appeal court overruled the paramount principle of the child's welfare in agreeing that the mother should be sent to prison for breach of a contact order. The judgment stated that 'the welfare of the child was a material but not the paramount consideration' (*A v N*: 533). The judgment also described the mother's objections to the father's contact with her 4-year-old daughter as 'flimsy', and her desire to protect her child as 'unwise' and 'misguided'. The judgment stated that the lower court judge was 'mindful of the distressing consequence of the [mother's] imprisonment on the child and indeed the other child of the mother, but that he had balanced this against the importance of this child knowing her father as she grows up and the long term damage she will suffer.' (p. 540). In this case (reported as the Dawn Austin case in the press, *Guardian* 11 October 1996) the father had served a prison sentence for breaking the jaw of his former wife, and had a history of serious violence against Ms Austin which the court accepted, but chose to disregard in compelling the father's contact.

Another case, *Re P*, is also an example of where the extreme unsuitability of the father has been overlooked and the mother's objections disregarded. This was an appeal by a father against a lower court's decision to allow him indirect contact only. In this case the father had attempted to strangle the mother and made attempts to kill the children for which he had received a 12-month prison sentence, 6 months of which was suspended (Re P: 318). On release from prison the father had eventually been allowed supervised contact at a contact centre, but the mother had applied for, and was granted, a variation of the order to the effect that there should be indirect contact only.

Psychiatric evidence was presented in favour of the mother's case which indicated that direct contact was causing distress to one of the children, and that this child did not want contact with the father. The mother argued that fear of the father's violence as a result of contact was affecting her health, and thus her ability to care for the children. There was also material evidence of the father's Nazi sympathies, including a photograph showing that when he had been involved with the children he had encouraged them to dress up in Nazi regalia. However, the lower court had accepted the father's explanation that this 'was only fancy dress' and his denials that he held racist beliefs. The father's behaviour at the supervised contact sessions was also described as 'exemplary'. The appeal court upheld the father's appeal on the grounds that the previous judge's decision had been 'plainly wrong'. The judgment argued that he had placed more weight than was justified by the evidence on the risk of emotional harm to the children due to the mother's deteriorating health resulting from her anxiety over contact. The principle that it is almost always in the best interest of children to have contact with both parents was stressed and the evidence was deemed not to justify a finding that the mother's hostility to direct contact would put the children at serious risk of major harm.

Positive resistance

As we have documented, changing notions of fatherhood in family law and policy have led to a greater involvement by violent and abusive fathers in children's, and consequently women's, lives post-separation of the parents. These trends can be seen in many Western and Australasian countries. However, the detrimental impacts on women and children are increasingly being met with resistance.

In the UK, following pressure from organizations such as Women's Aid, there has been some acknowledgement within public policy and local practice on child protection of the problems women and children face. An increasing number of social service departments have established policy and guidelines regarding the impact of domestic violence on children (SSI 1995; Hester et al. 1998). Women are also increasingly resisting decisions to allow fathers to have contact, where the father has been violent towards the mother and/or abused the children, with the grass-roots women's organization AMICA as a focal point of resistance. In cases where women are prepared to go to prison rather than allow an abusive father contact, an increasing trend has been for the courts to appoint the official solicitor to represent the interests of the child. A recent appeal case is indicative of a shift towards some consideration of the abusive impact of contact with violent fathers (*Re D*). In this instance, the mother's fear of the father's violence and the effects this might have on her son was recognized by the appeal court in denying the father contact. Commenting on this case Douglas (1997) argues that the court of appeal has made an important distinction between those cases of 'implacable hostility' that are unreasonable and those that are well founded. She tentatively suggests that in cases where there is serious risk of emotional harm to the child resulting from contact or where there is risk of violence to the carer and/or child from the parent seeking contact, the opposition to contact may succeed.[4]

From an international perspective there has also been some recognition that domestic violence can be a good enough reason to prevent fathers from having contact with children. New Zealand, Australia and a few states in North America now have statutes which either deny or limit fathers contact in situations of domestic violence.

Notes

1 Demands that men should become more involved with childcare in order to share the burden of this (unpaid) labour have long been made by some feminists (see Rowbotham 1989).
2 It should be noted that men report that they have a greater (shared) involvement in specific child-related tasks such as children's meals, washing and bedtime, than do women (Nordic Council 1990: 108).
3 It should also be noted that in the 'fatherhood reasearch' there has been a tendency to use research methodologies involving surveys or interviews with fathers without accompanying validity or reliability testing (Burgess and Ruxton 1996). As Marsiglio (1995) has pointed out, there is a problem with 'truth accounts' in such research with fathers, as father's accounts should be triangulated with data from mothers and children. Hearn (1996), talking specifically about research concerning men who have been violent to their partners, makes a similar point.
4 At the time of writing it remains to be seen whether this judgment will have a positive effect on subsequent appeal cases.

References

Abrahams, C. (1994) *The Hidden Victims – Children and Domestic Violence*. London: NCH Action for Children.

Amato, P.R. and Keith, B. (1991) Parental divorce and the well-being of children. A meta-analysis. *Psychological Bulletin*, 110: 26–46.

Anderson, L. (1997) *Contact Between Children and Violent Fathers: In whose Best Interests?* London: Rights of Women.

Aunbirk, A. (1993) *Forældreskab til forhandling* (Parenthood up for Negotiation). Copenhagen: Sociologi.

Barron, J. (1990) *Not Worth the Paper: the Effectiveness of Legal Protection for Women and Children Experiencing Domestic Violence*. Bristol: Women's Aid Federation.

Beail, N. and McGuire, J. (1982) *Fathers: Psychological Perspectives*. London: Junction Books.

Bertoia, C.E. and Drakich, J. (1995) The fathers' rights movement: contradictions in rhetoric and practice, in W. Marsiglio (ed.) *Fatherhood: Contemporary Theory, Research and Social Policy*. California and London: Sage.

Bradshaw, J. and Millar, J. (1991) *Lone Parent Families in the UK*. London: HMSO.

Bradshaw, J. and Stimson, C. (1996) *Fathers Apart in Britain*. Swindon: Economic and Social Research Council.

Brophy, J. (1989) Custody law, childcare and inequality in Britain, in C. Smart and S. Sevenhiujsen (eds) *Child Custody and the Politics of Gender*. London: Routledge.

Burgess, A. (1997) *Fatherhood Reclaimed: The Making of the Modern Father*. London: Vermilion.

Burgess, A. and Ruxton, S. (1996) *Men and their Children: Proposals for Public Policy*. London: Institute for Public Policy Research.

Burghes, L., Clarke, L. and Cronin, N. (1997) *Fathers and Fatherhood in Britain*. London: Family Policy Studies Centre.

Cacace, M. and d'Andrea, L. (1996) *Fathers in Services for Young Children*, EC Commission DG V 'Employment, Industrial Relations and Social Affairs'. Rome. Unit for Equal Opportunities.

Collier, R. (1995a) *Masculinity, Law and the Family*. London: Routledge.

Collier, R. (1995b) A father's 'normal' love?: Masculinities, criminology and the family, in R.E. Dobash, R.P. Dobash and Noaks, L. (eds) *Gender and Crime*. Cardiff: University of Wales Press.

Cretney, S.M. (1979) *Principles of Family Law*, 3rd edn. London: Sweet & Maxwell.

Crockett, M. and Tripp, J. (1994) *The Exeter Family Study. Family Breakdown and its Impact on Children*. Exeter: University of Exeter Press.

Dennis, N. and Erdos, G. (1992) *Families Without Fatherhood*. London: Institute of Economic Affairs.

Dobash, R., Dobash, R.E., Cavanagh, K. and Lewis, R. (1996) *Research Evaluation of Programmes for Violent Men*. Edinburgh: HMSO.

Dobash, R.E. and Dobash, R.P. (1992) *Women, Violence and Social Change*. London: Routledge.

Donovan, S., Tasker, F. and Murray, C. (1997) Children raised in fatherless families from infancy. *Journal of Child Psychology and Child Psychiatry*, 38 (7): 783–91.

Douglas, G. (1997) Re D (Contact: Reasons for Refusal) comment. *Family Law*, July 1997, 471.

Eekelaar, J. and Clive, E. (1977) *Custody After Divorce*. Oxford: Oxford Centre for Socio-legal Studies, Wolfson College.

Farmer, E. and Owen, M. (1995) *Child Protection Practice, Private Risks and Public Remedies: Decision Making, Intervention and Outcome in Child Protection*. London: HMSO.

Fuszara, M. (1997) Divorce in Poland: The Effects in the Opinion of the Divorced, in J. Kurczewski and M. Maclean (eds) *Family Law and Family Policy in the New Europe*. Dartmouth: Aldershot.

Gilbert, L.A. (1993) *Two Careers/One Family*. London: Sage.

Hague, G. and Malos, E. (1993) *Domestic Violence: Action for Change*. Cheltenham: New Clarion Press.

Harne, L. and Radford, J. (1994) Reinstating patriarchy: the politics of the family and the new legislation, in A. Mullender, and R. Morley, (eds) *Children Living with Domestic Violence*. London: Whiting and Birch.

Harne, L. and Rights of Women (1997) *Valued Families: The Lesbian Mothers Legal Handbook*. London: Women's Press.

Hearn, J. (1996) Men's violence to known women: men's accounts and men's policy developments, in B. Fawcett, B. Featherstone, J. Hearn and C. Toft (eds) *Violence and Gender Relations*. London: Sage.

Hester, M. and Pearson, C. (1998) *From Periphery to Centre: Domestic Violence in Work with Abused Children*. Bristol: The Policy Press.

Hester, M. and Radford, L. (1996) *Domestic Violence and Child Contact Arrangements in England and Denmark*. Bristol: The Policy Press.

Hester, M., Pearson, C. and Radford, L. (1997) *A National Survey of Court Welfare and Voluntary Sector Mediation*. Bristol: The Policy Press.

Hester, M., Pearson, C. and Harwin, N. (1998) *Making an Impact: Children and Domestic Violence. A Reader.* London. Barnardos in association with the Department of Health.

Hoggett, B. and Pearl, D. (1987) *The Family Law and Society: Cases and Materials*, 2nd edn. London: Butterworths.

HMSO (1990) *Social Trends*. London: HMSO.

HMSO (1996) Family Law Act. London: HMSO.

Hooper, C. (1994) Do families need fathers? The impact of divorce on children, in A. Mullender and R. Morley (eds) *Children Living with Domestic Violence*. London: Whiting and Birch.

Humphries, K. (1997) Child sexual abuse, allegations in the context of divorce: issues for mothers. *British Journal of Social Work*, 27: 529–44.

James, G. (1994) Discussion Report for ACPC Conference 1994: *Study of Working Together* 'Part 8' Reports. London: Department of Health, ACPC Series, Report no 1.

Jolly, S. (1995) Implacable hostility, contact and the limit of law. *Child and Family Law Quarterly*, 7 (4): 228–35.

Lewis, C. and O'Brien, M. (1987) Constraints on fathers: research, theory and clinical practice, in C. Lewis and M. O'Brien (eds) *Reassessing Fatherhood*. London: Sage.

Lund, M. (1987) The non-custodial father: common challenges in parenting after divorce, in C. Lewis and M. O'Brien (eds) *Reassessing Fatherhood*. London: Sage.

McKee, L. and O'Brien, M. (1982) *The Father Figure*. London: Tavistock.

McGuire, J. (1982) Gender – specific differences in early childhood: the impact of the father, in N. Beail and J. McGuire *Fathers: Psychological Perspective*. London: Junction Books.

Maidment, S. (1976) A study in child custody. *Family Law*, 6: 195–200, 236–41.

Mann, C. (1996) Girl's own story: the search for a sexual identity in times of family change, in J. Holland and L. Adkins (eds) *Sex, Sensibility and the Gendered Body*. Basingstoke: Macmillan.

Marsiglio, W. (1995) *Fatherhood: Contemporary Theory, Research and Social Policy*. London: Sage.

Mirrlees-Black, C. (1995) *Estimating the Extent of Domestic Violence from the 1992 BCS*, research bulletin no. 37, Home Office Research and Statistics Department. London: Whiting and Birch.

Mooney, J. (1993) *The Hidden Figure: Domestic Violence in North London*. London: Islington Police and Crime Prevention Unit.

Mott, F.L. (1993) *Absent fathers and child development: Emotional and cognitive effects at ages five to nine*, report for the National Institute of Child Health and Human Development. Columbus, OH: Centre for Human Resource Research, Ohio State University.

Murray, C. (1990) *The Emerging British Underclass*. London: IEA Health and Welfare Unit.

Nordborg, G. (ed.) (1995) Konstruktioner av moderskab och faderskab – genom reproducktions teknologin och ratten, in *13 Kvinnoperspektiv på ràtten*. (Constructions of motherhood and fatherhood – via reproductive technology and the law, in 13 Women Perspectives on the Law.) Uppsala: Instus Forlag.

Nordisk Ministerråd (1990) *Kærlighed og Ligestilling? (Love and Equality?)* Copenhagen: Nordisk Ministerråd.

Nordenfors, G. (1996) *Fadersratt: Kvinnofrid och Barns Sakerhet*. (Father right: women's freedom and children's safety.) Stockholm: ROKS.

O'Hara, M. (1994) Child deaths in the context of domestic violence: implications for professional practice, in M. Mullender and R. Marley (eds) *Children Living with Domestic Violence: Putting Men's Abuse of Women on the Child Care Agenda*. London: Whitting and Birch.

Richards, M. (1997) *The Needs of Children at Divorce*. Dartmouth: Aldershot.

Richards, M.P.M. (1982) Foreword, in N. Beail and J. McGuire *Fathers: Psychological Perspectives*. London: Junction Books.

Rights of Women (1984) *Lesbian Mothers on Trial*. London: Rights of Women.

Rowbotham, S. (1989) To be or not to be: the dilemmas of mothering. *Feminist Review*, 31: 1–11.

Sharpe, S. (1994) *Fathers and Daughters*. London: Routledge.

Simpson, B., McCarthy, P. and Walker, J. (1995) *Being There: Fathers after Divorce*. Newcastle upon Tyne: Relate Centre for Family Studies, University of Newcastle upon Tyne.

Smart, C. (1995) Losing the struggle for another voice: the case of family law. *Dalhousie Law Journal*, 18 (2): 173–195.

Smart, C. and Neale, B. (1997) Arguments against virtue: must contact be enforced? *Family Law*, May: 332–337.

Smart, C. and Neale, B. (1997) Experiments with parenthood. *Sociology*, 31 (2), 201–219.

Stark and Flitcraft (1985) Woman-battering, child abuse and social heredity: what is the relationship? in N. Johnson (ed.) *Marital Violence*. London: Routledge & Kegan Paul.

Wallerstein, J.S. and Kelly, J.B. (1980) *Surviving the Break-up*. London: Grant McIntyre.

Women's Aid Federation of England (1997) *Child Contact and Domestic Violence*. Bristol: Women's Aid Federation.

List of cases

BIC (1997) A v N (Committal: Refusal of Contact) [1997] 1 FLR 533

Re D (Contact: Reasons for Refusal) [1997] 2 FLR 48 CA

Re J (A Minor) (Contact) [1994] 1 FLR 729 at 736 B–C

Re O (Contact: Imposition of Conditions) [1995] 2 FLR 124

Re P [1996] 2 FLR 314

9

Mainstreaming equality

Teresa Rees[1]

The story of equal opportunities policies in the UK is one of simultaneous progression and regression. While some of the older equality agencies, such as the Equal Opportunities Commission (EOC) (set up in 1975) and the Commission for Race Equality (1976) have celebrated more than 20 years of progress, they have also testified to the need for vigilance. Other dimensions of equality, such as age, disability and sexual orientation are now receiving more attention with a variety of legislative formulations and institutional infrastructures. The new Labour government has now decided to incorporate the European Convention on Human Rights into domestic law which may give rise to a Human Rights Commission.

Yet, despite the legislative and institutional progress that has been made in recognizing and redressing some forms of discrimination and disadvantage, it remains the case that gender and ethnic origin, *inter alia*, continue to have a profound impact on the education, training, occupation, pay, health and other life chances of individuals. Equality policies appear to be remarkably limited in their effects. For this reason it is vital to monitor 'progress', to analyse the drivers of processes which incline towards or against equality and to theorize about the complex patterns of social relations which result in the efficacy or otherwise of equal opportunities policies.

This chapter reviews three approaches to equal opportunities: equal treatment, positive action and the most recent approach, 'mainstreaming' equality, giving special emphasis to the latter. Mainstreaming is essentially about *integrating* equality into all policies, programmes and actions, from the earliest stages of their formulation to their implementation and review. It means building the equality dimension into all policy making, even where, on the face of it, the issue may seem not to be relevant. It is more than an 'impact' study of likely effects of a policy on, say, gender equality. It represents a paradigm shift in conceptualizing equality within the context of both employment and service and product delivery.

Support for the mainstreaming approach is gaining ground both globally and nationally. It was supported at the United Nations Fourth World Conference on Women, held in Beijing in 1995. Various countries are taking further some elements of a platform for action agreed upon in Beijing, which included the idea of mainstreaming. In the UK, for example, mainstreaming is the subject of one of ten follow-up policy papers in the *National Agenda for Action* (Women's National Commission *et al.* 1996). The European Union (EU) has adopted mainstreaming as one of its strategic approaches: this is likely to have some influence upon the activities of member states. Sweden has been integrating equality into policy for years.

Mainstreaming as an approach already has as many critics as it does advocates. There are those, for example, who are concerned that if, as mainstreaming implies, equality becomes in effect everyone's responsibility, then the hard-won corners of equal opportunities, such as equality officers, special units and designated budgets, may be dismantled. Individuals employed for their expertise on one particular equality dimension may no longer be regarded as essential, and that expertise may then be lost. As in the USA and Canada, positive action and discrimination measures that take account of past disadvantage or discrimination may be sacrificed in the name of mainstreaming.

These are legitimate concerns. Essentially, mainstreaming is a long-term strategy that needs to be accompanied by the secure underpinning of equal treatment legislation and positive action measures. Equality experts should ideally become more centre-stage in the policy-making process, rather than dismissed. However, there is clearly a danger that in the name of mainstreaming hard won ground could be lost for no gain.

While the drive towards mainstreaming has been rooted in concerns about gender equality expressed at the Beijing conference, one of its potential advantages is that as an approach it has the capacity to move beyond gender to embrace other dimensions of inequality. By starting afresh, rather than being an 'add-on' policy, it affords the opportunity to rethink sets of assumptions. These include how public policy is formulated and delivered generally, and ways of organizing work and service delivery more specifically. It implies stepping back from the ways things have always been done, and the assumptions that have always been made, and thinking anew, recognizing difference and diversity. This brings the approach close to North American perspectives on managing diversity, although there are distinct differences too (see below). While this chapter focuses on the gender dimension of mainstreaming, because that is where most progress has been made, a similar analysis could be offered for race, disability, sexual orientation and age.

Mainstreaming gender equality begins with recognizing that our existing employment, tax and welfare systems are not gender-neutral and do not treat individuals as such. They are predicated upon a particular version of the 'gender contract', that of the male breadwinner and female homemaker. This model informs the design of legislation, public policy and practices even though it ignores substantial changes in family structures (in particular, reconstituted families), represents a smaller and smaller proportion of white families, never accurately described the families of Afro-Caribbean women, and has always been inappropriate for lesbian and single women. Moreover, while the gender contract was utilized by employers as a justification for keeping women's wages down (on the grounds they constituted a 'component' wage), relatively few males earn wages that can support an entire family unaided. The 'family wage' is something of a myth (Land 1994). Mainstreaming seeks to move away from assumptions about the breadwinner/homemaker gender contract and begin with equal status for men and women as individuals.

Although mainstreaming is gaining some political currency, it is as yet relatively undocumented as an approach. There are inevitably different conceptual understandings as to what the term may mean, both within the UK and across member states of the EU. Moreover, the concept of mainstreaming is open to opportunitistic perversion: some of the fears expressed about it are rooted in a concern that it may be used cynically and deliberately by management as an excuse for saving money on designated activities, rendering something that is intended to be all-encompassing into nothing at all.

This chapter explores mainstreaming as an approach to equal opportunities, focusing on three broad questions:

1 What is mainstreaming, and how does it differ from previous equal opportunities approaches?
2 What evidence is there that this approach is gaining ground in the UK and elsewhere?
3 How should mainstreaming be operationalized, taking into account the concerns raised by critics?

The first section provides some context by looking at the ways in which gender still impacts upon who gets what jobs, their pay, and prospects of training and promotion. The second section gives a brief, historical account of the development of previous approaches to equal opportunities (equal treatment, positive action and positive discrimination) and arrives at a definition of mainstreaming. The third section then goes on to explore the extent to which mainstreaming is taking root. There is support for it both from the EOC and the UK government. Moreover, the European Commission (EC) has recommended it as an approach to the Council of Ministers and is beginning to take it seriously in its policies and programmes. These developments give mainstreaming a higher profile.

The fourth section looks at how mainstreaming might be operationalized. It is necessarily speculative. It draws upon transnational pilot
projects to identify some lessons on how mainstreaming could be used
to reduce the impact of ascriptive characteristics such as gender and race
– not only on who gets what, but on how institutions are shaped and
structured, and how and what services are delivered.

The chapter ends with a few tentative conclusions on the extent to
which mainstreaming will be taken up in the future and the effect it
might have.

The context: equality indicators in the labour market

The labour market is characterized by deeply-rooted, and surprisingly
rigid, broad patterns of gender segregation. These take three forms:
horizontal segregation, where women and men work in different industries; vertical segregation where they are found at different levels of the
hierarchy in those industries; and contract segregation, whereby men are
more likely to enjoy full-time, permanent jobs with employer-sponsored
training and promotion prospects, and women are more likely to work
part-time, have temporary or no contracts, little or no investment made
in their skill development by their employers and poor terms and conditions of employment.

Despite the persistence of these general patterns however, women
now constitute half the workforce, and their level of post-school educational qualifications are similar to that of men. Nevertheless, new forms
of inequalities are emerging in the context of developing technologies
and the globalization of the workplace. There are shifts in the interaction
between new gender regimes and the dynamics of class and ethnicity
characterizing the economy (Walby 1997).

One of the most evident signs of gender differences in the labour
market is in pay. In 1996, roughly two decades after the equal pay
legislation, women working full-time in Britain earned on average only
80 per cent of male wages (Office for National Statistics 1996). Hourly
wage rates for part-time workers tend to be lower than those for full-
time workers, and many women earn rates below the threshold for
which figures are recorded, so even this percentage is an underestimate.

There have been successive attempts to develop theoretical explanations for the persistence and dynamics of these patterns of segregation,
in particular the pay gap (see Crompton and Sanderson 1990; Walby
1990, 1997). These have focused *inter alia* on the relationship between
patriarchal and capitalist relations, sex-role stereotyping and exclusionary
mechanisms operated by men (Rees 1992). While studies using quantit-
ative data have explored indices of segregation (Blackburn *et al.* 1993),
qualitative studies have examined in detail the effect of processes such
as recruitment (Collinson *et al.* 1990) and men's resistance to equal

opportunities policies introduced in the workplace (Cockburn 1991). These studies illustrate the complexities of gender dynamics in the workplace, their interrelationship with patriarchal relations in the home, and the severe limitations of equal opportunities policies. The next section draws on these and other studies to describe and critique approaches to equal opportunities at work.

Approaches to equal opportunities

Equal treatment

Early liberal feminist approaches to equal opportunities are couched in terms of equal treatment of men and women. Mary Wollstonecraft ([1792] 1967) was one of the first to draw attention to the omission of women from debates about citizens' rights at the time of the French Revolution. She was particularly concerned by the exclusion of women from education. The emphasis in this liberal feminist approach is on treating women and men the same.

Equal access and equal treatment have been the focus of many campaigns, and considerable advances in the law, perhaps most notably enfranchisement. During the nineteenth century, access to education generally and some of the professions specifically was barred to many women. Even women who successfully studied for degrees at some universities were denied the right to graduate (Delamont 1989). Legislation was eventually introduced (the *Sex Disqualification (Removal) Act* 1919) to remove such barriers. Then, the marriage bar, which prevented, for example, women civil servants from continuing in their careers after they married (which still pertained as late as 1972 in Northern Ireland and 1976 in the Foreign Office) was dismantled. In the 1970s the *Equal Pay Act* and *Sex Discrimination Act* were introduced and the EOC set up to monitor and recommend changes to the law, to back cases and to foster equal opportunities between men and women (see EOC 1996a for a report on progress in this work since the mid-1970s).

More recently, it has been recognized that indirect discrimination can occur, for example, if one factor applies more to one sex than another. This led to the abolition of age bars on entry to certain courses or jobs as it was recognized that one sex would be more affected than the other (women who took career breaks). However, while the law clearly has had an effect (see EOC 1996a), nevertheless the impact has been limited. It was found for example that as men and women are so segregated in the labour market, it was difficult for women to identify a man with whom she could claim equal pay. This led to the *Equal Pay for Work of Equal Value* (1986) amendment to the *Equal Pay Act*.

The issues of 'indirect discrimination', and 'equal worth' are both rather complex to be addressed satisfactorily by the law. These ideas start to point to the fact that there are differences between men and women. This is most evident in the subject choices they take in school and their subsequent education, training and occupational trajectories, and in the differences between men and women in their pattern of participation in paid work over the life cycle (Martin and Roberts 1984). The 'gender contract' referred to above influences the kinds of choices that are made: indeed, some would argue it severely constrains the notion of 'choice' altogether (Pilcher *et al.* 1988; Rees 1992, Ch. 3). Men will tend to have uninterrupted membership of the labour force from completion of full-time education until retirement (even if some of that period is spent as a member of the workforce without a job). For women, who bear a greater responsibility for domestic and caring work, career trajectories are much more likely to be fragmented. Relatively few have no interruptions whatsoever. Moreover, women are more likely to engage in 'atypical' work: part-time, short-term, temporary contracts (Meulders *et al.* 1994; Callender 1996).

Hence, treating people the same can at times produce very rough justice. Callender (1987), for example, shows how after calculating the redundancy pay due to men and women leaving the employment of a factory after exactly the same number of years' service, male employees received considerably more money than female employees. This was because the women had had breaks in their service and therefore only the last few years were factored in. Similarly, the idea of work of equal value proved difficult to operationalize because the gendering of work itself affects its valuation (Cockburn 1983). Job evaluation schemes have sought to disentangle the value put on work and its skill component from the gender of the majority of people who do that work.

Some of these complexities led to the recognition that there are differences between men and women and that always treating men and women the same could lead to women experiencing additional disadvantages. Equal treatment does not lead to equality of outcome or anything like it. This led to the notion of positive action.

Positive action and positive discrimination

The positive action approach to equal opportunities recognizes differences between men and women and seeks to create opportunities for women who have missed out in some way as a result of their gender. In education and training, this may take the form of special women-only courses in new technologies, for example, or access courses for women wanting to return to study or work after a period of child-rearing. There are courses too for women in middle management seeking positions in senior management. In employment, there are positive action measures which seek to take into account the fact that women have prime responsibility for childcare: these may take the form of flexible hours, part-time or shift work, career break and staying in touch schemes, working from home, job sharing, and childcare facilities. Strictly, these are 'family friendly' measures, but research consistently reports that it is women who undertake the major part of these responsibilities even when both partners are working (Warde and Hetherington 1993). As a result it tends to be women who benefit from such positive action measures most and it is in feminized sections of the labour market that such provisions are most likely to be found. Such measures are designed to facilitate women to 'balance' work and home demands, given the uneven domestic division of labour and the long-hours culture of work in the UK.

Positive action measures are of course welcome, but have some limitations. Positive action training schemes, while providing potentially excellent tailor-made training for women, tend to be precariously funded and the good practice they develop is not necessarily grafted onto mainstream provision. They tend to remain as special projects, despite their proven efficacy. Similarly, while employers may introduce and fund positive action employment measures, this is linked directly to the business case. They may be introduced in a bid to retain women employees: to save the costs of re-recruiting, inducting and training replacement staff. Indeed, many employers have testified that positive action measures can be highly cost-effective (Humphries and Rubery 1995). However, where such measures are so clearly linked to the business case, in a period where the labour supply is more plentiful or the sums work out differently, then the motivation to support them is lost.

Positive action, then, is welcome but may be precarious. It also in a sense cements the link between women and domestic responsibilities, unless men may and do take advantage of what is on offer. The *Parental Leave Directive*, currently working its way through the EU's decision-making structures, has built into it some leave that is sacrificed by the couple unless the father takes it. This is an attempt to encourage fathers to take time out of work to be with their young children. In some countries such as Sweden, fathers' caring role has already been institutionalized in parental leave policies (Hobson 1997). The potential eligibility of parents in other family forms for such leave is still being worked out.

Essentially, positive action recognizes difference between men and women and seeks to address some of the disadvantages faced by women in education, training and the labour market as a consequence of these differences. Positive discrimination goes further than this by specifying quotas (rather than targets) for numbers of women to be recruited to certain areas where they are under-represented or guaranteeing priority to the under-represented sex.[2] Positive discrimination is illegal in the UK although it has existed for some time in North America. However, even there, it is now being challenged and partially withdrawn.

European law on positive discrimination is somewhat complex. A European Court of Justice case decided that the practice of the City of Bremen Parks Department (*Kalanke* v. *Hansestadt Bremen* 1995) in using employment quotas as a 'positive action' measure went too far and was incompatible with the 1976 EC *Equal Treatment Directive*. This decision reversed some ground that had been gained. However, in November 1997, the same court decided that where there are fewer women than men in a particular post in the public sector, it is not contrary to the *Equal Treatment Directive* to give priority to a woman, provided suitably qualified men are guaranteed serious consideration on criteria which do not discriminate against women (*Marschall* v. *Land Nordrhein Westfalen* 1997).

The essence of positive action and positive discrimination is the recognition of difference and the introduction of special measures to address past discrimination or disadvantage. The weaknesses of these approaches lies in their precariousness, and their treating women as 'special'.

Mainstreaming equality

The mainstreaming approach also recognizes that there are differences between men and women. Indeed, it goes further than this and acknowledges that there are differences among men, and among women. It argues that existing structures are not gender-neutral, but privilege people with certain ascriptive characteristics. Maybe not as obviously as in the case of the marriage bar, or the prevention of women from training as accountants or doctors, but all the same, the dice are loaded.

Hence, the 'norm' is in effect a male norm. We have already seen some examples of this. Redundancy pay calculations, rooted in the law, are predicated upon a typical male pattern of working. The curriculum for some courses for women in middle management on how to be senior managers include topics such as 'how to develop a killer instinct', 'how to cope with sexual harassment' and 'how to be heard in meetings' (see Rees 1998). The use of the term 'atypical' (in common currency in the EC) to describe part-time, temporary work indicates that the male pattern of participation is being taken as the yardstick against which these various forms are measured. Atypical work is however, of course, all too typical of the daily lives of many millions of women throughout the EU.[3]

One of the criticisms of the positive action model is that it may be operating, albeit subconsciously, with a 'deficit' model of women. Such measures seek to turn women into surrogate men, better able to cope with the demands of a world fashioned for a (particular) male lifestyle. Hence, the courses designed for middle managers privilege a particular version of male management style, and prepare women better to cope with it. Marshall's (1995) work on women high-fliers who drop out reveals that it is the culture, not the work that causes them difficulties. It could be argued that some positive action measures, by assisting women better to cope with the male culture of the boardroom, are in effect contributing to its sustenance while reassuring workplaces that they have cracked the equal opportunities 'problem'.

In essence, equal treatment and positive action approaches are limited in that they do not tackle the gender contract which is at the root of organizational and institutional structures which embed male advantage and female disadvantage. While the law may chip away at some of the grosser manifestations of this, and while positive action measures may create ways of coping or generate a parallel opportunity of experiencing a world more geared to women's needs, the edifices of an androcentric world order remain unchallenged. 'Progress' can only be muted. It is in this context that mainstreaming may have something to offer. It seeks to recognize and shift those male-centred biases and to establish new values. This approach is rooted in the post-modern approach of valuing diversity and difference (see Hallett 1996). At the same time as challenging male-centred ways of seeing and doing, mainstreaming seeks to accommodate differences among women and among men.

The mainstreaming agenda in the European Union and UK

The mainstreaming agenda has its roots in Swedish approaches to equality where the division of the Ministry of Health and Social Affairs has the following responsibilities (EOC 1996b: 5):

- to ensure that the terms of reference for government committees and commissions require them to analyse the gender perspective in their work and the gender impact of any proposal made;
- to scrutinize, from an equal opportunities point of view, all proposals for government bills and other government decisions emanating from various ministries prior to discussion by cabinet;
- to approve public appointments to public boards and committees, including an evaluation of a particular recommended appointment against the targets and timetable to achieve equality on that body;
- to initiate promotional activities on equality.

This integration work is complemented by a major programme of gender disaggregation of statistics by the official statistics service *Statistics Sweden*, which started in the early 1980s. This was seen as vital for awareness-raising and making transparent the role gender played in the organization of Swedish society. Monitoring of statistics is a major part of the mainstreaming agenda.

The approach of the EU to equal opportunities has been based on the legal framework of the 1957 commitment to equal pay for women and men, followed up by a series of directives in the 1970s to plug the gaps where women were omitted from consideration under the legislation (such as family workers) and in allied areas such as pensions and social security. In the 1980s, the EC also began to sponsor a series of positive action measures known as medium-term community action programmes on equal opportunities for women and men, the most recent of which runs from 1996–2000. A shift in approach from positive action to mainstreaming can be traced within these programmes (and other EC initiatives, see Rees 1998). The third programme, which ran in the early 1990s, spoke of 'integrating' equality into policy formulation and implementation. The fourth is more overtly about mainstreaming. It called for annual reports to be produced on equal opportunities within the EU, the first of which was published in 1997 (see EC 1997).

At the same time, there was growing political concern about skill shortages, unemployment and the need to develop a flexible, trained workforce and commensurate employment opportunities. White Papers on economic (EC 1994a), social (EC 1994b) and teaching and learning policy (EC 1996) were produced. All three express a commitment to equal opportunities but are not based on a gendered analysis of the labour market and social issues. The Equal Opportunities Unit of the EC commissioned seven 'wise women' to prepare a 'feminist critique' of the economic White Paper (EC 1995). The contributions all pointed to the 'malestreamism' underlying the analysis of the White Paper and made recommendations for how a more integrated approach might work.

The EC issued a communication to the Council of Ministers advocating mainstreaming of equality into all EU policies, programmes and actions (CEC 1996). The addition of new member states (in particular Sweden), and a new intake of MEPs, some of whom were both committed to and experienced in equality issues, provided political weight to the agenda. Responsibility for equal opportunities moved from one commissioner to a committee of five commissioners, chaired by the president, Jacques Santer. This committee and the influence of its members across a number of directorate generals has the potential to provide a highly significant driver for the mainstreaming agenda. This is because member states, and organizations of all kinds within them (central, regional and local government, employers and trade unions, non-governmental organizations, the voluntary sectors, education and training providers), all depend upon the EC for finance for the development of infrastructure and activities. In future, applicants will increasingly need to demonstrate that they are mainstreaming equality within their projects. Monika Wulf-Matheis, the regional affairs commissioner (and one of the members of the equal opportunities committee) has already made it clear she will not be funding projects that have not integrated an equality dimension (Wulf-Matheis 1997). By insisting upon the mainstreaming of equality for men and women in the structural funds, a significant carrot is being provided for the member states to act.

Finally, the 1997 *Treaty of Amsterdam* gave a further commitment to equal opportunities between men and women. It also brought into the legislation capacity for positive action which institutionalizes it. It extended commitment to equal treatment of people on the grounds of ethnic origin, race, religious belief, sexual orientation, disability and age.

This will need to be followed up by directives or guidelines to member states to have any effect; however, the basis has been laid to extend human rights in this way.

The Organization for Economic Cooperation and Development (OECD) (1994) has backed mainstreaming and individual member states have been developing their own approaches to mainstreaming to a greater or lesser extent following the Beijing conference. In the platform for action developed at the United Nations conference, specific emphasis was placed on the generation and dissemination of gender disaggregated statistics (Section 209) and the use of gender impact analysis in the development, monitoring and evaluation of policies (Section 167).

In the UK, the EOC adopted mainstreaming as its long-term strategic approach to fostering equal opportunities between men and women in the mid-1990s. It launched a major study on the economics of equal opportunities to draw attention to the business case for equality (Humphries and Rubery 1995) and has also been advising the Department for Education and Employment, the first Government department to pilot mainstreaming in its employment practices and service delivery.

Guidance on policy appraisal for different social groups was issued to Government departments in 1992. The Department for Education and Employment subsequently revised and updated these in 1996 as *Guidance on Policy Appraisal for Equal Treatment*. In Northern Ireland, guidelines on policy appraisal and fair treatment (PAFT) were introduced with effect from January 1994, and these are more far-reaching than those that pertain in Britain. The aim of the guidelines is to ensure that questions of equality of opportunity and equity of treatment for all sectors of the community are addressed and inform policy making and action at all levels of government activity. While PAFT is clearly driven by concerns about providing equality of opportunity on the grounds of religion, it nevertheless includes other equality dimensions and is an interesting example of a mainstreaming instrument.

In June 1997, a Cabinet sub-committee was set up to examine the effects of all proposed legislation on women. Responsibility for gender equality now stretches beyond the race and sex equality division of the Department for Education and Employment to the Department for Social Security, where the secretary of state is also minister for women's issues. In addition, there are ministers with responsibility for women and for childcare within Whitehall, the Scottish Office and the Welsh Office. This raises the public profile of gender equality issues, puts a clear emphasis on the government's concerns with women's issues and indicates some support for mainstreaming.

Operationalizing mainstreaming

Despite the indications at the European level and within the UK of support for a more radical approach towards gender equality, as yet it is early days in terms of working out what mainstreaming might mean in practice. However, there are a number of EC-funded pilot projects which have provided some indications of how mainstreaming might be operationalized.[4]

Recognizing androcentricity

The first stage is to recognize the androcentricity of existing provision and to remove or adapt policies and programmes which in their design or their implementation are leading to further discrimination. One example of this is documented in an EOC report on compulsory competitive tendering (CCT) (Escott and Whitfield 1995). While this policy of itself is not necessarily androcentric, the way in which it was implemented impacted far more upon women than men. The decision was made by local authorities in the UK to apply CCT to catering and cleaning services. Service providers sought to provide competitive contracts by reducing wages. This led to a disproportionate cut in women's wages and in sectors that were already low paid.

Patterns of work organization which rely upon a long-hours culture are discriminatory, both to the vast majority of women who take the major share of domestic responsibilities and to single parents and some men. Anticipating the gendered effect of proposed policies should ensure that fewer become embedded in practice.

Gender disaggregation of statistics

Providing statistics disaggregated by gender can be a powerful tool of transparency and the results can be fed into policy-making processes. It is the first step taken by many organizations seeking to enhance equal opportunities among their staff. But clearly, public policy organizations need to look beyond their own house to the delivery of goods and services. Who are the consumers? To what extent do the clients reached reflect need?

It is noticeable that many employers are unable to provide a gender breakdown of their consumers or clients. Training and enterprise councils (TECs) in England and Wales, for example, are charged with the delivery of services to both men and women in their areas. However, a study of post-compulsory education and training in Wales which requested a gender breakdown of TEC-funded training in Wales revealed that few TECs could access the data and certainly none were using it in their performance monitoring and review procedures (Istance and Rees 1994). Boddy (1995) found a similar situation with regard to TEC services for ethnic minorities. Regular statistical breakdowns disaggregated by gender (and race) that are known, understood and used by organizations are vital.

Visioning

This is the hardest part of mainstreaming because it means imagining doing things differently. The argument is that public service providers fall into a pattern of service provision. But how does this match need? The health service would need almost unlimited resources to match potential demand. Rationing already takes place but in a rather *ad hoc* fashion. How should need be measured in a way that is not necessarily influenced by what has always been? It means that some groups who have grown accustomed to receiving certain goods and services may have to do without, or pay for them. Other needs which have not been met in the past might need to be so in the future.

Similarly, in terms of patterns of work organization, criteria for establishing 'merit' would have to be revisited. In Northern Ireland, until recently, one of the large employing authorities for schools used continuity of service as a criterion for promotion (this has now ceased) (Deloitte and Touche 1997). Several police forces insisted upon a candidate having a number of years continuous service before earning eligibility to apply for promotion above a certain grade. Some trade unions too have ruled that members must have a minimum number of years' active service before being eligible to apply for certain senior officer posts. These practices, of course, discriminate indirectly against women, who are most likely to have had career breaks. Visioning demands starting again from basics and recognizing the diversity of the people the organization wishes to employ and to serve.

Participation and democracy

Some public-sector organizations, in recognition of the fact that they serve a sub-section of the population, have taken the step of asking their clients what they want. Participation and consultative exercises were a strong feature of the work undertaken as part of the EOC's pilot project on mainstreaming in local government. The partners reported how, rather than continuing to provide services in the established fashion, they consulted local people about their priorities, and policy decisions were informed by this exercise. Accountability was thus built-in to a greater extent (EOC 1997b).

In Wales, for example, the EOC has worked with black and ethnic minority women, including some who do not speak English, to try to facilitate them in networking and communicating their needs to bodies such as local authorities and health trusts which might be in a position to respond to them. Up to this time their voices had been silenced by the language barrier and their needs were unknown and ignored. Nasir (1996) has drawn attention to the way in which social policies are either inappropriate to the needs of ethnic minority women, or ignore such needs completely. Such policies are also often inappropriate for white women. Where black and ethnic minority women are remembered, stereotypes rather than consultative exercises often inform policy decision making. Participation is therefore an essential element of mainstreaming.

Awareness-raising and training in mainstreaming

All this implies a massive programme in awareness-raising and training. This goes far beyond the minimalist, 'keep within the law' equal opportunities training that is already provided in many organizations. Training is needed particularly in using statistics for strategic planning, in visioning and in conducting and using consultative exercises. This means an investment of resources, human and monetary, which will be necessary to equip staff to deliver mainstreaming and in order to ensure that staff 'own' the mainstreaming agenda (EOC 1997b).

If mainstreaming is to be effective, rather than, as is widely feared, an excuse for doing nothing, then skills in lateral thinking need to be developed. One of the advantages however is that if equality can be mainstreamed, then other 'transversals' such as the environmental agenda can also be mainstreamed. It is in considering the task of challenging an entire organization to rethink ways of seeing and doing that the long term nature of mainstreaming becomes evident. Some authorities have sought to pilot mainstreaming in specific departments in order to make the task manageable and to be able to feed-back specific results to encourage others.

Unfortunately, equal opportunities is a highly complex concept and a little learning can induce complacency. If a few women have penetrated the upper corridors, notwithstanding the cost to themselves, then it is assumed that there is no equal opportunities 'problem' in an organization. Similarly, all too often, if an organization has a wheel ramp, it is assumed that the needs of disabled users or employees have been adequately addressed. To make a serious difference, awareness-raising would need to be a constant activity and sufficiently sophisticated to address the complexity of the subject. The pay-off, however, might well go far beyond the workplace: employees may take their new thinking into their homes and other places of association.

Monitoring and evaluation, processes and procedures

Mainstreaming is an approach rather than a one-off event and therefore monitoring and evaluation procedures need to be set in place. Gender disaggregated statistics can play a role here. Community profiles are useful as a check against service delivery and recruitment. Additional processes and procedures can help to develop the mainstreaming agenda, such as insisting on certain standards of equal opportunities practices as part of contract compliance requirements for suppliers. Building performance on mainstreaming into staff development and review processes can motivate a desire to learn and implement good practice. It can also help in the development of ownership and in offsetting backlash.

Conclusion

While there appears to be a level of political enthusiasm for mainstreaming as an approach to equal opportunities that goes beyond the law and piecemeal positive action measures, there is little consensus as yet as to what mainstreaming means. For some, it is little more than building a gender-impact process into policy making. For others it is a far more radical approach towards employment practice and service delivery which seeks to undo the raft of disadvantages experienced by women as employees, citizens and consumers as a result of the breadwinner/homemaker gender contract that sets patriarchal relations in law, custom and practice. It is far too early to tell whether mainstreaming can deliver a real challenge to old orders and power relations. Moreover, as yet, most of the focus in the mainstreaming discussion has been about gender relations; implications for other forms of inequality such as race and ethnic origin have not been developed or tested.

Some aspects of mainstreaming are likely to prove more acceptable than others. Few are arguing against gender disaggregation and publishing of statistics although there are, of course, cost implications. This is the 'safe' side of mainstreaming. Some local authorities have introduced equalities audits and government departments have a duty to appraise the impact of proposed policies on equal treatment. The area where there is least debate and progress is that of visioning, which is the most significant element of the mainstreaming approach.

Alongside discussions about developments in equal opportunities, there is a parallel debate about a human resource management approach: managing diversity (Kandola and Fullerton 1994; Liff 1996). Mainstreaming as an approach comes closest to managing diversity in that it works with difference. In the USA there has been some enthusiasm for recruiting a diverse workforce among companies that are persuaded that it leads to better decision making by opening up processes to people with other experiences. In particular there has been some enthusiasm for bringing women into management for the different skills that they are presumed to have (Liff 1996). There are also examples of companies anxious to increase their markets by ensuring that their services reach a wider section of the population. In one of the case study companies in the MOSAIC project (in Sweden), this commercial approach is being adopted. A telecommunications company wanting to expand its market recruited operators from ethnic minorities to facilitate callers to and from their countries of origin who do not speak Swedish. This is clearly linked to the business case.

While there are differences in the approaches (managing diversity and mainstreaming) there are common elements. Both purport to move away from the investment of power and resources in a limited section of the population, determined to a large extent by ascriptive characteristics and gender/race (and other) power relations and towards the allocation of opportunities that better reflect the diversity of populations. Both recognize the significance of difference. However, there are strong and legitimate criticisms of market-driven mainstreaming and diversity approaches, not least for reinforcing the ideology of individualism (Webb 1997). They can be regarded as simply restructuring the inequality map. The issue of difference needs to be separated out from that of disadvantage in designing employment and service delivery agendas.

As yet, while the mainstreaming and managing diversity approaches are much debated, there is little empirical evidence of what they deliver and to whom. There are widespread concerns beginning to emerge in research such as the MOSAIC project (4) about the dismantling of equality units and dismissal of equality experts in the name of mainstreaming. There are also concerns that by making it everyone's responsibility, nothing will happen. The focus on the procedural integration of mainstreaming in the processes of policy development and delivery in local government, and on consultative exercises, has largely left the organizational structures, culture and ideologies which reproduce inequalities untouched.

It is arguable that for the UK, membership of the EU has been an effective catalyst to the development of equal opportunities policies over the years. The most recent developments, whereby applicants for structural funds need to demonstrate that they have an equal opportunities policy and that equal opportunities issues have been taken into account in their bids, combined with a more favourable political climate for equality in the UK, are likely to keep mainstreaming high on the agenda. The extent to which it results in changes that significantly affect the occupational life chances of women, however, remains to be seen.

Notes

1 The author is a consultant to the European Commission on equal opportunities and the Equal Opportunities Commissioner for Wales. However, the views expressed in this chapter do not necessarily represent those of either organization.
2 This made a significant impact on the number of women returned to the House of Commons in the 1997 general election where Labour operated a limited form of positive discrimination through all-women shortlists for candidature adopted in selected constituencies, until the practice was challenged on legal grounds. The subsequent European Court of Justice judgment in the *Marschall* v. *Land Nordrhein Westfalen* case makes the legal situation for political parties seeking to achieve a better balance of men and women in the UK and Scottish Parliaments and the Welsh Assembly very unclear (see EOC 1997a).

3 People working part-time (the vast majority of whom are women) have only recently been granted entitlement to the same employment protection rights as full-time workers.

4 The projects include MOSAIC, a surveys and analysis project on managing diversity in the UK, Ireland, Sweden, Italy and The Netherlands, funded under the EC's LEONARDO DA VINCI action programme on training (co-ordinated by the author) and one on mainstreaming in local government, funded under the EC's fourth medium-term action programme on equal opportunities for men and women. The EOC coordinated the project and the technical work was conducted by ECOTEC of Birmingham and Brussels. The transnational partners were from Ireland, Italy and Sweden. In addition, a project funded by the Economic and Social Research Council on *'Gender Relations and the Local State'* being conducted at the University of Edinburgh is examining the equality agenda in Scottish and Welsh local government following reorganization. It, too, has a focus on mainstreaming (see Mackay *et al.* 1996; Webb, forthcoming).

References

Blackburn, R.M., Jarman, J. and Siltanen, J. (1993) The analysis of occupational segregation over time and place: considerations of measurement and some new evidence. *Work Employment and Society,* 7 (3): 335–62

Boddy, M. (1995) *TECs and Racial Equality: Training and Work Experience for Ethnic Minorities.* Bristol: University of Bristol School for Advanced Urban Studies (SAUS) Publications.

Callender, C. (1987) Women seeking work, in S. Fineman (ed.) *Unemployment: Personal and Social Consequences.* London: Tavistock.

Callender, C. (1996) Women and employment, in C. Hallett (ed.) *Women and Social Policy: An Introduction.* Hemel Hempstead: Prentice Hall Europe.

CEC (Commission of the European Communities) (1996) *Communication from the Commission: Incorporating Equal Opportunities for Women into all Community Policies and Activities,* COM(96) final. Brussels: CEC.

Cockburn, C. (1983) *Brothers: Male Dominance and Technological Change.* London: Pluto Press.

Cockburn, C. (1991) *In the Way of Women: Men's Resistance to Sex Equality in Organisations.* London: Macmillan.

Collinson, D., Knights, D. and Collinson, M. (1990) *Managing to Discriminate* London: Routledge.

Crompton, R. and Sanderson, K. (1990) *Gendered Jobs and Social Change.* London: Unwin Hyman.

Delamont, S. (1989) *Knowledgeable Women: Structuralism and the Reproduction of Elites.* London: Routledge.

Deloitte and Touche (1997) *Women in Teaching: Equal Opportunities.* Belfast: Department of Education, Northern Ireland.

Department for Education and Employment (1996) Guidance on Policy Appraisal for Equal Treatment. London: DfEE.

EC (European Commission) (1994a) *Growth, Competitiveness, Employment: The Challenges and Ways Forward into the 21st Century,* White Paper, bulletin of the

Commission of the European Communities Supplement 6/93. Luxembourg: Office for Official Publications of the European Communities.

EC (European Commission) (1994b) *European Social Policy: A Way Forward for the Union*. Luxembourg: Office for Official Publications of the European Communities.

EC (European Commission) (1995) *Equal Opportunities for Women and Men: Follow-up to the White Paper on Growth, Competitiveness and Employment*, report to the European Commission's Task Force (DGV). Brussels: European Commission V/5538/96-EN.

EC (European Commission) (1996) *Teaching and Learning: Towards the Learning Society*. Luxembourg: Office for Official Publications of the European Communities.

EC (European Commission) (1997) *Equal Opportunities for Women and Men in the European Union 1996* (DGV). Luxembourg: Office for Official Publications of the European Communities.

EOC (Equal Opportunities Commission) (1996a) *Challenging Inequalities Between Women and Men: Twenty Years of Progress 1976–1996*. Manchester: EOC.

EOC (Equal Opportunities Commission) (1996b) *Briefing on Mainstreaming*. Manchester: EOC.

EOC (Equal Opportunities Commission) (1997a) *Improving the Representation of Women in Parliament – EOC Briefing*. Manchester: EOC.

EOC (Equal Opportunities Commission) (1997b) *Mainstreaming Gender Equality in Local Government*, project no. UK1/52/96, final report to ANIMA. Manchester: EOC.

Escott, K. and Whitfield, D. (1995) *The Gender Impact of CCT in Local Government*, research discussion series no. 12. Manchester: EOC.

Hallett, C. (1996) Social policies: continuities and change, in C. Hallett (ed.) *Women and Social Policy: An Introduction*. Hemel Hempstead: Prentice Hall Europe.

Hobson, B. (1997) Cross national dialogues and the emergence of new waves of comparative gender research in Sweden, in E. Hemlin (ed.) *"Det har ändå hänt fantastiskt mycket": Vad har jämställdhetsforskningen uppnått?* Stockholm: Riksbankens Julieumsfonf & Gidlunds For"lag.

Humphries, J. and Rubery, J. (eds) (1995) *The Economics of Equal Opportunities*. Manchester: EOC.

Istance, D. and Rees, T. (1994) *Women in Post-Compulsory Education and Training in Wales, research discussion series no. 8*. Manchester: EOC.

Kandola, R. and Fullerton, J. (1994) *Managing the Mosaic: Diversity in Action*. London: Institute of Personnel Development.

Land, H. (1994) The demise of the male breadwinner – in practice but not in theory: a challenge for social security systems, in S. Baldwin and J. Falkingham (eds) *Social Security and Social Change: New Challenges to the Beveridge Model*. Hemel Hempstead: Harvester Wheatsheaf.

Liff, S. (1996) *Managing Diversity: New Opportunities for Women? Warwick papers in industrial relations* no. 57. Coventry: Industrial Relations Research Unit, Warwick Business School, University of Warwick.

Mackay, F., Breitenbach, E., Webb, J. and Brown, A. (1996) *Early Days: Local Government Reorganization and Equal Opportunities Practice*, Department of Politics Waverley Paper. Edinburgh: University of Edinburgh.

Marshall, J. (1995) *Women Managers Moving On: Exploring Career and Life Choices*. London: Routledge.

Martin, J. and Roberts, C. (1984) *The Women and Employment Survey: A Lifetime Perspective*. London: HMSO.

Meulders, D., Plasman, G. and Plasman, R. (1994) *Atypical Employment in the EC*. Aldershot: Dartmouth Publishing.

Nasir, S. (1996) 'Race', gender and social policy, in C. Hallett (ed.) *Women and Social Policy: An Introduction*. Hemel Hempstead: Prentice Hall Europe.

OECD (Organization for Economic Cooperation and Development) (1994) *Women and Structural Change: New Perspectives*. Paris: OECD.

Office for National Statistics (1996) *New Earnings Survey*. London: ONS.

Pilcher, J., Delamont, S., Powell, G. and Rees, T. (1988) Women's training roadshows and the 'manipulation' of schoolgirls' career choices. *British Journal of Education and Work*, 2 (2): 61–6.

Rees, T. (1992) *Women and the Labour Market*. London: Routledge.

Rees, T. (1998) *Mainstreaming Equality in the European Union*. London: Routledge.

Walby, S. (1990) *Theorising Patriarchy*. Oxford: Blackwell.

Walby, S. (1997) *Transforming Gender*. London: Routledge.

Warde, A. and Hetherington, K. (1993) A changing domestic division of labour? Issues of measurement and interpretation. *Work, Employment and Society*, 7 (1) 23–45.

Webb, J. (1997) The politics of equal opportunity. *Gender, Work and Organization*, 4 (3): 159–69.

Webb, J. (forthcoming) Mainstreaming at mid-shire: a case study of equal opportunities in the new local authorities, in C. Clegg, K. Legge, and S. Walsh (eds) *The Experience of Managing: A Skills Workbook*. Basingstoke: Macmillan.

Wollstonecraft, M. ([1792] 1967) *A Vindication of the Rights of Women*. New York: W.W. Norton & Co.

Women's National Commission, Equal Opportunities Commission, Equal Opportunities Commission for Northern Ireland (1996) *In Pursuit of Equality: A National Agenda for Action Policy Papers*. London: WNC, EOC, EOCNI.

Wulf-Matheis, M. (1997) The structural funds and equal opportunities, in Chwarae Teg (Fair Play) (eds) *Women, Players in Regional Development*. Cardiff: Chwarae Teg.

10

'Dangerous and different': reconstructions of madness in the 1990s and the role of mental health policy

Sarah Payne

There have been a number of developments in mental health policy in Britain in recent years. These include an increasing emphasis on care in the community for those suffering from mental disorders, the run-down and closure of large-scale psychiatric institutions and the transfer of inpatient beds to smaller units often located in general hospitals. New legislation has also been introduced which increases the degree of medical control over discharged psychiatric patients amidst widespread debate over issues of supervision, coercion and civil liberties. Over the same period there have been changes in the ways in which people diagnosed as suffering from mental disorder are perceived, particularly when they are in the public arena. This has involved a growing fear of the dangerous psychiatric patient released prematurely into the community. While those suffering from illnesses within the milder range of mental disorders are still recognized as mentally ill, greater attention has been paid in public discourse to the smaller group of the severely mentally ill, and in particular to those seen as representing a threat to the public.

At the same time, there has been a gendered shift in the discursive construction of madness and the mentally ill. The major mechanism by which this shift occurred was through media representations of the dangerously mad which were prominent particularly in the early 1990s. While media coverage of the mentally ill has long been negative (Glasgow Media Group 1997), notorious cases of mad killers before the early 1990s – for example, Myra Hindley, Denis Nilson and Peter Sutcliffe – involved those defined as mentally disordered only after they had committed their crimes. As such, they were largely distinct from those who were already being treated by the psychiatric services. The questions which surrounded them were not about the failure of treatment but about the deficiencies of individuals, usually blamed on a mixture of unhappy family homes and individual pathology, and the failure of those around them to recognize their 'evil'. In contrast, during the first part of the 1990s, the diagnosed 'mad' – those who were receiving psychiatric treatment or who had recently been discharged from treatment – increasingly became a figure to fear.

This reconstruction of madness as dangerous and different centred largely on the young, schizophrenic male. At a time when young men were becoming more likely to receive psychiatric in-patient treatment, or to be caught up in the criminal justice system, and were increasingly disengaged from both the family and the workplace (Campbell 1993; Payne 1996a), they were also increasingly represented among the violently mad, threatening the everyday world.

Thus despite women's long over-representation in the mental health system, particular gendered shifts have occurred in recent years both in location of treatment and in the construction of madness.

While the media played a major role in this reconstruction, other influences were also significant. One of these was the formulation of mental health policy itself, with reductions in psychiatric beds and the increasing emphasis on community psychiatric treatment combined with the introduction of greater control and surveillance of the mentally disordered in the community. This chapter explores media representations of madness and danger in the early 1990s, and the role of mental health policy in reflecting and reconstructing notions of the mentally disordered in this period. How did young dangerous men become central figures in the landscape of madness during this period, and how did mental health policy play a part both in the creation of this new spectre and in the subsequent re-creation of the danger posed by this figure?

Discourse, madness and mental health policy

One way of explaining shifts in how the mentally ill were perceived during the early 1990s is through an analysis of discursive constructions of madness. Discourse analysis begins with the understanding that 'our presumed stable realities are in fact realised within variable discursive constructs' (Nettleton 1995: 21). There are two theoretical strands drawn on in this chapter which suggest that madness can be understood as discursively constructed. The first argues that 'medicine's objects are created through the language and practices which surround them' (Nettleton 1995: 23), while the second explores the value of discourse analysis as a tool in social policy analysis.

In the field of mental illness, discursive constructs include the language and practice of psychiatry, but also those discursive practices which are found elsewhere. Prior (1989) argues that familiar objects of the social world, including madness, are 'realised only in and through the discursive elements which surround the objects in question' (p. 3). As the discourse changes, so too do the objects of attention. A discourse, moreover, is not merely a narrow set of linguistic practices which reports on the world, but is 'composed of a whole assemblage of activities, events, objects, settings and epistemological precepts' (Prior 1989: 3). Psychiatry has played a key role in this, through the claim to recognize what is constituted as illness (as opposed to distress), the claim to differentiate between forms of madness, and the claim to be able to provide appropriate cures in appropriate settings. In so doing, the discourse has also been gendered: psychiatric texts, for example, spell out the sex ratio of different diagnostic groups, while pharmaceutical adverts also depict women and men in the context of distinct disorders (Ettore and Riska 1995).

While disease has been increasingly located in the socially constructed body, medicine has also extended its gaze from the abnormal to the normal, from that part of the population diagnosed as ill to the general population (Prior 1989; Nettleton 1992, 1995). This process has been particularly evident within psychiatry, partly with the increasing number of forms of mental ill-health under psychiatric scrutiny (the inclusion of pre-menstrual syndrome being one of the more recent) and partly with the physical move of psychiatry 'over the walls of the asylum' into the community (Prior 1989; Pilgrim 1993). Nettleton (1995) describes this process in terms of Armstrong's 'dispensary' power in which 'there was a demise of a binary separation between the normal and abnormal, the ill and the healthy, the mad and the sane' (Nettleton 1995: 248). The move towards non-institutional treatment has not been straightforward, as professional groups other than psychiatry have increased their representation, and these struggles have contributed to the redirection of madness and mental health. Part of this struggle is visible in media representations of the mad, as individual psychiatrists seek to explain their treatment and discharge decisions, and as the professional body seeks to regain lost ground.

How well can a discursive analysis explain developments in social policy? Such an approach has been used more often in criminology, as well as in some feminist analysis. Discursive analysis in more general social policy literature has highlighted the failure of universal accounts of policy development to explain the apparent disunity and lack of coherence of many policy solutions to problems: as Pringle and Watson (1992) argued, the state has to be seen as 'disconnected and erratic', as 'a plurality of discursive forms' (p. 63). Hillyard and Watson (1996) suggest that a post-modern social policy analysis allows recognition of the many contradictions of policy, both in how it is made and implemented, and the consequences which result. Smart's (1989) exploration of feminism and law offers a distinction between woman and Woman which highlights the way in which legal discourse both produces different kinds of women within the criminal justice system, and constructs the category Woman as other to Man. Similarly, psychiatric discourse produces different kinds of women (the depressed housewife, the postnatal mother, the senile woman) and also constructs Woman as other, in which Woman is inherently closer to depression while Man is closer to other disorders – those relating to substance abuse and the rare, violent psychopathic disorders. But these categories are constructed from other sources as well as psychiatry. In particular, in the early 1990s, media portrayals of the 'dangerous and different' mad man and the ways in which this was responded to by mental health policy are significant contributions.

In the early part of the 1990s psychiatric discourse increasingly focused on notions of risk. Two reports – the Reed Report on mentally disordered offenders (Department of Health/Home Office 1992) and the Boyd Report on suicide and homicides committed by the mentally ill (Royal College of Psychiatrists 1996) – serve to reinforce the connection between mental illness and categories of risk. In professional discourse, psychiatry increasingly discusses risk – how to recognize it, how to measure it against other risks – as though risk itself is an object rather than a constituted category. This process mirrors legal discourse, in which risk becomes something to be calculated by both victim and offender (Garland 1996) and within which 'the political uses of danger' (Douglas 1992: 10) become increasingly obvious. Garland (1996: 461) argues that since the early 1990s there has been a growth in a criminology of:

> essentialized difference: a criminology of the alien other which represents criminals as dangerous members of distinct racial and social groups which bear little resemblance to 'us'. It is, moreover, a 'criminology' which trades in images, archetypes and anxieties, rather than in careful analyses and research findings.

Garland's description of such a criminology also works as a description for an increasingly prominent mental disorder discourse during this same period. This discourse – focused on the potential risk of a particular subgroup of those who were diagnosed as mentally ill – constituted the mad as alien and dangerous, in which two distinguishing features, youth and masculinity, came to dominate the discourse through a variety of means.

Women, men and the mental health landscape

Women far outnumber men in the figures for treated mental illness, both in the UK and around the developed world (Showalter 1987; Ussher 1991). This over-representation of women in treatment for psychiatric disorders is long-standing, although it is difficult to determine when women began to outnumber men (Busfield 1996). More women than men receive psychiatric treatment in every setting, from the hospital to community care, although the ratio of female to male patients differs, being least marked in institutional settings and most marked in treatment outside the hospital. In a recent UK survey of the general population, one in seven adults was seen as suffering symptoms of mental ill-health, and the majority of these were women (Meltzer *et al.* 1995).

However, although there are more women than men in psychiatric treatment overall, the extent to which women outnumber men varies with different diagnostic groups. Thus women dominate in figures for the treatment of depression and anxiety, both as in-patients and in the community, while in both hospital and the community, more men than women are treated for problems related to alcohol and drug misuse (Miles 1988; Department of Health 1995; Meltzer *et al.* 1995). Men and women are diagnosed in roughly equal proportions for psychotic illness, and in particular for schizophrenia – although age patterns vary, with more younger men and older women in this diagnostic group (Busfield 1996; Payne 1996a).

These differences in patterns of diagnoses are important for a number of reasons. Depression and anxiety-related disorders are more frequently treated in primary healthcare settings, while the more severe psychotic illnesses more often lead to in-patient admission. Thus the greater proportion of women diagnosed as depressed, compared with the more equal representation of men and women in the psychotic diagnostic groups, helps to explain why women outnumber men more in community treatment than they do in hospital. Changes in the ways in which mental health services for different kinds of mental illness are delivered are therefore likely to affect men and women differently.

Women's dominance in particular diagnostic groups and men's dominance in others helps to construct ideas about the gendered nature of these illnesses. The prevalence of diagnoses of depression and anxiety among women compared with men means that these illnesses are more readily understood in mental health discourse as women's illnesses: depression becomes in essence a female disorder, more rarely suffered by men. Pharmaceutical adverts in medical journals more frequently show women when selling drugs for depression, while men are more often portrayed as misusing alcohol and drugs and as suffering from substance-related psychiatric disorders (Ettore and Riska 1995). This is reinforced by the medical textbooks used in psychiatric training which spell out the sex ratio of cases for different diagnostic groups. In the wider public arena, depression is discussed in women's magazines, on morning television programmes aimed at women and appears in the story-line of soap operas, particularly in the context of biological changes associated with childbirth and the menopause.

Such a gendered construction of mental ill-health is not new. Men's and women's mental health problems have long been perceived in different ways, both in terms of the origins of mental disorder and the ways in which disorder manifests itself (Skultans 1975; Showalter 1987). The discursive construction of mental disorder reflects and incorporates a range of voices, both professional and lay. In Victorian psychiatry, textbooks and journals pictured mad women as distinct from mad men in both the origins of their disorder and the diagnostic labels attached to these troubles. Again, these gendered identifications of madness were reinforced in literature and art – Charlotte Brontë's *Jane Eyre* for example.

However, madness is not a one-off construction but one which continually changes in reaction to different discursive elements. An increasingly significant influence on these changes is the delivery of mental health services within the healthcare system. This influence began with the identification of mental disorder as a medical phenomenon and the creation of psychiatry as a profession to manage the those seen as mad in Victorian society (Foucault 1967). Thus, for Foucault, psychiatry developed and continues as a discursive practice aimed at the regulation of society. From this perspective it is not only the psychiatrists themselves who are significant, but other contributors. The enlarging role of central government in determining the management of the mentally disordered population in the mid-1800s resulted in an increase in the number of large institutions for the insane, which required not only staff and the professional expertise of psychiatrists but also patients.

Similarly, in the 1990s, policy arrangements do not simply create a structure in which the care of those suffering from mental distress is to be organized. Thus mental health policy helps to determine who is seen as mentally ill: the provision and accessibility of mental health services affects demand for those services, how such services are seen and also the use made of those services by different groups of people with different levels of illness. Mental health policy in the latter half of this century has helped to generate what was being seen by the early years of the 1990s as a crisis in psychiatric care.

There are two ways in which the design and delivery of mental health services are important in these discursive shifts in the face of madness. The first reflects the way in which policy contributed to a situation in which these incidents became not only possible but, to some degree, probable. The second concerns the way in which violent acts by the mentally disordered, and public reaction to them, helped to shape mental health policy and how these new developments in policy, and the debate surrounding them, further reinforced the shift in the construction of madness.

No particular place to go: the closure of the asylum and the arrival of community care

The most significant development in the latter part of this century in the delivery of mental health services has been the closure of large-scale institutions and the increasing use of psychiatric services in community settings. The number of psychiatric beds available has decreased by more than half since 1959 (Chew 1992) and the number of psychiatric in-patients by nearly 300 per cent (House of Commons 1994). In-patient treatment is now found mainly in smaller units, often as part of the district general hospital (Pilgrim 1993). Taken alone this might simply reflect improved mental health status or improved community care treatment. But despite reductions in the number of psychiatric beds, the number of psychiatric admissions taking place each year has increased (Department of Health 1969; Department of Health 1995), with shorter in-patient stays and earlier discharge. The vast majority of those admitted as psychiatric in-patients in the 1990s have been readmissions – those people who have been treated for mental illness inside a hospital before, and are likely to return at a later date.

Meanwhile, more and more people are treated outside hospital either in the primary healthcare system, by the general practitioner (GP) or by specialist community mental health teams (CMHTs). Most people with what are diagnosed as minor mental disorders are treated by their GP, and this has long been the case (Strathdee *et al.* 1990). The real shift in mental health policy has been the increasing role of community care for those with severe and enduring mental health problems. This means that there has been an attempt to provide care outside the institution for those who would in the past have been admitted, many of whom would have remained incarcerated for a number of years. These are the patients who are seen as being failed by the community care system, and who have been at the fulcrum of the debate over alternatives to in-patient care and the threat posed by the mentally disordered.

Community psychiatric care is perceived by many as having failed because it is massively underfunded, and cannot provide care at an appropriate level for all of those who need it (Tyrer *et al.* 1998). Thus the Royal College of Psychiatrists, the Mental Health Commission, the National Schizophrenia Fellowship, MIND and SANE (Schizophrenia: A National Crisis) have all argued that community care is inadequate for the demands which are placed on it (Hogman 1992; Mental Health Commission 1993). All contributed to a debate in the popular press highlighting this failure, and the consequences as they saw them.

In line with these criticisms, existing community mental health services have been increasingly blamed for shifting their focus from the severely ill to the less ill (Shanks 1991; Jackson *et al.* 1993), and this too added to the problems suffered by those with the most disabling mental illness (Hogman 1992; Pilgrim 1992). Again, this criticism was picked up and repeated in the national press in the early 1990s.

By the 1980s and 1990s those policy changes had produced a system which was verging on collapse, with too few beds for emergency admissions without the precipitous discharge of other, severely ill patients, and too little money to provide community psychiatric care for all those in need (Mental Health Commission 1993). The services which were provided were often fragmented and seen as directed to the wrong group of patients. For many of the mental health pressure groups a further problem was that community psychiatric services were provided within a medical framework in which the curative model was not challenged (Pilgrim 1992; Pilgrim and Rogers 1993). However, the dilemma facing the psychiatric profession was how to regain and retain control in the community setting (Tyrer 1993).

The effects of these changes have not been experienced equally by male and female patients. In the 1980s there was a reduction in the extent to which women dominated psychiatric admission figures. Indeed in some age groups (under 35 and over 75) the number of men admitted to hospital was greater than the number of women (Payne 1996a). The requirement to provide adequate community care on discharge following the 1991 NHS and Community Care Act is problematic with a shortage of psychiatric beds, which speeds discharges to the point where the pressure on community care in some areas is substantially beyond what can be provided and is often inadvisable at that stage of the patient's recovery (Geddes and Juszczak 1995; Mental Health Commission 1993). Psychiatric admissions have increasingly been reserved for those who are seen as a threat to themselves or others – a bill which men, and in particular young men, increasingly fit. Mirroring this process, women remain more often in the community than before, either with GP care or care from the CMHT.

This then is the policy backdrop to the emerging portrayal in the media of the 'dangerous mad'. There is an increasing emphasis on community care but what is provided is seen by many as too little and inappropriate (Pilgrim and Rogers 1993; Payne 1996b). Community care has other critics: feminists have highlighted the implicit assumption of community care that families and women in particular are both willing and able to provide unpaid labour in the home (Finch and Groves 1983; Pascall 1997). In addition, mental health survivors and pressure groups like MIND have pointed out that as a result 'care in the community' for people with psychiatric difficulties in the 1980s and 1990s has usually been provided by the sufferers themselves (Pilgrim 1992).

The reduction in in-patient provision has left discharged patients at large in the community. Many of these are young men who have been admitted as psychiatric in-patients, and discharged after a shorter in-patient stay, often with inadequate care in community settings. In the early 1990s these discharged mentally-ill patients were increasingly seen as dangerous to the general public, and the psychiatric services were increasingly seen as unable to cope. And there was a gendered dimension to this fear: while women patients who commit acts of extreme violence do so inside the privacy of the family, the random, violent acts which fuel public fear rather than private concern are committed by young men in the community.

The beast unleashed: discursive constructions of madness in the 1990s

During the early 1990s a string of highly publicized events drew media and public attention towards the mentally ill. While the focus of attention during this period varied, with the debate moving across a number of different themes, the arguments centred around the care of a specific sub-group of those with severe levels of psychiatric disorder. The development of this discourse of the dangerous madman can be traced through a number of different sources. However, national newspapers made a significant contribution. This section draws on a search of the main broadsheets during the first six years of the decade after two serious incidents involving people in receipt of community psychiatric care, in late 1992 and early 1993. The time frame includes the three years on either side of what became a turning point in mental health policy in the decade. The focus is on the broadsheets, for while the tabloids were carrying the same stories with less temperate language, it is revealing that the more 'respectable' newspapers also frequently resorted to language which was both extreme and sensational. When *The Times* used the phrase, 'knife-crazy mental patient' (29 June 1993) it was all the more powerful by contrast with the other, more restrained articles in the same paper.

A search of the *Guardian*, *The Times*, the *Observer* and *The Sunday Times* over the period 1990 to 1995 reveals a number of references to violent actions and crimes by people defined, both in the headlines and in the text, as mentally ill. However, alongside the 'dangerous' mad is the discourse around the threat patients pose to themselves. Both of these threads suggest an increasing risk posed by the mentally ill, who are represented as a danger to themselves, and a danger to the public at large. Other aspects of this debate, however, identify this risk more explicitly in terms of gender and race, so that the politicized discourse also features the young, mad, black male as the alien emerging from the rhetoric. What develops during this period is a dualized psychiatric discourse, in which the mad are characterized by the spectre of the dangerous madman who is beyond control and represents a threat to us all, while the mentally ill are characterized by the depressed female suffering in private.

This mirrors an increasingly dualized criminology of the time, in which the criminology of the self characterizes the criminal as the rational consumer, committing largely economic crimes, who is essentially the same as the rest of us, while the criminology of the 'other' constructs the criminal as the threatening outcast (Garland 1996: 461). In both discourses, there is a duality in which one element is rational and represents little threat and the other is increasingly pushed outside as 'other'.

Mad, bad and dangerous

A major part of the debate over psychiatric care in the early 1990s was about the question of the danger presented to the general public by discharged mental health patients. This debate was conducted in a highly charged public setting and centred on issues of safety, violence and danger within a specific framework. The safety being discussed, however, was often the safety of the general public and the violence feared was violence carried out by the ill person, not violent acts towards the mentally ill. Questions were also rarely posed regarding the safety of the mentally-ill individual as a result of drugs being administered, or the danger of removing civil liberties from such individuals. The beast was constructed as 'other', as external to society, and increasingly as in need of physical rather than moral restraint.

In the opening years of the 1990s the psychiatric disorder of those who have committed violent crime is central to the story presented. In 1990 we read:

Killer mother sent to hospital – a woman suffering from paranoid schizophrenia strangled her two children.
(*Guardian*, 27 March 1990: 4)

Mentally-ill man accused of running amok with a shotgun.
(*Guardian*, 2 May 1990: 3)

Mrs Ngai was suffering from an acute psychotic illness, possibly schizophrenia, when she strangled her young children.
(*Guardian*, 21 July 1990: 4)

Schizophrenic . . . battered cab driver Peter Lewis . . . to death.
(*Guardian*, 17 August 1990: 8)

Paranoid woman killed girl.
(*Guardian*, 1 September 1990: 2)

Man who killed baby with machete sent to Broadmoor.
(*Guardian*, 4 September 1990: 5)

Similar reports of violent crimes by those defined as mentally ill continue in later years:

Mental patient released by wife kills her and sons with scissors.
(*Guardian*, 15 October 1991: 3)

Gunman 'mentally ill' when he killed.
(*The Times*, 26 March 1992: 2)

Family's anger at insane killer.
(*Guardian*, 28 May 1993: 7)

Schizophrenic raped three.
(*Guardian*, 6 June 1993: 2)

Schizophrenic who killed an 83-year-old grandfather.

(*Guardian*, 17 July 1993: 4)

Schizophrenic who killed father while on bail.

(*Guardian*, 13 November 1993: 12)

This reporting of crimes committed by the mentally ill (as opposed to crimes by people, without reference to their mental health status) is not new (Glasgow Media Group 1997). However, in the first years of the 1990s there was an increasingly recurrent debate surrounding such crimes, fuelled by a number of high-profile incidents. One of these incidents, in early December 1992, was the murder of Jonathon Zito by 30-year-old Christopher Clunis, later described by *The Times* as a 'knife-crazy mental patient' (29 June 1993: 3). Clunis was later convicted of killing Zito in an apparently random act of violence, and cover of his trial repeatedly referred to his identification as 'a schizophrenic with violent tendencies' who 'had been released into the community with little medical supervision' (*Guardian*, 22 July 1993: 5). Zito's widow – a mental health therapist – argued that Clunis had been failed by the mental health system, and added to the calls for better care for people suffering severe mental illness, and better supervision after discharge.

Clunis, and the debate over the murder of Jonathan Zito, was undoubtedly one of the central cases in the development of the public image of the mentally ill as young and dangerous. However, the construction of the threat posed by young men occurs within an existing context which is also significant. In the six-year period between 1990 and 1995 the *Guardian*, for example, reported on 31 murders carried out by people defined as severely mentally ill. Of these, 20 cases were men, 11 were women, and nearly all were under 40 years of age. In more than a third of the cases reported, the murder was either of someone chosen at random or relatively unknown to the person committing the crime. In each of these random attacks, the person committing the crime was male and under 30.

In addition, the paper reported on nine further cases of harm towards others committed by people defined as seriously mentally ill. In eight of these incidents the person accused was male, and the crime was towards a stranger. The crimes included rape and attempted rape, kidnap and abuse of a child, and attempted murder. The tone of these reports emphasizes the inexplicable nature of the assailants' actions, other than by reference to their psychiatric condition.

While cases relating to both women and men are reported in the pages of the same newspapers, the cases of women invariably involve their close family – and in particular their children – and the women are frequently reported in the context of their familial role: as loving mothers who failed to cope or as mothers who were, in their own minds, acting in the child's interests.

The overall impact of reading these stories is a rendering of the un-controlled and unsupervised madman as a serious threat to the public. Indeed, in reporting court cases, newspapers often report the judge's words in summing up, which refer to the defendant's danger to the public. Over and over again throughout the 1990s we are warned of this danger posed to us – the general public rather than the immediate family – by the young schizophrenic at loose in the community.

A risk to themselves

The second theme during this period is the risk of patients in the mental health system inflicting self-harm. There are a number of reports of the suicide of discharged patients, and of in-patients in situations of inadequate supervision: 'Risk patient kills himself in hospital' (*Guardian*, 8 August 1991: 3). Part of the debate over psychiatric care which developed in this period concerned the inability of existing services to provide the level of support which was required. The mentally ill were described as 'falling through holes in the community care net' (*Guardian*, 7 August 1991: 17) while ' "Little help" [is] given to discharged schizo-phrenics' (*Guardian*, 25 October 1991: 6) and 'Psychiatric patient [is] driven to suicide by hospital failure' (*Guardian*, 26 March 1991: 3).

On New Year's Day in 1993 the debate over the adequacy of community care for Britain's mentally ill took on a new dimension, when Ben Silcock climbed into the lion's den at London Zoo and was mauled by the lions. Although the debate over the risk posed by mental health patients to both themselves and to others had been growing in previous years, Silcock's actions that day had a huge discursive impact, and major policy changes followed. The case was significant because it was highly publicized, partly due to the day itself, when there was little else to report, and partly because Silcock's action and subsequent rescue were captured on amateur video and subsequently fed to the waiting public in their homes. Although the Silcock case also hit the headlines because of the Zito murder scarcely a month earlier, the violence of this act, compared with the earlier one, was seen to be directed inwards, hence the discussion which ensued focused on the failure of psychiatric care to protect Silcock against the danger he presented to himself rather than on any danger he might present to the public.

We were left in no doubt, however, of Ben Silcock's mental disorder. Headlines and reports in the days after his action highlighted his mental illness: 'Mauling victim "a schizophrenic" ' (*Guardian*, 2 January 1993: 4). Silcock's family were highly critical of the failure of the psychiatric services to care for their son. His father is reported to have said: 'There is no care in the community. Ben's just dumped'. The *Guardian* added that 'there has been no suggestion that Ben Silcock had been failing to take medication', and his father is also quoted as saying he had managed on his own 'fairly successfully' in the past 18 months (4 January 1993: 1).

The cases of Clunis and Silcock – both of whom were described as having been let down by the system – shifted the debate over the failure of community care, and the consequences of that failure for ordinary members of the public, into new territory. As we shall see, the debate had now reached a level in which Conservative health minister Virginia Bottomley felt the need to respond almost immediately, with new suggestions for mental health policy. The debate over the adequacy and appropriateness of this policy response further fed back into, and fuelled, the debate over the dangerousness of the discharged mentally ill.

'Big, Black and Dangerous': the representation of young Afro-Caribbean men[1]

The other significant shift in the discursive construction of madness is the representation of young black men in the media. Some of the young men described in articles on violent unprovoked attacks are also black. The text of articles in the broadsheets largely ignores this, although accompanying photographs keep the public informed (Francis 1996). In the tabloids there is less delicacy, and reports carry full details of the ethnicity of these dangerous young men.

However, the theme is present in other ways which also add to the discursive construction of young black men as representing a greater threat. There was a debate during this period about the over-representation of young Afro-Caribbean men in mental health treatment, and in particular in the secure mental health system (Knowles 1991; Prins *et al.* 1993; Browne 1995). Newspapers in the early 1990s carried several conflicting accounts of explanations of this over-representation of people of Afro-Caribbean origin among those receiving a diagnosis of schizophrenia, and in particular the high number of young black men given this diagnosis. Articles reported the words of those psychiatrists who supported the idea that there is an inherent susceptibility to schizophrenia among people of Afro-Caribbean origins, and those who did not.

Alongside these debates, however, there was a longer-running series of articles covering the death of three young black men in Broadmoor. In 1992 Orville Blackwood died as a result of a fatal injection of a cocktail of drugs to control his violence – the third young Afro-Caribbean man to die in Broadmoor in this way. Newspaper reports of the inquiries into Blackwood's death described him as suffering from 'either manic depression or schizophrenia', and his behaviour as 'either jovial and likeable or menacing and, increasingly, violent' (*Guardian*, 11 September 1993: 2). They also refer to his size and his weight, which reinforces the underlying message of threat. When Blackwood received the medication which killed him, he was being restrained by up to seven nurses, and the fear of his violence is a constant theme in the accounts of his death and of the earlier deaths and maltreatment of young black men. This image is repeated and reinforced in part of the title of the report of the private inquiry into Blackwood's death: 'Big, Black and Dangerous', a reference to the ways in which the predominantly white staff viewed patients like Blackwood. The report discussed questions of racism within the mental health services in some detail, pointing out, for example, the high proportion of Broadmoor inmates from minority ethnic groups and the predominantly white staff in the hospital (Prins *et al.* 1993). The inquiry team also highlighted the impact of the 'macho culture' on the regime and the way this in turn reinforced the idea of the potential violence of patients, which is repeated in the newspapers: '"This sense of danger is exaggerated and may be "hyped up" by some members of the nursing staff because it tends to reinforce the need for a more custodial rather than therapeutic regime", the inquiry team says' (*Guardian*, 1 September 1993. 2).

The climate of fear and the voice of psychiatry

> Rightly or wrongly, there is a public perception that insane people are being let out on to the streets to kill.
>
> (*Guardian*, 5 February 1992: 19)

> Since [January] there have been a number of isolated but tragic cases in which mentally disordered patients have assaulted – even killed – people in the community. With each new case in the spotlight, public anxiety has grown.
>
> (Leader article, *Guardian*, 13 August 1993: 19)

During 1992 and 1993 newspapers reflected and contributed to the growing view of the danger resulting from the failure of the mental health services to control patients and former patients. In February 1992 a feature article described the random killing of a pensioner by a young man diagnosed as schizophrenic under the headline 'Fear on the streets – the potential danger in releasing psychiatric patients from hospital without the back-up of proper community care' (*Guardian*, 5 February 1992: 19). The *Guardian* subsequently referred to thousands of mentally-ill patients who had been 'freed' under the government's community care policies (14 September 1994: 4), while *The Times* described London psychiatric services as 'under huge strain because of the increasing number of mentally ill people picked up from the streets by the police' (27 July 1992: 4).

However, it was not only the press who feared the consequences of the changing mental health services, and expert opinions were used to bolster the fear:

> More people will die in incidents involving schizophrenics unless the Government legislates to tighten controls on community care, the leader of the Royal College of Psychiatrists warned yesterday.
>
> (*Guardian*, 7 July 1993: 6)

The National Schizophrenia Fellowship says more than 40 people have been killed by mentally ill people in the past two years and at least 100 mentally ill people have committed suicide.

(*Guardian*, 13 August 1993: 3)

The closure of long-stay large-scale psychiatric institutions and the transfer of psychiatric treatment to community services over the past 20 years was seen by the psychiatric profession as a threat to their position in the services (Tyrer 1993). In addition, in the debate over inadequate funding of mental health services and the shortage of in-patient beds, psychiatrists sought to avoid blame in high-profile cases. Both public enquiries and the High Court were asking why psychiatrists appeared to have discharged patients prematurely and inappropriately, when these patients had gone on to commit acts of violence against the general public. Not surprisingly, the psychiatric profession acted to defend their role, and a number of press releases followed. Such contributions by the medical profession and the Royal College of Psychiatrists were widely reported in the early 1990s, as the issue of public safety gathered pace in media debates over community care for the mentally ill:

London psychiatrists barely able to cope – the government's plans to improve the country's mental health will fail unless money is provided to employ more consultants.

(*The Times*, 27 July 1992: 4)

Crisis in acute mental care – patients being discharged prematurely.

(*Guardian*, 16 June 1994: 6)

Mentally ill arsonist is jailed for life after hospital care is refused.

(*Guardian*, 2 July 1994: 10)

Beds crisis hits psychiatric patients.

(*Observer*, 13 November 1994: 11)

Psychiatrist goes in fear of schizophrenics on the loose.

(*Observer*, 24 September 1995: 7)

By 1995 psychiatrists were arguing that the development of community care had not only transferred care to the 'worried well' – leaving those with severe acute illness untreated – but also that psychiatry itself had been diverted towards less serious and 'more socially acceptable' illness, with more difficult illness pushed aside in medical training. The argument recurs in both psychiatric texts and in the more widely-read media: 'The desperate seriousness of serious mental illness was systematically devalued' (*Guardian*, 22 January 1995: 23). The emerging argument was for a seamless web of community care in which psychiatry played a leading role and in which patients did not 'fall through the net'. Thus the Royal College of Psychiatrists supported supervised discharge and care registers as a way to monitor mental health patients in the community, with the medical profession in charge. What then was the impact on policy of the intensification of this public debate over the dangers of poorly funded and inadequate community care?

The policy response: the end of moral restraint?

Virginia Bottomley, then Conservative health secretary, responded to Ben Silcock's actions in January 1993 with an announcement of a review of mental health law, and in particular the question of compulsory treatment in the community. 'Community treatment orders' (CTOs) had been suggested by the Royal College of Psychiatrists in 1987 as a means of ensuring that people with severe mental disorders in the community remained on medication to prevent relapse. At that time opposition from patients' groups and pressure groups such as MIND over the threat such compulsory treatment presented to the civil liberties of discharged patients had meant the idea was not taken further (Harrison 1995). However, in the light of new public concern over the danger posed by psychiatric patients in the community the idea was revived by Virginia Bottomley.

The Royal College of Psychiatrists had by this time, however, had what they described as a 'rethink' and were advocating a lesser stage of constraint – community supervision orders (CSOs) – which would not mean enforced treatment in the community, but enforced readmission of patients who continually refused medication. In the early months of 1993, after Bottomley's hasty announcement of the introduction of CTOs immediately after Silcock had climbed into the lion's den, health ministers listened to the Royal College and swiftly moved on to describe proposals for CSOs rather than CTOs. Other groups, such as MIND, were firmly opposed to both CSOs and CTOs and continued to voice their opposition throughout the period up to the passing of the Mental Health (Care in the Community) Act in 1995 in which such supervision was introduced (OpenMind 1995). This debate was reported in the press, under such headlines as 'Bottomley unveils plan to protect public from mental patients' (*The Sunday Times*, 25 July 1993: 1). The leader of a two-year Royal College of Psychiatrists' working party on community care was quoted as welcoming 'the concept of supervised discharge, which he said was in line with the community supervision orders his team had proposed' (*The Times*, 25 July 1993: 1).

Over the months following Bottomley's announcement of changes to mental health law, issues surrounding the care of people with severe mental illness in the community continued to be discussed up to the enactment and introduction of the new legislation. This discussion around policy to contain and control patients in the community added to the discursive construction of the dangerous psychiatric patient at large and this patient continued to be personified as young and male through consistent reminders of both Clunis and Silcock. The *Guardian* reported: 'Mrs Bottomley has favoured a change in the mental health law since Ben Silcock, a schizophrenic, was severely mauled after leaping into a lion's enclosure at London Zoo' (13 May 1993: 2), while *The Sunday Times* (25 July 1993: 16) in a discussion of the new measures, mentioned '40 murders since the programme of closing long-stay psychiatric beds began two years ago' and '100 mentally ill people [who] have committed suicide' before going on to mention both Silcock and Clunis.

Attention was further encouraged by continuing reports of violent crime carried out by mentally disordered people (former patients of the system) in which the picture of random violence against unknown others continued to be a male phenomenon. Relatives of the victims of these crimes were also given a voice, quoted as saying the care and supervision given to discharged patients was inadequate.

In 1994, the junior health minister John Bowis promised more money for secure psychiatric beds in response to a report on community care published by the Mental Health Foundation (1994). The *Sun's* headline, 'Four million pounds to lock up schizos' (Philo, 1997: 7), summed up both public panic and the health ministry's response. However, this response was in spite of the content of the report itself, which argued that the majority of those with severe mental illness did not present a risk to the public, and that the needs of these people had been overlooked as a result of the focus on a few potentially violent patients.

Clearly the incidents of violence committed by those diagnosed as mentally ill in the early part of the 1990s, and the reporting of these by the press, had a significant impact on public perceptions of madness and the danger represented by the severely mentally ill. Fears were also fuelled in that these dangers were personified: the severely mentally ill were given a face, the face of young, often black, men who were pictured alongside these stories. If we now knew what to fear from the mad, we also knew who to be afraid of. As policy responded in the way it did, and this too was reported in its turn, the discursive production of the madman as 'Big, Black and Dangerous' continued.

Conclusion

By the time the 1995 Mental Health (Patients in the Community) Act came into force in April 1996 the debate had subsided considerably, although there continues to be disquiet over the new measures among some groups. The focus in the late 1990s has returned to issues of underfunding and the inability of existing services – whether they are in the community or hospital-based – to give help to all of those who need it (Mental Health Commission 1993). The Labour government's injection of £3m, announced in the autumn of 1997, for additional healthcare spending is to be spread over the National Health Service as a whole, and it seems unlikely that it will significantly alter the problem of resource shortage in the mental healthcare sector.

Mental health policy took the specific direction it did – greater restraint rather than increased funding – for a variety of reasons. The timing of the changes was the cumulative result of highly-publicized incidents involving young mentally disordered men. There were other factors which became important in this period and which increased the difficulties being faced by young men: higher rates of youth unemployment, increased levels of involvement with the criminal justice system, dramatic increases in suicide and changes in the structure of family life. These were also part of the public debate over young men and shifting masculinity at the time. The representation of the danger of the mentally disordered during the early years of the 1990s was one in which mentally disordered young men were the focus and this coincided with representations of young men elsewhere. The re-creation of this discourse by a shift in mental health policy which focused on the dangers presented by the mad and which clearly grew from the acts of young mentally disordered men meant that madness also became re-created in gendered terms. By the late 1990s we have two manifestations: the mentally disordered young man, in need of control lest the public are harmed, and the depressed neurotic woman who has always been present, but who continues to suffer in private, at home.

Neither men nor women benefit from this reconstruction. The danger which exists for most people with mental health problems is the danger to themselves of the medicine they are prescribed and the dangers for families who have to cope with too little support from the mental health services. Ben Silcock did climb into the lion's enclosure, to be severely mauled, Christopher Clunis did kill Jonathon Zito and many others have suffered, both as victims and as those who are suffering from severe and enduring mental disorder. We cannot transform these incidents so that this is forgotten, as we concentrate on a discursive rendering of the dangerous madman. However, this shift in discourse led to a development in mental health policy in which a small group of people – more often men, more often black – have lost their civil liberties, while still receiving too little of the care and support they need.

Note

1 Big, Black and Dangerous' is the astonishing – and apparently ironic – title given to the report of the inquiry into the death of Orville Blackwood in Broadmoor (Prins *et al.* 1993). The inquiry uses the phrase to convey the climate of fear which is seen as over-exaggerated by staff at Broadmoor. None the less, the title also reinforces notions of the danger posed by Afro-Caribbean patients in the mental health system.

References

Browne, D. (1995) Sectioning: the black experience, in S. Fernando (ed.) *Mental Health in a Multi-Ethnic Society: A Multi-Disciplinary Handbook*, pp. 62–72. London: Routledge.

Busfield, J. (1996) *Men, Women and Madness: Understanding Gender and Mental Disorder*. London: Macmillan.

Campbell, B. (1993) *Goliath: Britain's Dangerous Places*. London: Methuen.

Chew, R. (1992) *Compendium of Health Statistics*, 8th edn. London: Office of Health Economics.

Department of Health (1969) *Digest of Health Statistics for England and Wales*. London: Department of Health.

Department of Health (1995) *Mental Health in England from Calendar Year 1982 to Financial Year Ending March 1992*. London: Government Statistical Service.

Department of Health/Home Office (1992) *Review of Health and Social Services for Mentally Disordered Offenders and Others Requiring Similar Services* (The Reed Report). London: DoH/Home Office.

Douglas, M. (1992) *Risk and Blame: Essays in Cultural Theory*. London: Routledge.

Ettore, E. and Riska, E. (1995) *Gendered Moods: Psychotropics and Society*. London: Routledge.

Finch, J. and Groves, D. (eds) (1983) *A Labour of Love: Women, Work, and Caring*. London: Routledge & Kegan Paul.

Foucault, M. (1967) *Madness and Civilization: A History of Insanity in the Age of Reason* (translated from the French by Richard Howard). London: Tavistock.

Francis, E. (1996) Community care, danger and black people. *OpenMind*, 80: 4–5.

Garland, D. (1996) The limits of the sovereign State: strategies of crime control in contemporary society. *British Journal of Criminology*, 36 (4): 445–71.

Geddes, J.R. and Juszczak, E. (1995) Period trends in rate of suicide in first 28 days after discharge from psychiatric hospital in Scotland, 1968–1992. *British Medical Journal*, 311 (7001): 357–60.

Glasgow Media Group (1997) *Media and Mental Distress*, edited by G. Philo. Harlow: Longman.

Harrison, K. (1995) Growing opposition to 'uncontroversial' bill. *OpenMind*, 74: 5.

Hillyard, P. and Watson, S. (1996) Postmodern social policy: a contradiction in terms? *Journal of Social Policy*, 25 (3): 321–346.

Hogman, G. (1992) *Window Dressing: The Care Programme Approach and the Mental Illness Specific Grant April 1991–April 1992: The First Year. A Research Analysis of the Implementation of the Care Programme Approach and the Mental Illness Specific Grant in a representative group of 14 Local Authorities and 14 Corresponding District Health Authorities*. Kingston-upon-Thames: National Schizophrenia Fellowship.

House of Commons (1994) *House of Commons Health Committee: Better Off in the Community? The Care of People who are Seriously Mentally Ill, First Report*. London: HMSO.

Jackson, G., Rater, R., Goldberg, D., Tantam, D., Loftus, L. and Taylor, H. (1993) A new community mental health team based in primary care: a description of the service and its effect on service use in the first year. *British Journal of Psychiatry*, 162: 375–84.

Knowles, C. (1991) Afro-Caribbeans and schizophrenia: how does psychiatry deal with issues of race, culture and ethnicity? *Journal of Social Policy*, 20: 173–90.

Meltzer, H., Gill, B. and Pettigrew, M. (1995) *OPCS Surveys of Psychiatric Morbidity in Great Britain, report no. 1: The Prevalence of Psychiatric Morbidity Among Adults Aged 16–64 Living in Private Households in Great Britain*. London: OPCS.

Mental Health Commission (1993) *Fifth Biennial Report of the Mental Health Commission*. London: HMSO.

Miles, A. (1988) *Women and Mental Illness: The Social Context of Female Neurosis*. Brighton: Wheatsheaf.

Nettleton, S. (1992) *Power, Pain and Dentistry*. Buckingham: Open University Press.

Nettleton, S. (1995) *The Sociology of Health and Illness* Cambridge: Polity Press.

OpenMind (1995) Care not coercion. 77: 4–5.

Pascall, G. (1997) *Social Policy: A New Feminist Analysis*. London: Routledge.

Payne, S. (1996a) Masculinity and the redundant male: explaining the increasing incarceration of young men. *Social and Legal Studies*, 5 (2): 159–77.

Payne, S. (1996b) Psychiatric care in the community: is it failing young men? *Policy and Politics*, 24 (2): 193–205.

Pilgrim, D. (1992) Rhetoric and nihilism in mental health policy: a reply to Chapman *et al. Critical Social Policy*, 34: 106–13.

Pilgrim, D. (1993) Mental health services in the twenty-first century: the user-professional divide, in J. Bornea, C. Pereira, D. Pilgrim and F. Williams (eds) *Community Care: A Reader*. Milton Keynes: OU/Macmillan.

Pilgrim, D. and Rogers, A. (1993) *A Sociology of Mental Health and Illness*. Buckingham: Open University Press.

Pringle, R. and Watson, S. (1992) Women's interests and the post-structuralist state, in M. Barrett and A. Phillips (eds) *Destabilizing Theory: Contemporary Feminist Debates*. Cambridge: Polity Press.

Prins, H., Blacker-Holst, T., Francis, E. and Keitch, I. (1993) *Report of the Committee of Inquiry Into the Death in Broadmoor Hospital of Orville Blackwood and a Review of the Deaths of Two Other Afro-Caribbean Patients: Big, Black and Dangerous?* London: Special Hospitals Service Authority.

Prior, L. (1989) *The Social Organisation of Death: Medical Discourses and Social Practices in Belfast*. London: Macmillan.

Royal College of Psychiatrists (1996) *Report of the Confidential Inquiry into Homicides and Suicides by Mentally Ill People* (the Boyd Report). London: Royal College of Psychiatrists.

Shanks, J. (1991) Services for patients with chronic mental illness: results of research and experience, in H. Freeman and J. Henderson (eds) *Evaluation of Comprehensive Care of the Mentally Ill*. London: Gaskell.

Showalter, E. (1987) *The Female Malady: Women, Madness and English Culture 1830–1980*. London: Virago.

Skultans, V. (1975) *Madness and Morals: Ideas on Insanity in the Nineteenth Century*. London: Routledge & Kegan Paul.

Smart, C. (1989) *Feminism and the Power of Law*. London: Routledge.

Strathdee, G., Brown, R.M.A. and Doig, R.J. (1990) Psychiatric clinics in primary care: the effect on general practitioner referral patterns. *Social Psychiatry and Psychiatric Epidemiology*, 25: 95–100.

Tyrer, P. (1993) Who is failing the mentally ill? *British Medical Journal*, 307 (6897): 1199–201.

Tyrer, P., Evans, K., Ghandi, N., Lamont, A., Harrison-Read, P. and Johnson, T. (1998) Randomised controlled trial of two models of care for discharged psychiatric patients. *British Medical Journal*, 316 (7125): 106–9.

Ussher, J. (1991) *Women's Madness: Misogyny or Mental Illness?* Hemel Hempstead: Harvester Wheatsheaf.

Index

Page numbers in italic refer to tables.